PERFORMANCE-BASED STRATEGY

Tools and Techniques for Successful Decisions

This 'how-to' guide has worked well and will work for any group seriously wanting to change direction, change culture, and deliver results. The authors have done a very good job in a straight-forward, understandable and, most importantly, executable way to provide the roadmap to develop a strategy for your organization that will work, and with a deep commitment to communication, lead to results early in the first year of execution.

— Doug Oberhelman, Former Chairman and CEO,
Caterpillar Inc.

It is rare to see practice and theory combine as completely as they have in this book. Having had the pleasure of working with Steve and his team, and more importantly, having benefited directly as an investor, I can attest to the quality of his work. What is so terrific about this book is the clarity of thought and broader framework the authors provide as a scaffold for their very practical advice.

— David Steinglass, Partner,
Northlane Capital Partners, LLC

Your key customers and partners will also want to know if your strategy is sound. These tools will give the user command of their situation, and provide a powerful way to communicate it to both internal and external stakeholders.

— George Taylor, CEO,
Professional Cowboy Rodeo Association

The authors take the esoteric out of strategy development, which can be paralyzing for many leadership teams. Their actionable tools enable companies to quickly improve their strategy and ultimately their company's value. I have seen first-hand the power of these techniques in practice, and the results were amazing.

— Arthur R. Monaghan, Co-Founder,
Granite Equity Partners LLC

At a time when development of strategies in organizations is characterized by broad-brush, jargon-laden, vacuous discussions, this easy-to-read book reminds readers that crafting meaningful strategies is a challenging task that mandates paying attention to details. The authors also make the tools come alive by providing interesting anecdotes related to the particular tool in question. In brief, strategic decision makers and students of strategy can benefit greatly from reading this book.

— Dr. B. Ram Baliga, Professor of Strategy and
International Business, Wake Forest University

PERFORMANCE-BASED STRATEGY

Tools and Techniques for Successful Decisions

BY

STEVE FAIRBANKS

AARON BUCHKO

United Kingdom – North America – Japan
India – Malaysia – China

Emerald Publishing Limited
Howard House, Wagon Lane, Bingley BD16 1WA, UK

First edition 2018

Reprints and permissions service
Contact: permissions@emeraldinsight.com

British Library Cataloguing in Publication Data
A catalogue record for this book is available from the British Library

ISBN: 978-1-78743-796-8 (Print)
ISBN: 978-1-78743-795-1 (Online)
ISBN: 978-1-78743-982-5 (Epub)

Printed and bound by CPI Group (UK) Ltd, Croydon, CR0 4YY

ISOQAR certified
Management System,
awarded to Emerald
for adherence to
Environmental
standard
ISO 14001:2004.

Certificate Number 1985
ISO 14001

INVESTOR IN PEOPLE

To the memory of my father, Dr. Larry James Fairbanks.
I miss you every day.
SCF

To Kathy, Alex and Andrej, for making me a better person.
AAB

Contents

List of Figures   *xi*

List of Tables   *xvii*

Foreword   *xix*

Acknowledgments   *xxi*

Introduction   *1*

1. What Is Strategy?   *5*
   Is there a simple "real-world" definition of strategy?

2. The Market and Four P Tool   *15*
   Is there a simple way to structure my strategy effort?

3. The Bottom-Up Market Sizing Tool   *23*
   How do we figure out the size of our market in the
   absence of hard data?

4. The Market Segmentation Tool   *35*
   How do I better understand the make-up of my overall market?

5. The Segment Niching Tool   *49*
   Now that my market is sized and segmented, how do I better
   understand segment niches?

6. The Market Map Tool   61
   *Is there a simple yet comprehensive way to characterize the
   business health of my markets, segments, and niches?*

7. The Strategic Environmental Scan Tool   71
   *How do I develop an effective plan and strategy in an
   environment that is highly uncertain, turbulent, and unpredictable?*

8. The Product Volume Margin (PVM) Chart Tool   91
   How do I assess the "business health" of my products or services?

9. The Strategic Market Portfolio Matrix Tool   101
   How do I assess the "market health" of my products or services?

10. The Customer Value Analysis Tool   121
    What do our customers really value in our products or services?

11. The Willingness to Pay (WTP) Ranking Tool   143
    *How do I understand my customers' "willingness to Pay"
    for my products or services?*

12. The Product/Service Portfolio Matrix Tool   157
    *How do we determine and prioritize which products/services
    need action?*

13. The Poor Man's Quality Function Deployment (QFD) Tool   171
    *How do I get the right product/service specification defined
    in timely fashion?*

14. The Process Improvement Guidance Tool   189
    *How should we approach our internal cost reduction/value
    enhancement efforts?*

15. The Strategic Outsourcing Matrix Tool   197
    Are we properly outsourcing key elements of our cost structure?

16. The Critical to Customer Mindset Tool: Where Are
     We Causing You Pain?   209
     How can we enhance our reputation with our customers in the
     most effective and efficient manner?

17. The Brand Perception Tool   221
     How do we effectively communicate our brand to our
     customers and our market?

18. The Opportunity Sourcing Matrix   233
     How can I prioritize among all the potential opportunities
     in front of me?

19. Milestone Project Management Tool   241
     How do we successfully manage our product/service
     improvement projects?

20. The Visual Waterfall Chart Tool   257
     How can I track the status of multiple initiatives in a timely and
     easily understood fashion?

21. The 90-Day Bucket Tool   263
     How can I keep my performance goals relevant and continually
     driving proper action and achievement?

22. The Communication Matrix Tool   277
     How do I keep everyone on the same page?

23. The 10-Quarter Tool   283
     Is there a way to help me follow through on the changes
     I personally need to make?

About the Authors   287

Index   289

List of Figures

Chapter 2

Figure 2.1   The Market and Four P Approach. *15*

Chapter 3

Figure 3.1   The Bottom-Up Market Sizing Matrix. *25*

Chapter 4

Figure 4.1   A Typical Market Segmentation Tool Output   *35*

Figure 4.2   Bottom-Up Calculation of Market Segment
              Sizes.   *42*

Figure 4.3   Market Segmentation for Business Unit. . . .   *46*

Figure 4.4   Expanded Opportunity Using the Market
              Segmentation Tool. *47*

Chapter 5

Figure 5.1   A Completed "Size, Segment and Niche"
              Effort. *49*

Figure 5.2   Niching on the "Why They Buy?" Question. .   *52*

Figure 5.3   Constructing the Size, Segment, and Niche
              Market Map. *54*

Chapter 6

Figure 6.1   The Completed Market Map Tool. *61*

Figure 6.2   Assigning a "Business Health" Ranking to
              Segments. *64*

Chapter 7

Figure 7.1   The Environments of Organizations. *76*

Figure 7.2   Strategic Environmental Scan: One-Page
              Framework. *79*

Figure 7.3   Issue Prioritization Matrix. *83*

Figure 7.4   Commercial Banking — Strategic
              Environmental Scan. *88*

Chapter 8

Figure 8.1   A Typical Product Volume Margin Chart. . .   *91*

Figure 8.2   Strategic Implications of the PVM Tool. . . .   *97*

Figure 8.3   PVM Analysis of Manufacturing Company. .   *98*

Chapter 9

Figure 9.1   The Strategic Market Portfolio Matrix. *105*

Figure 9.2   SMPM for the Example Firm.. . . . .   *112*

Figure 9.3   SMPM — Service Lines, Returns, and
              Share of Population. *114*

Figure 9.4   SMPM — Products, Margins, Forecasted
              Growth, and Product Complementarity.. . .   *115*

Figure 9.5   SMPM — Midwest Community Hospital. . .   *118*

Chapter 10

Figure 10.1   The CVA Model. *131*

Figure 10.2   Customer Groups: Price by Ease of Use. . . .   *137*

Chapter 11

Figure 11.1   The WTP Ranking Tool. *143*

Figure 11.2   WTP Ranking Example. *149*

Figure 11.3   WTP Ranking for Homebuilder Example. . .   *150*

Figure 11.4   WTP for a Manufacturing Company. *154*

Chapter 12

Figure 12.1   The Product/Service Portfolio Matrix Tool. .   *157*

Figure 12.2   Strategic Questions from the Product
Portfolio Matrix Tool. *164*

Figure 12.3   Market Map and Product Portfolio Matrix for
Manufacturing Company A. *168*

Chapter 13

Figure 13.1   Example of the Poor Man's QFD Tool. *171*

Chapter 14

Figure 14.1   The Process Improvement Guidance Tool. . .   *189*

Figure 14.2   Techniques Associated with Three Process
Improvement Approaches. *192*

Figure 14.3   Examples of the Progressive Use of the Three
Approaches. *193*

Chapter 15

Figure 15.1   A Typical Strategic Outsourcing Matrix. . . .   *197*

Figure 15.2   Considering Changes from Current State. . .   *204*

Figure 15.3   Working Strategic Outsourcing
Matrix Result. *207*

Chapter 16

Figure 16.1   CTC Process Improvement Example.. . . . .   *218*

Chapter 17

Figure 17.1   The Brand Perception Chart. *221*

Figure 17.2   Charitable Organizations' Brand Perception
Chart.   *231*

Chapter 18

Figure 18.1   A Typical Opportunity Sorting Matrix
Framework. *233*

Figure 18.2   Typical Opportunity Sorting Matrix Tool
Output. *238*

Chapter 19

Figure 19.1   The Milestone Project Management Tool. . .   *241*

Figure 19.2   Ineffective and Effective Stage Gate
Resource Use. *250*

Figure 19.3   Detailed Milestone Project
Management Tool. *252*

Figure 19.4   Positive Impact on Time to Market
using the Milestone Project Management
Tool.   *254*

Chapter 20

Figure 20.1   The Visual Waterfall Tool. *257*

Figure 20.2   Strategic Information from The Visual
Waterfall Chart Tool. *261*

Chapter 21

Figure 21.1   The 90-Day Bucket Tool. *263*

Figure 21.2   Using the 90-Day Bucket Tool to
Adjust and Monitor Resource Allocation. . .   *274*

Figure 21.3   90-Day Buckets for CEO Organizational
Transformation. *275*

List of Tables

Chapter 9

Table 9.1   Sample Market Attractiveness Assessment. .   *110*

Table 9.2   Sample Competitive Position Assessment. . .   *111*

Chapter 10

Table 10.1   Key Purchase Criteria/Purchase Process Factors.   *134*

Table 10.2   Example: Customer Value Analysis — Key Purchase Criteria/Purchase Process Factors..   *136*

Chapter 13

Table 13.1   Examples of Feature and Requirement Definition.   *178*

Table 13.2   Poor Man's QFD for a Production Constrained Situation. *184*

Chapter 19

Table 19.1   Potential Stage Gate Structures. *245*

Chapter 21

Table 21.1   Examples of Defining 90-Day Bucket Tasks. .   *267*

Chapter 22

Table 22.1   A Typical Communication Matrix. *277*

Foreword

Steve and Aaron have addressed "strategy" in a simple and understandable way. Too many strategic consultants make it too hard. It's not. As the authors so eloquently point out, if you know your markets and your business, using the practical tools discussed in the book will lead to results in a fairly short time. That's also my experience — do it quick, measure it as often as practicable and keep communicating, consistently. Far too often I would visit a Caterpillar plant or office and see "strategy" on the walls from years before, and some with pictures of prior management teams. How can leaders expect their team to execute a strategy if they don't know what it is, understand it, and then live it?

This "how to" guide has worked and will work for any group seriously wanting to change direction, change culture, and deliver results. The authors have done a very good job, in a straightforward, understandable, and most importantly executable way to provide the roadmap to develop a strategy for your organization that will work, and with a deep commitment to communication, lead to results early in the first year of execution.

I particularly was impressed by "The 90-day Bucket Tool," in which "Get it Done" is the driver. This is absolutely imperative in a company that needs change, and rapid moves reinforce leadership's commitment to that change.

I applaud Steve and Aaron in compiling a lifetime of learning from a very practical academic and a proven turnaround CEO. This is a strong combination and one that has impressed me. I've no doubt this book will change how companies think about strategy, from development, execution, coordination, and most importantly — results.

This book, *Performance-based Strategy: Tools and Techniques for Successful Decisions*, incorporates tried and true philosophies, exercises, and tactical recommendations to guide any kind of organization, of any size to identify and implement a strategic direction and then *deliver results*.

There are unknown quantities of books, articles, and scholarly academic productions written over the years to do what this book actually does — know your business, know your markets, know your customers, and then devise a direction based on deep core knowledge. All of this won't work unless all levels of management truly believe and then communicate to all constituents. This includes all the leaders, team members, key suppliers, and key customers! Everyone in the chain has to be knowledgeable and then believe in it! Then deliver!

Doug Oberhelman,
Former Chairman and CEO, Caterpillar Inc.

Acknowledgments

From Steve Fairbanks

The genesis of this book began one day at a corporate meeting about 10 years ago. I learned that Dr. Ram Baliga, Professor of Strategy at Wake Forest University, was in attendance. I corralled him between the meeting and dinner to review a just completed strategic plan for the company I was with. I asked him for his honest feedback — or any comment — since I rarely got the chance to consult such an academic expert on strategy. He remained quiet as I reviewed a series of tools I used to complete the plan for the constrained and failing organization. I thought I'd laid an egg. When finished he simply said, "Why are you asking me? This is one of the best uses of strategy tools I've ever seen — and would you consider coming to Winston-Salem and presenting these to my MBA students." What an honor. And I actually got invited back! My thanks to Ram for his generous support and eventual contributions to this book.

A year later, I was reacquainted with another business school professor, Dr. Aaron Buchko from Bradley University. Upon learning of my speaking with WFU's MBA students, and my subsequent sharing of that presentation, he similarly asked if I'd come to Bradley and share it with his Executive MBA students. Again, another honor and multiple repeat annual visits. The tools seemed to resonate even more strongly with the EMBA's — those students with full-time executive jobs under a variety of time and resource constraints. The feedback from them was very encouraging. It was Aaron who first suggested that the presentation would actually make a great book. We both served on a company Board together, and after a couple of years of pushing, and to get me off-center, he said "Look, I'll co-author it with you. This stuff needs to get out into the public." After I completed my last turnaround project, I took him up on his offer. And I'm glad I did. Having worked with Aaron in the past, I always described him as a great academic thinker who actually understood the real world. That combination has been vital to this book. He has also turned out to be a great writing partner. My sincere thanks to Aaron for his indispensable help on this project and friendship over the years.

Along the way, I have been blessed to work with a wide variety of people and have endeavored to learn something from each boss, peer, and associate I've met on the shop floor. Without you, the tools in this book could not have been honed to the point that we felt they were mature enough to share. My hope is that your efforts here will truly help others. Rest assured there is a little bit of all of you in this book.

I'd like to thank Don Rimes for not only being a great mentor, but seeing something in me worth investing in and starting me on my servant leadership path. Likewise, I am indebted to Ken Blanchard and the Lead Like Jesus movement for helping me evolve further on that journey, and I would also like to thank Jim Mudd and Phil Hodges for showing me an incredible kindness at a particularly difficult time.

In my Private Equity life, I am thankful to have crossed paths with David Steinglass, Art Monaghan, and Brett Keith, all leaders in their respective firms, for their help, encouragement, and support as owners and Board members. I would also like to recognize and thank Judy Bland, Randy Ingram, Bob Kuch, Maria Oelke, Jeff Ingles, Earl White, Luke Livingston, and Rodney Crim — as executives and team members I was honored to count you as colleagues. I'd also like to recognize Greg Flint and the Anderson Center, an executive training group in St. Cloud, MN, for their thinking on the definition of strategy — which we adapted herein to round out our vision.

I'd like to thank my Mom and Dad for giving me a great foundation in my formative years. My Dad was also a college professor and I remember walking around the ping-pong table as a kid in our basement hand collating stacks of pages for a book he had written. I've had writing a book on my bucket list ever since and am proud to follow in those footsteps.

I'd also like to thank my children, Craig, Corey, Allyse, and Evan for all their love and support through the years. In addition to their Dad working long hours at times, they also put up with more than their fair share of family moves. I am so proud of the men and women you've become, and the families you have started. I am forever in your debt and now look forward to the opportunity of trying to repay it.

Lastly, and most importantly, I am eternally grateful to my wife Lori. Any modicum of success I've had in the business world pales in comparison to the fact I've somehow been able to hold on to one of the most wonderful women in the world for 36 years. Thank you for your sacrifices, your tireless devotion to our children, your support and patience with me, and for keeping me grounded in those things that really matter the most in life.

From Aaron Buchko

Getting a book together and published is not an easy task and is the result of the efforts of numerous individuals. Trying to acknowledge everyone is like trying to get the speech right at the Academy Awards — you're going to forget someone, and then the music will start playing. Nonetheless, I'd be remiss if I didn't acknowledge some key people who made this possible.

First of all, I owe a huge debt of gratitude to Steve for allowing me to be his wingman on this journey. We've known each other for about 12 years now, and every chance I've had to work with him and watch him in action with a group of executives never ceases to amaze me at his ability to grasp the needs of his audience (whether a management team or students), then take really tough challenges and reduce these to simple tools that people can get their heads around and lead to good decisions and better results. In my view, he is a genius at strategy, and it has been a privilege to have been able to learn from him over the years we've worked together.

This book would not have been possible without the thousands of executives I've worked with over the years who have been the "test lab" for many of these ideas. Some worked, some didn't; and they let me know which was which! Their time, energy, and effort helped to refine many of these concepts and make these tools better. Some of them are used as anonymous anecdotes; hopefully, they will recognize themselves in the book. I hope that, in some small way, their use of these tools helped pay them back in part for letting me into their companies to learn and work with their people. In particular, I would like to acknowledge a debt of gratitude to Alan Sadler, CEO of Triple S, who has been a true friend as well as a brilliant strategist, and Gordon Honegger, the Chairman of Hometown Community Banks, who is a master at strategic market insights.

Likewise, I've benefitted over the years from my colleagues at Bradley University, especially Dr. Larry Weinzimmer, my "partner in strategic management" and golfing idol, who has helped shape my views of the practice of strategy. My students at Bradley, both graduate and undergraduate, have applied these tools to various situations and helped improve the quality of these techniques in hundreds of classroom interactions; their questions and enthusiasm remind me why I became a professor.

None of us gets to where we are in life on our own, we are indebted to countless people who have influenced. In my case, my biggest influence in management was Dr. Eugene Jennings of Michigan State University. Gene was the most brilliant management scholar and thinker I've ever known. He died in 2016, and I miss being able to have him as a mentor, colleague, and friend to challenge my thinking and development. The management faculty at Michigan State in the late 80s turned me from a manager into a strategy professor, and I particularly want to thank Jim Skivington, John Wagner III, Glenn Omura, Harry Perlstadt, and Michael Moch. Before that, the faculty in the College of Business at Ferris State University set me on a path of intellectual fascination with business management. I've also been blessed to have had wonderful parents who encouraged me to pursue education and business management as a field of study. They supported us during my days as a Ph.D. student and taught me more about life than anyone else. There's not a day goes by I don't miss them; I know they'd be happy to see my name on the book.

Finally, my family. Kathy, my wonderful wife, has stayed by my side for 36 years, 2 major moves, career changes, and children. Somehow during all of that she managed to get her own Ph.D. as a counseling psychologist, and I've learned a lot from her. She is the solid foundation of our family and makes it possible for me to pursue all of the academic and organizational work, and she was there for me along the path to getting this book done. I can't adequately express my thanks for her support. My daughter Alex, has Dad wrapped around her little finger; she's a terrific person and makes me proud every day that I had a part in her upbringing. My son Andrej is my golfing partner, flyfishing buddy, hockey hero, and friend. It's an honor to be their Dad. They put up with my long hours in the study working on books, articles, classes, etc. I could not be where I am without their support. I'll be forever indebted to them for their love.

Joint Acknowledgments from Steve and Aaron
Aaron's daughter, Alex, spent hours of her time and applied her English degree to read through the manuscript for us while still in draft and make numerous corrections to improve the writing quality. She spent hours going over the book line by line and cleaning up our material, and we can't thank her enough for her efforts. (Aaron did promise her she would never have to read the word "strategy" again in anything he wrote.)

We would both like to extend a special thanks to our team at Emerald. Our Editor, Charlotte Maiorana, believed in the concept early on and went to bat for us in getting the book accepted for publication; her enthusiasm and positive attitude were invaluable in keeping us going through the process. Nick Wolterman, our

Assistant Editor at Emerald, likewise hung in there with us and made sure we successfully navigated through the steps in getting the book into print. They felt the tools and stories were as relevant to today's business world as we do, and we appreciate their hard work in bringing this book to fruition.

Introduction

In September 2004, Steve Fairbanks walked into a medium-sized manufacturing company in northern Iowa as the new CEO. The private equity firm that owned the company had hired him to turn around a business that had been going downhill for two and a half years; the value of the company was decreasing fast. The usual slash and burn efforts had been tried — budgets had been cut, assets reduced, and capital frozen — with little effect. There was no strategy or plan. All Steve had to do was reverse the trend of 10 consecutive quarters of company devaluation by the first quarter of 2005. That, and rescue a business that was vital to the local community. The pressure was clearly on.

Fortunately for the firm that hired him, they got a CEO who was prepared for the challenge. In his career, Steve had already demonstrated success at running similar manufacturing businesses. During that time, he'd developed a set of tools that had proven to be effective and valuable in generating significant improvements in company results. Now, if he could just apply those tools to the current business, maybe the company would have a chance.

Steve called his team together and began to share the tools he'd developed. They analyzed the market and identified the strategic customer segments. Processes were reviewed and improvements identified. Milestones were established. Critical factors were set and programs put in place to address these needs. In 90 days, the team had put together a comprehensive strategic plan for the Board of Directors to review. The Board's take: "Looks great on paper — now execute it." More tools were applied to drive action, and the team delivered. After 6 months, the company showed positive market share growth and an increase in quarterly valuation.

They didn't stop there. After 2 years, revenues had increased by 50%, almost FOUR TIMES the industry average, and earnings had doubled. In 2008, the Great Recession hit — yet the company continued to grow revenues and earnings in an economy that was destroying other manufacturers. In 2009, in the depths of the recession, when hundreds of business were being shuttered and factories closed, the company actually OPENED a new plant to handle the growth. By 2011, the business had doubled sales and tripled earnings. The Compound Annual Growth Rate (CAGR) for 2004 through 2011 — including the Great Recession period — was over 10% for revenues and over 16% for earnings (keep in mind that the U.S. economy was growing less than 4% during this same time period). The owners were very, very happy with the results.

This wasn't the only time the tools had been used effectively. In another situation, Steve was appointed CEO of a company that was in what the banks termed (in their usual understated manner) a "distressed situation." Lending covenants had been broken, the company's future was in jeopardy, and the situation required immediate reversal if the business was to be saved. In the same way, and within 90 days, the tools were used again to construct a winning strategy and plan. The lead bank retained one of the largest consulting firms in the United States to review and test the plan. The consultants' response? The tools used to develop the plan were "fantastic," and this was one of the few companies in this situation the consultants had seen who actually "got it." The results? Over the next 5 years, revenues grew at a compounded rate of nearly 10% per year, gross margins grew by nearly 25% per year, and earnings grew almost 70% per year. The bank went from being the harshest critic to the company's strongest advocate, even encouraging the firm to now borrow more money to support further growth.

Every manager who has walked into a new job or a new company and has been charged with improving business performance and increasing results understands these stories. The manager comes in, sits down at their desk, and says, "What do I do now?" The challenges are significant and the problems are real. Resources are constrained and the clock is ticking; bosses and owners expect results now. Managers don't have years to figure out what to do. They need real, practical tools and processes that will enable them to analyze the situation and make the right decisions to drive future success right away.

That's why we wrote this book. It's for every manager who has ever been put into a situation where they were expected to quickly and effectively improve organization results — and we're betting that describes most managers. They were put there because they have the knowledge and experience to do the job. Now they need to apply that knowledge and experience effectively and quickly. How can we make it easier for them to do so? That's what the tools in the book are intended to do.

The bases for many of these tools aren't necessarily new; many of these concepts have been available in the business literature for some time. The real-world need was to embrace and adapt the powerful strategy ideas that were out there into a framework that would work in organizations that are constrained in both time and resources (which, if you think about it, describes virtually all organizations). *The goal for each of the tools is meaningful and actionable results in hours and days, rather than the more typical weeks or months.*

The positive feedback we've received from those who have been exposed to and employed these tools has been eye opening. The success that has been achieved by organizations that use these tools speaks for itself. It has been especially gratifying to see these tools applied across public and private organizations, small-cap and Fortune 500 companies, service and manufacturing firms, for-profit, not-for-profit, governmental, and charitable organizations. These tools are universally applicable — and they work.

We think we can create value not only by sharing the tools with the reader, but by demonstrating how to construct and use the tools. And we provide real-world anecdotes of how each tool has been successfully applied. This is not a conceptual or theoretical discussion of strategy and planning. It is a practical book with proven tools and the guidance on how to properly use them to drive business results. If even one of these tools resonates with the reader and helps them make a better business decision, the pay-back can be substantial. We know, because we've done it.

What Is Strategy?

Strategy Question: *Is there a simple "real-world" definition of strategy?*

The Definition

This is a guide to using various tools for strategic analysis and planning purposes, so we need to first define what we mean by using the word *strategy*. It is a good word, an old concept, but it has been overused so much throughout the years that it has lost a lot of its meaning. Before we get too far into the tools, we want to present an overall framework for understanding strategy, both to provide a clear understanding of the concept and to provide a framework for the tools.

The word "strategy" comes from the Greek word "*strategos*," literally meaning "general of an army." Strategy has its roots in the military; originally it meant the decisions and directions of the general commander of a military force in conflict with an enemy. The dictionary defines strategy as "the commitment of resources to support adopted policies, usually in time of war." So the basis for strategy is conflict. It involves making decisions and directing resources and actions toward a desired end goal.

Fortunately, in most organizations, we're not in armed conflict with our competitors. But we are competing for customers, revenues, and market share. Or in a not-for-profit organization, we're competing for funding or grants, for clients and services. Inherent in strategy is this idea of a competitive environment in which firms struggle for access to the resources necessary to survive, grow, and prosper. This idea of competition for scarce, limited resources is fundamental to understanding the reason for strategy in organizations.

Unfortunately, executives seem to like the word "strategy" or "strategic" so much that it has become overused in their organizations. Today we have marketing strategies, human resource (HR) strategies, information technology (IT) strategies, operational strategies, financial strategies, and more. We have a strategy for this market or that group of customers, a strategy for dealing with the government, and a strategy for growth. We strive for strategic leadership in our industry, with strategic product placement and strategic innovation based on strategic research and development activities. The problem is, when everything is a strategy, nothing is strategic. Our ability to communicate and to understand our management decisions and actions becomes difficult due to the confusion created by our use or misuse of this single word.

Having multiple "strategies," like a supply chain strategy and an advertising strategy and a growth strategy and an innovation strategy, doesn't mean your organization is strategy rich. In our opinion, the more "strategies" you have, the less likely it is that your organization has a strategy at all. There's a quick acid test for strategy: if every manager in the organization can state, clearly and succinctly, what the organization's strategy is, then odds are good you have a strategy. If no one can state in a clear, simple, and easily understood manner what the strategy is, then you probably don't have one. It doesn't matter what your official documents say; if the people in the organization cannot state a common strategy for the enterprise, then the organization doesn't have a strategy, because the actions that individuals are taking are not bound together in an integrated way toward a common, shared objective. There may be nice words on paper, and they may make managers feel good, but there's no strategy.

Over the years, and with experience and time, we have narrowed down the definition of strategy into one that captures both the competitive nature of organizations and the essence of strategic decision-making and execution. We've worked with and talked to countless managers in diverse organizations. We've seen all kinds of conceptualizations and definitions of strategy. We've seen numerous strategy statements, the good, the bad, and the ugly. And we've studied the works of the major writers, researchers, and strategy consultants. From this, we believe we have been able to distill it all down to a practical definition of strategy:

> *Strategy is an integrated set of resource commitments and actions that position an organization within the competitive environment so as to generate superior results over time.*

We'd like to break that definition down to be sure that we begin by having a shared understanding of what these tools are intended to produce and support.

Integrated — The first thing that needs to be understood is that strategy is purposely intended to integrate all the various functions and activities of the organization. By nature, strategy is inherently integrative, involving all the elements of the firm.

Nothing happens in isolation in an organization. Every activity, every function, is inherently linked to everything else. A decision to increase market share requires product or service development and expansion, HR commitments, financing to support growth, and information support. Reducing costs affects HRs, operations, finance, marketing, and so on. Hence, integration across the various functional areas or disciplines of the enterprise is fundamental to strategy.

The activities are not just integrated, though, the activities are integrated in varied, complex, and numerous ways. So even if it were possible to isolate the actions of each functional area, it isn't possible to isolate the relationships among these because of their complexity. As a result, every strategy will touch all aspects of the enterprise, and therefore all elements of the organization have to be considered in developing a strategy.

Set of Resource Commitments — Like the classic dictionary definition, strategy involves the commitment of resources — human,
financial, and capital. These are the basic resources of any organization: people, money, and assets. Strategy requires that the managers of the organization make decisions about how to apply
these resources, and it is the commitment of those resources that
comes to define the strategy of the organization. We want to distinguish, then, between an organization's stated strategy and the
actual strategy. Organizations make a lot of statements about
what their strategy is, but the commitment of resources is what
operationalizes the strategy and makes it real. An organization
that claims to be pursuing a strategy of innovation yet never com-
mits people, money, or assets to innovation isn't likely to come up
with too many innovative ideas. No resources, no strategy.

As economists constantly remind us, these resources are scarce,
limited, and finite. That's what gives rise to competition: the struggle for scarce and limited resources, which in turn defines the
nature of market competition. But it is this property of resources
that also necessitates the development of strategy, because it is not
possible for firms to do everything. No organization has an unlim-
ited amount of resources. Since resources are scarce and limited,
strategy involves making tradeoffs — making decisions about
where, when, and in what amount to apply the limited resources
available to the manager. The old strategy truism "an organization
cannot be all things to all people" is based on this innate requirement of tradeoffs among resource commitments. Executives have
to decide how to allocate a fixed set of resources among alternative potential uses in order to drive the right behaviors and outcomes. This is the nature of strategy.

Actions — Strategy is not a concept; it is not words on paper, it is
not a three-ring binder with charts and tables and graphs, and it is
not a list of Critical Success Factors or project plans. At the end of
the day, strategy is about people DOING things. Strategy requires
actions, actions that involve the use of people, money, and assets
(hence the commitment of resources). If, at the end of the strategy
development process, the organization has nothing but words on

paper, or if no one actually does anything, then the process (and the strategy) will be a failure.

Strategy is not passive; it is active. It is real people spending time, energy, and effort on various activities that cause things to happen and that create meaningful change in an organization. These activities, as we've noted, are integrated with hundreds and thousands of other activities in the organization in complex ways, but ultimately it is these actions that define what the strategy is in practice. We distinguish, then, between an organization's strategy CONCEPT (what we say) with the strategy PRACTICE (what we do). Of these, it is the latter, the actual practice of the strategy, that is in fact the real strategy of the organization.

Position — Since strategy is by nature competitive and occurs within a competitive environment, then it follows that the goal of strategy is to secure for the firm a particular location within that environment, based on the unique commitments of resources and the integrated actions undertaken by the organization. This location is defined relative to all other organizations by the distinctive application of those resources and the resulting activities that occur based on those resources.

It is these unique commitments of resources and actions that give rise to such traditional strategy concepts as "distinctive competence" or "competitive advantage." What we are trying to describe through these terms is the manner in which an organization is different from all others — but different in what space? At some level, all organizations have products or services, people, money, and assets. All organizations "do" marketing. All organizations have operations that need to be managed. The uniqueness of differentiation of an organization cannot be relative to these common resources and actions. Positioning comes about as a result of the distinct manner in which resources are applied and actions are performed.

Competitive Environment — The uniqueness of the organization must therefore lie in its position — but a position relative to what? Since competition and conflict are inherent in strategy, the position must refer to the competitive space, that arena in which firms must compete. In business organizations, the arena is the market. In not-for-profit organizations, the arena is the firm's external environment. In any case, the essential point to note is that strategy is intended to enable the firm to occupy a unique space within the competitive arena, distinct from all others. This presumes that the organization understandings the environment and market(s) in which firm is trying to compete. There must be a way of evaluating or assessing the competitive space that aids managers in determining if the resource commitments and actions are effective in enabling the firm to identify and secure that space within the environment relative to others.

Superior Performance — By achieving a unique position within the competitive environment, an organization will be able to generate superior performance. In the case of the for-profit business enterprise, superior performance can be measured as returns to the owners, profitability, return on investment, cash flows, economic value added, or any of several measures. For the not-for-profit entity, performance can be measured by clients served, services provided, outcomes produced, return on philanthropy, and several other metrics. The essential point is that a successful strategy enables a firm to generate superior performance in the competitive arena through the ability to stake out a defensible, unique position based on an integrated set of resources commitments and actions.

Wow; what a long-winded, technical definition. What is it we're really trying to say? The point we're trying to make with all of this is that the proper application of strategy tools requires that we have a framework to "hang" the tools on. If we don't know what we mean by strategy, then virtually any technique or activity can be viewed as strategic. It's like trying to build a house: if you don't have a blueprint for the home you're trying to construct, then you don't know how to develop a plan to build the home and which tools to apply at which times. You're likely to wind up with a mess and a lot of frustration. But if we have a clear sense of what it is we're trying to create, then we can develop a process to achieve the goal and we can determine which tools to apply along the process to enable us to reach the desired end state.

Unfortunately, all too often we've seen organizations and executives with no sense of strategy, just this vague notion that "we need a strategy" (usually because performance is suffering or some Board member or consultant told them they needed one, or because there's some significant change in the organization's circumstances). In these situations, organizations usually hire consultants to perform various analyses or to develop a strategy for the firm based on the consultant's models and tools. The problem is that the consultant's toolkit is usually limited to a few key models or concepts, and the resulting analyses and strategies are likewise limited as a result. To continue the analogy, it is like only hiring a carpenter to build a house; you'll get a nice structure, but you might also want a plumber and an electrician to really have a livable space. Many times, strategies look like the house built only by a carpenter: a nice structure, but no way of actually doing anything.

So if it seems like we're being a bit "anally retentive" in insisting on this precise understanding of what strategy really is, it's only because our intention in providing a strategy framework relies on having an accurate conceptualization of strategy in the first place. Once we have a common concept and definition, we can begin to talk about HOW to go about developing an effective strategy. That's where we'll turn our attention next.

Practical Strategy Tools

Let's assume (now that you know what strategy really is) that you're aware that your organization doesn't really have a strategy. Or perhaps you have a strategy, but it is not effective; it doesn't tell you what your unique position is in the environment, and it isn't creating superior returns or outcomes for the organization. You know that your organization needs an effective strategy, one that can be shared among the members of the enterprise and that will guide decisions and behaviors. But you're not sure how to go about developing a strategy, and you don't want (or can't afford) to hire a consultant to develop one for you. You know the questions you need to have answered, but aren't sure how to go about getting those answers. If this sounds like your situation, then you are the target of this book. You are the person or organization for whom this book was written. No one outside of your firm can develop a strategy for your organization; there's no way an outsider can possibly understand all of the complex interrelationships among people, assets, processes, and systems that are necessary for your company to be successful. You know that ultimately, *effective strategies need to be developed by the members of the organization.* You can't hire this out or look to consultants for the necessary experience if you want to be truly effective in your business situation. It takes intelligent, committed, and capable people inside the enterprise to develop an organization's strategy.

But you also know that your abilities to do so are limited. Most organizations don't hire people because they are great strategists or strategic thinkers; they hire them because they are extremely capable of performing the tasks necessary for the organization to be successful. However, the essential strategic question is not "How can we perform our organization's tasks better?" The essential strategy question is this: "What tasks do we need to perform well?" These are two different questions. And the skills that make a person very good at determining a better way to market a product, to lower manufacturing costs, or to improve processes over time are very different from the skills needed to analyze the future of the business and determine how to allocate resources and actions in creating the future.

How does the organization determine which position to secure in the market? How does the organization decide which tasks need to be performed in order to achieve success in the competitive marketplace? How does the business allocate resources to those tasks? These are crucial strategy questions, yet most managers in organizations have limited experience in addressing these issues. They need help, but they are justifiably leery of having people from outside the organization make these decisions for the business — managers realize that no outsider ever understands the business in the same way an insider does. Outsiders simply can't; they lack the knowledge that comes from years of experience in dealing with customers, vendors, and service providers. They are not immersed in the organization in such a way that allows them to be able to see the web of interrelated systems and to understand how those systems and processes interact with one another to yield results. You want to do it yourself, with your own people, because no one can know your organization as you do. You want to involve others in the organization for the knowledge and experience they can lend to the decision-making process.

This book is intended to provide you with a set of analytic and decision-making tools that will help you and your team assess your situation, analyze the information, ask the right questions, and develop an effective strategy. This is for the senior leader or executive who is a type of "do it yourself-er" when it comes to strategy. You believe in your people and your organization, but you want to be able to guide them in a way that will enable you to develop an effective strategy. You just want some proven, effective tools to help people see the situation in a strategic manner and make effective strategic decisions.

We present tools in this book with this need in mind. The tools cover each area of our strategy definition. We start with tools that help with understanding the competitive environment. Next, we offer tools that will help define your current position within the competitive environment and continue with tools to help discern what, if any, actions you need to take to make your products or services more competitive. More tools are then offered to help provide understanding of the resources needed compared to the resources available, and even more tools to help with prioritization amongst actions if it is necessary (we've never had a case where it wasn't). Lastly, once the plan is defined, we offer tools to help with the execution phase; without execution on the actions defined, you don't have a working strategy — just that three-ring binder sitting on the shelf.

We have written this book so that the tools can be used individually or collectively. The chapter for each tool is actually titled by the typical strategy problem you may encounter. You can jump to any of the 23 chapters individually in any order and get the benefit of our thinking on that particular strategy problem. If, however, you are new to strategy (especially if this is your first planning effort), consider using the structured approach defined in Chapter 2. In fact, Chapters 2–23 are actually ordered to provide helpful tools from a typical beginning to end of a typical strategic planning process.

In the remainder of this book, we are going to take you through of each of the tools one by one and explain how each tool is used. Your selection of the tool should be based on the strategic question that you want to answer. The tool and its strategic question are provided for you in the Contents. You can either select only those tools you feel you need for the strategy job at hand, or you can learn about all of the tools and, in the process, perhaps discover additional questions and tools that will help you develop a more effective strategy for your organization. However, you approach the problem, eventually you will want to learn about all of the tools available to you for strategy development. The greater your knowledge and perspective, the greater the likelihood that you will be able to develop a strategy that will enable your organization to achieve superior results.

The Market and Four P Tool

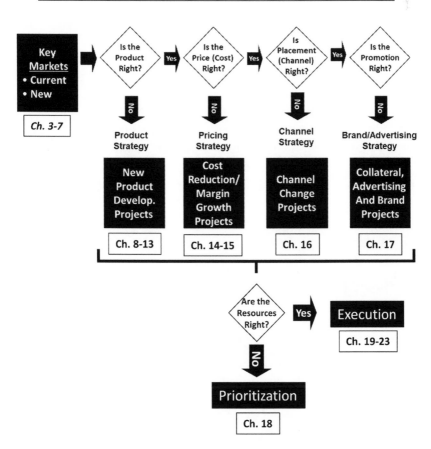

> **Strategy Question:** *Is there a simple way to structure my strategy effort?*

Figure 2.1: The Market and Four P Approach.

Introduction

The extent to which people try to complicate the strategy process amazes us. In our mind, the framework for developing a strategy really is as simple as Marketing 101 and the classic Four P model with which we are all familiar. We have found the Market and Four P framework helps effectively guide the analysis and initiative development process, and we have used it as the framework to introduce and present the tools in this book. As with anything, you need to start somewhere. All of our experience leads us to the conclusion that in most cases there is only one place to start — the Markets.

Markets First

We believe every strategy effort begins by identifying your Markets. Markets shift. Markets morph. Technology advances. Markets adapt. How do you assess your market environment? How big are your markets? How do you segment and niche them? What is your share? Which markets are the most attractive? Which will allow you growth opportunity? Where would it be best for you to compete? *Understanding your evolving markets is the first and, in our opinion, the most critical step in your strategy development*. We spend significant time on helpful tools to do this in Chapters 3–7.

The Four P's

Once the market and segment solutions are clear, your strategy challenges unfold very quickly using the Four P model. Consider the flowchart in Figure 2.1. The process is pretty simple. For a given market, we ask four questions:

- Product — Do we have the right product/service for this market? If not, the new product/service development queue begins to be defined. As we feel the product/service is the most important of the Four P's, we rank it first in priority and have dedicated a number of tools to help in Chapters 8–13.

- Price/Cost — Do we have the right price for said product/ service? If not, the value proposition issues (price side) and/ or production issues (cost side) need to be studied. We feel price/cost follows closely behind product/service in priority and dedicate Chapters 14 and 15 for tools to help in this area.

- Placement (Channel) — Do we have the right channel for said product? If not, channel issues begin to be defined. We spend time in Chapter 16 with tools to become more valuable to your channel partners.

- Promotion — Do we have the right activities in place to properly promote our brand? If not, we need to put in place the right activities to ensure the customer awareness. Chapter 17 provides a tool to help identify those key brand elements for such promotional activities.

Again, our experience leads us to prioritize the Four P effort in just this way: Product, Price/Cost, Placement/Channel, and Promotion. If you are working a strategic plan for the first time, we recommend you follow this path. If you are further along in your planning expertise, or your specific situation clearly calls for switching the order of the process around, feel free to do so — it is your plan, after all. But we do recommend that once you have defined the right order for your circumstance, you undertake each area in that defined order.

Resources and Execution

Once you have made it through the aforementioned phases of evaluation, you must next consider the resource allocation and execution issues. You will note that the preceding strategy tools help put focus not only on what to do, but also on the equally important what *not* to do; we've never seen a situation where resources are infinite. You must be effective in resourcing and executing your action items.

- Resourcing/Prioritizing — If you are following the flow of previous chapters, prioritization and integration of activities naturally evolve from the process — and resource needs for them can be tracked. However, there are times when you need to make a prioritization call among numerous options, with minimal time and imperfect information. What then? We share Chapter 18 (The Opportunity Sourcing Matrix) as a tool we've found extremely helpful in resource prioritization.

- Execution — Once you have a prioritized set of initiatives, how do you ensure you keep the momentum going and execute properly? It is here where motivating and managing the people and process are imperative. We offer some unique tools in Chapters 19–23 that we have found to be very effective.

We have found the Market and Four P tool to provide successful results more quickly than any other approach. We begin our trek here. On to understanding our markets!

Our Favorite Anecdote Using This Tool

A CEO, facing a turnaround situation at his new company, was working quickly to get to know his new organization. He found a state of mediocrity and a marginal-at-best strategic planning effort. He also found a very siloed organization that didn't have a clue about the other functional areas — and no desire to understand them. It was easy to see why the organization was floundering in both revenue and profitability areas. There was a glaring need for a strategic plan and even some basic analysis, yet there was little understanding in the organization of what that really meant.

With those organizational shortfalls in mind, the CEO decided to use his Market and Four P Tool approach to understand their marketplace issues, positioning shortfalls, and their competitive situation with their products and services. He also needed a mechanism to do some team-building. So, he pulled a key team of his executives, managers, and floor supervisors together and reviewed the Market and Four P Tool approach he was taking with them. The flowchart was easy for this team (the members of which were new to a structured planning approach) to understand.

He then commandeered a conference room and dedicated it for the strategic plan. He asked his maintenance group to go out and buy 10, 4-foot by 8-foot by 1-1/2 inch sheets of Styrofoam insulation and deliver them to the "planning room." Prior to his first official team meeting, he stood up the boards around the conference room. On the top of each, he posted a functional department: Marketing, Sales, Finance, Engineering, Purchasing, Operations, IT, Human Resources, etc. The team entered the room and basically saw 10 empty boards with only a group designation at the top. The CEO said that during the course of the next few weeks, he was giving the team concurrent assignments and the resulting charts, graphs, and information would be posted via pushpins on their boards for all to see and discuss.

He then gave out the first assignments, actually using the tools in this book. His initial charge looked something like this:

Round One

- Market Sizing (Chapter 3) — The company actually had great trade associations, so market size was pretty easy to determine. *Sales* was to validate the trade association assumptions and deliver their best definition of true market size.

- Segmenting and Niching the Markets (Chapters 4 and 5) — This company had not considered further breaking down the overall market. *Marketing* was charged to segment and niche the overall market.

- Overall Strategic Environment (Chapter 7) — Nothing serious had been done here. The *Executives* of the company were charged with this exercise.

- Product/Service Business Health (Chapter 8) — *Finance and Operations* were charged to create a Product-Volume-Margin chart for the company's product and service forms to understand their comparative revenue and profitability (price/cost) levels.

The team went about their tasks, and within 7–10 days, the results from each tool were reviewed and refined. Each iteration (and supporting data) was posted on the board. There were many informal stand up meetings springing up in the conference room, centered around the Styrofoam boards and the information posted on them. The different functional groups were starting to interact. Once the round one deliverables were solid enough to build on, the CEO defined the next round of tasks.

Round Two

- Market Map (Chapter 6) — Each of the defined market segments and niches from (from Chapters 4 to 5) were now to be evaluated for business health (growth rate, margin potential) and prioritized for attractiveness for the company's efforts. *Marketing and Finance* were given this task.

- Market Portfolio Matrix (Chapter 9) was done to evaluate the market health of each of the company's product and service forms. *Sales, Marketing, and Engineering* were charged with this task.

We'll stop here as you probably get the idea. The tools and analyses built upon each other, each function got progressively more detailed in their areas, and their Styrofoam board postings became more insightful as supporting documentation was generated. Operations had added all the major issues supporting why margins, if below company gross margin averages (PVM Tool) were dilutive. Engineering added their analyses of competitors' products and services along with their conclusions of what improvements would need to be made to the company's offerings. Other functions provided similarly helpful information.

After 3 weeks, the essence of their situation was becoming clearer. Formal update meetings were routinely called where each functional representative would stand in front of their board and bring the team up to speed on the newest information and conclusions.

The team was growing and learning fast. It became evident to everyone when the most change-resistant (30-year seniority) plant supervisor on the team, in listening to the updates, scratched his chin, and stood to ask a question. He walked over to the Finance board and said, "Product X here has a dilutive gross margin. In fact, we are losing money on it." Then he walked to the Engineering board, pointed to Product X, and said, "And here it is the least attractive in the marketplace," and then to the Operations board and said, "And it is our biggest source of warranty returns, and it sucks up more operating line hours to make than any product we have." Further, he concluded, "We could make five units of Product Y, which (pointing at the Engineering board) the market loves, in the time it takes to do one Product X, and (pointing to the Finance board) we could make a whole lot more money. Why don't we do that?"

The CEO smiled to himself, said it sounded like a great idea to pursue, and asked permission to add it to the growing initiative list. At that point, the CEO gave them a jolt. He reminded them they had started from no knowledge and completely empty Styrofoam boards. Now they had essentially completed a competitive environment analysis and understood their markets and segments, as well as their positioning within each. And they knew a whole lot more about each other. He asked them to remind him again of the Market and Four P meeting kick-off date. They were shocked at how far they had come — in exactly 30 days.

The Bottom-Up
Market Sizing Tool

> **Strategy Question:** How do we figure out the size of our market in the absence of hard data?

Introduction

You can't approach strategy if you don't have a grasp of your customers. It is extremely important to understand how big your addressable market is. Strange as it may seem, our experience is that many companies do not have a good handle on this information. This is critical because in our Market and Four P model, different markets, segments, and niches will have different Product, Price, and Placement needs. We have developed the ensuing four tools in a methodology we call *"Size, Segment, and Niche"* to help the strategist define and clarify the spectrum of their customers.

We will deal with "Sizing" the market here in Chapter 3. The Market Segmentation Tool of Chapter 4 and the Segment Niching Tool of Chapter 5 will further help with the "Segment" and "Niche" aspects. Lastly, Chapter 6 will add ways to "assess the business health" of each segment. The culmination of this work is one-page Market Map (building upon and combining the results of Chapters 3–6) that we have found extremely helpful in communicating what could be complex information in a simple and straightforward way.

We'll take a moment to put this methodology into perspective. When we say size, segment, and niche, what do we actually mean? Suppose we use the automotive world as an example. Let's assume that there will be 17 million new vehicles sold this year in the United States. This would be helpful information, especially if we had no clue what the market "size" really was. Once the market size is known, it becomes clear that a better definition would be of added benefit. Suppose we then "segment" this overall market and use five major categories: small car, mid/large car, luxury/sport car, light truck, and crossover vehicles. We are making progress, especially if one of those segments is closer to our particular product or service offering.

But we still could use more definition. So, let's "niche" each segment further. Suppose we niche out the light truck segment. Let's use niche categories of pick-up trucks, mini-vans, and sport utility vehicles (SUV's). You see where this is going? And, once we have logically "sized, segmented, and niched" our market, we now have defined areas we can investigate and "assess the business health" of. Suppose we research and find the following historical and forecasted trends for the U.S. automobile market within our 2017–2020 planning horizon:

New Car Market Share by Segment	Model Year 2007–2016 (%)	Model Year 2017–2020 (%)
Crossover	21	31
Light truck	21	27
Small car	21	18
Mid/large car	22	15
Luxury/sport car	8	9
Others	7	–

Now we're getting somewhere. We know market and segment size. We have two segments growing considerably, two shrinking,

Product of Service Form Listing	General Area 1				General Area 2				Additional General Areas as Needed				Market Totals	
	Our Units	Area 1 Units	Price per Unit	Area 1 Dollars	Our Units	Area 2 Units	Price per Unit	Area 2 Dollars	Our Units	Area X Units	Price per Unit	Area X Dollars	Total Industry Units	Total Industry Dollars
Product Form A														
Product Form B														
Product Form C														
Product Form D														
Product Form E														
Product Form F														
Product Form G														
Product Form H														
Product Form J														
Product Form K														
Product Form L														
Additional Forms														
General Area Total														

Figure 3.1: The Bottom-Up Market Sizing Matrix.

one holding flat, and one being absorbed in some way into the others. Pretty good insight to have as you begin thinking about where to focus.

So, do you have this type of knowledge about your marketplace? Do you know its overall size? Do you have defined segments and niches? Do you know the respective business health of each? If not, in our experience, you are by all means not alone!

Let's get started then in helping you to get there.

Overview

The Bottom-Up Market Sizing Tool provides a method to estimate market size in the absence of hard data, or confidence in existing market intelligence. It is a structured approach that builds market size through definition of "General Areas" the business currently has defined or already uses. A series of sources and methods for identifying and estimating the size of each general area (in units and dollars) are provided. Review and refinement of estimates by internal and external experts provide triangulation toward a final market size definition. The tool is somewhat iterative in nature and 2–3 revisions from the first pass is common.

Time to Complete This Tool

A first pass using this tool can easily be completed in 1 day. With subject-matter expert availability, an effective working version for strategy planning can be ready in 3 days.

Discussion

There are a variety of starting points for this task. If you don't have a trade association that provides market information to its members, or your market isn't tied directly to commonly reported mainstream economic data, you will have to size your market from the bottom-up yourself. This tool can be used for this purpose.

If this is your first time estimating your market size, it is important to know up front that even with infinite resources, you will not get it perfect, and that is all right. What you are after is a timely estimate that is accurate enough to give you solid directional guidance.

This tool provides a structured way to size your market. No tool will be perfect, but the intelligent use of internal experts tempered with help from external sources such as end-users, dealer/distributors, trade associations, and competitors will go a long way to helping you define your market size.

What You Will Need to Construct the Tool

- A structure and/or a set of "General Areas" upon which to build your sizing estimates.

- Any information that can help provide initial perspective to market size (macro-economic sources).

- Any existing external intelligence relevant to framing market size (industry experts, purchased market studies or forecasts, suppliers).

- A listing of major competitors for each of your products or services, along with an estimate, or ability to estimate, their sales (in units or dollars).

- An understanding or an ability to estimate how many units are sold or performed annually into each "General Area" category (closely correlated data, application assumptions).

- A way to estimate the price of said product/service.

- A network of internal and external "experts" to help validate your assumptions.

Where to Get the Information

Structure and General Areas to Build the Estimate — This is the important starting place. What is the best way for you to begin your process of sizing the market? We need a structure around which to build our estimate. We call these our "General Areas." We will use Figure 3.1 as our tool to build and compile our estimate.

You have already seen that our process is going to drive toward segmentation. If you have ideas about or already use some form of market segmentation, we'd encourage you use them as your "General Areas."

But if you don't have a good feel for your segments yet, or how to best define them, there are other ways to begin the sizing exercise. You will need to define your "General Areas" a different way. A good place to start may be with the way you currently group your sales results. These can be defined as your "general areas." Or, perhaps you have salespeople who sell into certain areas or have particular expertise and customers. You can use the expertise categories or the customer types. Another idea might be to think about the territories that you are selling into and use geography breakdowns as your "general areas." However you decide to begin, you'll likely naturally begin to evolve into better defining business segments as you work this exercise.

Macro-Economic Metrics — Many helpful metrics are part of normal governmental or macro-economic reporting. Items such as the number of housing starts, number of automobiles produced annually, and number of oil rigs in the field are commonly available. Census data for many geographical areas also exists courtesy of your tax dollar (www.census.gov or www.commerce.gov). Additionally, your bank, lending institution, investment Banks, or even personal wealth management groups have access to this material and routinely compile and share it in many forms with commentary through monthly or quarterly update reports to their clients.

Industry or Trade Associations — Information can also come from industry-related associations. If your industry does provide this type of information and you are not a member, it might make sense to join for a year to obtain it and assess whether it has value going forward. Trade associations may supply compiled and summed marketplace production totals from confidential, voluntarily submitted production figures from its members (in essence, this can also form the denominator of a market share calculation).

One note on trade association data: in our experience, this data must be reviewed to ensure it represents your best picture of the market. We have rarely used this type of information at face value. You will need to ensure you know who is reporting. For instance, if the subset of companies reporting encompasses only 50% of all industry players, the number supplied will need to be multiplied by 2 to get a feel for total market size. You must also take into consideration the ethics of those companies reporting the data; there are no safeguards to ensure they are being truthful with their submittal. All in all, we believe trade association data is valuable, but it must be massaged for accuracy by your best judgement.

Lastly, trade associations usually have a companion trade publication that follows the industry. These magazines may be helpful, especially after national industry conventions or trade shows where presentations and predictions of industry performance by experts are summarized in article form.

Industry Experts — Many times retired executives from competitors form some type of consulting practice or end up on industry or trade association Boards. In some cases, a one-day engagement may provide general market information that will help (you should obviously not expect to extract confidential information, but the general observations on market size and trends may be useful).

Purchased Market Studies or Market Forecasts — These are prepared and supplied by independent market research firms. There are many of them out there, especially in B2B (business to business) situations. These may or may not be helpful, and they can be very expensive. We know firsthand of one report that was sold for about $5,000 a copy. The purchaser, in this case the recognized share leader with over 25% of the market, wasn't even listed as a player in the report on their industry. How accurate do you think the accompanying information was? As previously mentioned, we do not know of a circumstance where we've used these at face value. If you need to go this route, be sure you dig into the numbers before assuming them to be accurate.

Suppliers — Suppliers can also provide perspective here. They are usually assessing their business relative to you and your peer companies. For example, your first pass has your market sized at 100,000 units. You ask your component supplier, who you know provides to roughly half your competitors in the market, and she says her business looks like 75,000 units this year. You've just gotten insight suggesting you undersized your market by 50,000 units.

List of Competitors (and estimated sales in each Segment/Group Sales Area) — Again, initially, in-house sales or product management people are an obvious source of information here.

Closely Correlated Data — Correlations based on information you know can be helpful. For instance, if you exclusively supply 100,000 gallons of cleaning product annually to a 200-bed hospital, you can arrive at typical correlation of 500 gallons per bed per year. Multiplying that by the number of hospital beds in your market area gives you a good feel for market size.

Application Knowledge — It probably seems obvious by now, but those who know the general rules of thumb for your products/services will be of help here. For instance, "we receive on average 30 physical visits per year from a retail banking customer," or "we average 3.5 lab tests per patient visit and each takes an average of 15 minutes," or "every engine of said type produced in the United States needs an average of 8 linear feet of drive belt and 16 major gaskets."

Price or Value per Unit/Service — Again, your sales or similar group should be of help in this area. If you have a formal pricing department, they obviously are a source of information. You can always use your price as a default to begin the exercise if you are starting the process from scratch.

External Experts for Validating Assumptions — This information can come from a variety of places. The aforementioned list (industry professionals, suppliers, etc.) can provide a wealth of help. In addition, consider your channel partners (dealers, distributors, wholesalers, etc.) as well as key end-users.

How to Construct the Tool

The best way we've found is to use a simple spreadsheet as the base document. Here is our checklist of steps for this tool:

- Define your "general areas" for use in building up your estimate.

- Set up a "four-column group" for each "general area" you have chosen. Title the first column "Our Units," the second "Area Units," the third "Price per Unit," and the last "Area Dollars." There will probably be 5–10 of these four-column groups given your particular situation, depending on the number of "general areas" you sell into and choose to use (consider including general areas that you may not sell into but your competitors do, to better capture the true market size).

- Set each line item row as a product or service form that you sell. It is likely you will sell the same product form into multiple general areas. This structure allows you to capture that aspect (this also gives us a head start in the Chapter 4 segmenting exercise).

- Create on the far right of the spreadsheet total industry columns for both units and dollars. These columns will provide the overall market size. The final spreadsheet format should resemble Figure 3.1.

- For each product/service line item, estimate the total number of "general area" occurrences (column 2) per year. Input and use your sales numbers in column 1 as an initial starting point reference for a first pass (i.e. we provide 10,000 of this "Product Form A" per year to "General Area 1," and we estimate we are one of five equal-sized competitors; hence, the line item for "area units" would be 50,000 occurrences per year and be input into column 2 for General Area 1 on the Product Form A line).

- Insert your unit price (or estimated unit price) for each product form in each general area in the appropriate line in column 3 of each four-column general area grouping.

- Set up your spreadsheet to show column 4 as the product of columns 2 and 3. This will provide the dollar value of units in column 2 for each line item.

- Complete the unit estimate for each row line item and four-column "general area" group as appropriate.

- Total the results of columns 2 and 4 in each "four-column area group" to get the number of units and the dollar value of those units per year to obtain your total general area size.

- Sum the total of all "General Area" line items in the far-right two columns to begin building the market total size by product/service form line item.

- Calculate total market size by summing the far two right columns to calculate overall market size in units and dollars.

- Check this number against the summed totals of each column 2 and 4 in each "four-column segment group" as a check of overall industry size in both units and dollars.

- Perform a reasonableness test on the overall result with your team. We find projecting the spreadsheet on a screen with a core team of internal experts is a great way to wade through and create/validate your best first pass assumptions. It also gives that group perspective on where the soft areas are and enough process knowledge that they can efficiently pursue further refinement with internal or external experts.

- Once the team has tweaked a first pass, solicit external expert comment and feedback on the result. Focus on areas that you see as needing more validation.

- Adjust the spreadsheet as needed until you get a final result you feel is representative.

If your iterations start falling within 3–5% of each other, we'd suggest ending the exercise there. At this point, your resulting information is far more accurate than where you initially started, and it should be more than directional enough for you to move forward in timely fashion. If you are doubtful of stopping here, consider the payback on spending extra resources (money and time) for the increased accuracy in what likely will be a diminishing returns type of scenario. Regardless, remember you have the coming year to further research any areas in question during the normal course of business. And now that you have a structured tool, you will now think in terms of that structure and will likely be more effective and alert to information you might have dismissed in the past.

Key Strategic Questions

There are a number of strategic questions elicited by this exercise. Here are a few we'd likely pursue:

- Is the market size developed significantly larger or smaller than you originally thought? What were you assuming incorrectly, and is it an issue with other parts of the business?

- Are you confident in the external sources used?

- What areas or assumptions used in the build-up do you feel need to be more accurate? What can you do moving forward to build confidence or improve the accuracy in those areas?

- Are any of the sources you used published routinely enough (census data, trade association data, etc.) such that you can use them in "real-time" to track overall market changes (monthly, quarterly, annually, forecast revisions, etc.)?

- How reflective are the "General Areas" you used of an actual market segmentation you would want to use going forward?

Our Favorite Anecdote Using This Tool

We are fond of the story of a MBA student in the mid-1980s (it even might have been one of us!). The marketing class was mired in a group exercise they were trying to be extremely precise on. Frustrated with the class missing the bigger picture, the professor informed the group he was changing that day's class material. He assigned the class a task and informed them it was due in 30 minutes. The accuracy of the answer would account for a major portion of their grade. The task: estimate the number of piano tuners in a particular large metropolitan city. The professor referenced the current time, said the task started now, and immediately left the room.

The class, a bit stunned, got down to work. Now this was before the Internet search capabilities available today (in fact, fax machines were the new technological marvel). The class broke the task down logically. Of the students in class, how many total families could they think of? How many of them had pianos? How many estimated families in that city? How many pianos does that imply? How many times does a piano need to be tuned? How long does it take to tune a piano? You get the picture. Each time an educated guess had to be made, tempered with reasonable challenges, and agreed upon to move to the next step.

Exactly, 30 minutes later the professor came in and asked for their answer. The class said to the best of their estimates there were 50 piano tuners in that city. The professor smiled and then dropped a 7-inch-thick book called the Yellow Pages for that city on a desk (those of you under 35 years of age can Google "Yellow Pages"). The professor asked one of the students to find the listing for piano tuners and count them. The answer equally stunned the class — it was 52.

The Market Segmentation Tool

Strategy Question: *How do I better understand the make-up of my overall market?*

Segment 1	Segment 2	Segment 3	Seg. 4	Seg. 5	Seg. 6

$400 Million	$200 Million	$200 Million	$100 M	$50 M	$50 M

Total Market Size = $1 Billion

Figure 4.1: A Typical Market Segmentation Tool Output.

Overview

Now that we have our market sized, it is important to also spend similar efforts on defining segments and sizing them appropriately. This tool basically mirrors and builds on the result from the Bottom-Up Market Sizing Tool. At this stage, emphasis turns to breaking the overall market into actionable segments. The tool output casts the segments in a rectangular graphic, made up of one column for each segment. Segment width is representative of its size relative to the other segments. The width of all segment columns, added together, ties back and equals the overall size of the market. The tool output is a powerful start toward further niching of markets that we address in Chapter 5.

Time to Complete This Tool

A first pass can be completed within 2–3 hours. A final pass can usually be completed in 2–3 days with subject-matter expert availability and good team interaction and input.

Introduction

You understand the size of your organization's market, and that is an important starting point. But no entity can be all things to all people. It is critical to dig deeper to understand the different segments and niches within your market. In our Four P approach, understanding these segments is critical because each will have different needs for Product, Pricing, or Placement.

If you have come to this chapter first, you are likely in a position where you understand how big your market is. You have a trade association or other means that provide the market size for you, which is a good place to start. But the total market is normally way too big to act upon. You also likely understand that you need to know more.

Consistent with the "size, segment, and niche" approach discussed in Chapter 3's introduction, you are now at the stage where you need to "segment" the overall market in some way. What does that mean? It means starting the process of breaking your overall market into smaller and more defined groupings. It is important we get this stage right before we delve into further "niching" detail.

What You Will Need to Construct the Tool

- The total market size you are working in relevant metrics (units, dollars, etc.).

- Definition of your segments.

- A method to allocate your total market across the defined segments.

- A team of internal and external experts to help you validate your assumptions.

- A simple spreadsheet software.

Where to Get the Information

Total Market Size — The total market size can come from a number of areas. If you have good trade association data, or your total market is directly related to regularly reported statistics (housing starts, automobiles produced, etc.), you have a well-defined source. If not, we encourage you to reference Chapter 3, where we discuss how to develop your market size in the absence of the aforementioned hard data. Please note that if you purchased and are using some type of market study or industry evaluation, be sure you review it for accuracy. As we discuss in Chapter 3, we rarely take these numbers at face value, as we find they usually need some refinement for accuracy in our particular situations.

Definition of Segments — Creativity in assigning segments and niches is important, but don't get carried away and overthink it. It is easy to do and many fall into that trap. You already know we approach the tools in this book with the mindset of a time and resource constrained leader — and we can't afford to waste time and effort. So how do you efficiently define the best way to segment your overall market. Here are a few thoughts.

First, start with what you already know. Having been in the business, you probably have inherently split your business or organization into what may be a logical set of groupings (or "general areas" from Chapter 3). Start here. Use those groupings (especially if they seem to fall into the logic discussed below) as segments as we move toward sizing them. The test on whether they are the right groupings will come when we try to niche them with the simple criteria we use in Chapter 5. If they aren't, then circle back and try again with the following guidance.

Second, are you B2C (business to consumer) or B2B (business to business)? This is important and can help expedite your effort if you are segmenting for the first time. If you are primarily selling to individual consumers, your segmentation criteria will be different than if you are selling to other businesses. In general, here are some thought starters for B2C or B2B customers.

Business to Consumer — Personal consumer characteristics will be relevant to the grouping segments you choose. Typical segments that may be appropriate are:

- Demographics — income, age, gender, health, etc.
- Lifestyle — groupings based on lifestyle. Some popular groupings are: DINK (dual income no kids), SINK (single income no kids), SITKOM (single income two kids oppressive mortgage), GLAM (graying, leisured, and moneyed), YUPPY (young, upwardly mobile, prosperous, professional), MUPPY (middle age, upwardly mobile, professional, prosperous), etc.
- Consumption — none, minor, occasional, average, heavy, etc.
- User status — first time, light user, regular user, never use.

You get the idea. Many times you will see a related term called "Psychographics" in B2C segmentation literature, which basically means arranging consumers into some type of group or cluster based on criteria like these.

Business to Business — The grouping categories may be similar, but the criteria are different, as we are shifting from personal to organizational. Here are some thoughts:

- Demographic — size of the business, number of employees, etc.

- NAICS (North American Industry Classification System) or the older SIC (Standard Industrial Classification) codes. NAICS was adopted by the U.S. Office of Management and Budget in 2004, superseding SIC codes. Both were designed to facilitate government reporting and tracking. They are different, so both may be helpful in visioning segmentation approaches.

- Generic Industry — classifications that reflect broad application of your products or services (i.e., automotive, oil & gas, medical, agricultural, etc.).

- Geography — where is the business located (i.e., regional, state, national, international).

- Application — ranges in equipment size, use or capacity, residential/commercial/industrial classification (i.e., low/moderate/heavy duty cycles), etc.

Going back to our example in Chapter 3, what B2C criteria do you think the automotive companies used to arrive at the five major segments we discussed in the introduction? While they are very sophisticated in their market research, conceptually we could make a case for some type of "lifestyle" approach as a segmentation method. It could look something like this:

New Car Market Segment	Lifestyle	Comment
Crossover	DINK	Nice vehicle to haul our bikes and kayaks
Light truck	SITKOM	I need to haul stuff myself (kids, home repair items)

(Continued)

New Car Market Segment	Lifestyle	Comment
Small car	SINK	New, environmentally conscious college grad
Mid/large car	MUPPY	Working empty nesters
Luxury/sport car	GLAM	Retired and enjoying life

Purely speculation on our part here, but the point is you can see thinking being used to narrow the overall market into smaller segments. Note other criteria could also have been used (how about income demographics?). Again, don't overthink it. There is no right or wrong answer. Among your team, pick the approach you best feel represents your business and go from there.

If B2C or B2B does not accurately portray your organization, try applying the concepts to your situation. If you are a charitable or social service, use the B2C mindset if your primary mission is focused on individuals, and the B2B mindset if your focus is on groups.

Method to allocate the total market across defined segments — This one is straightforward and relatively simple with the right structure. If you have completed Chapter 3, you'll see we've already set you up. If not, we are going to use the tool in Chapter 3 in reverse.

In Chapter 3, we used the Bottom-Up Market Sizing Tool to estimate our total market size. We did this by defining each of our product or service line items by what we called "general areas" at that time. By listing each product or service line item in Figure 3.1, we worked — from left to right — by "general area" of the business to establish the far two right-hand columns defining the total market size in units and dollars. Now having that total market established, we want to work back to the left, replacing the "general area" groupings with your new "segment" groupings. If you used your thinking on segments for the general area categories, you are already done (how's that for saving time?)! If not, we'll want to work backwards to break down the total market size — by your product or service forms — into the segments you have newly defined. The resulting totals for each four-column segment grouping provide that insight. Figure 4.2 illustrates how the Bottom-Up Market Sizing Tool is now used for segment sizing.

Team of internal and external experts to triangulate data — Similar to the process of sizing the market by general areas from Chapter 3, we use the same process to ensure we have agreement on the proper unit allocation to our new segments. Be prepared; this may be harder than you think. For example, your trade association reports the market consists of 1 million units for B2B line item Product Form A in Figure 4.2. Allocating them backwards across the segments (which now replace the general areas) may require team input to arrive at a conclusion.

Or, say you worked through Chapter 3, used geographic criteria for your general areas, and arrived at that 1 million units for Product Form A (let's call it a steering wheel). But, by now replacing the general areas with your newly defined segments (suppose we call them automotive, light duty truck, classes 3–5 truck, classes 6–7 truck, and class 8 truck), you now estimate, with better accuracy, 1.5 million units for that steering wheel line item. You may want to go back, apply the new segments to the market sizing tool, and concurrently work to resize the market by the newly defined segments.

Sizing the market and allocating by segment is an iterative process, and it will need a core team to help get you there. The good news is that the results will converge quickly. We find that 2–3 iterations pretty much get us to a solid conclusion. And as mentioned in Chapter 3, if your iterations are converging to within 3–5%, the law of diminishing returns would imply this is probably a good place to stop.

Simple Spreadsheet Program — This can be Excel or any other like program. You will need this for the spreadsheet exercise of Figure 4.2 and construction of the summary chart of Figure 4.1.

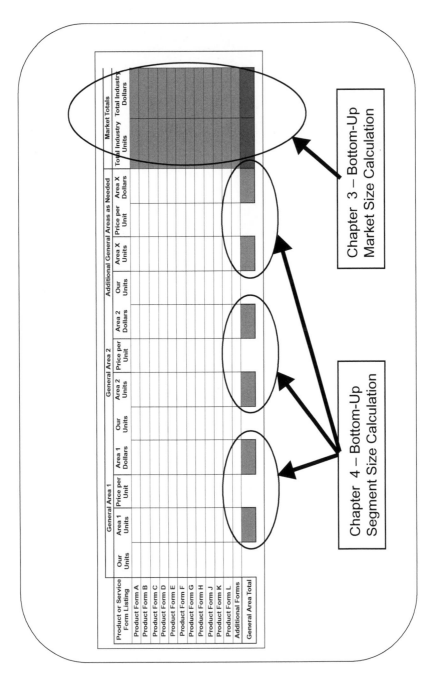

Figure 4.2: Bottom-Up Calculation of Market Segment Sizes.

How to Construct the Tool

- If you have already defined your segments and their sizes, jump below to the "Construct Figure 4.1" bullet. If you have not, continue on here.

- If you haven't worked through Chapter 3, construct Figure 3.1 consistent with instructions there. However, use your newly defined segments in place of the "general areas" for the four-column groupings.

- Define (or revisit appropriateness of) the product/service form line items you provide and list them on the far left of the spreadsheet.

- Ensure the far-right "Market Total" columns are reflective of your current thinking. This is the starting point for sizing your newly defined segments. (If you have worked through Chapter 3, simply use and/or tweak the values you have already developed there.)

- Begin allocating, now right to left, the total number of units or dollars from the Market Total columns for each line item back through the defined segments.

- You are finished when the sum totals of the four-column segment groupings equal the total market size numbers in the far-right columns.

- Construct Figure 4.1 with the output from the completed Figure 4.2 evaluation.

- In your spreadsheet program, proportion columns by size corresponding with the size of the segments (i.e., if Segment 1 was $400 million size the column width to say 40, Segment 2 at $200 million size it at 20, etc.).

- Label each column with the segment name.

- Reference the total market size at the bottom of the columns (merge and center this label). You can identify and label each segment size (in dollars, units, or whatever metric you chose); we typically do this.

- You should then have a graphic resembling Figure 4.1.

Strategy Implications

Believe it or not, this simple effort you went through and the summary chart in the form of Figure 4.1 convey a wealth of information and perspective. We like this chart format for so many reasons. First, it is simple and powerful; it conveys the overall market size, and each segment size is reflected in width relative to the entire market and the other segments. Suddenly, the entire market is broken into intelligent segments that better reflect the customer base. And it is so simple to understand that you can get your team, executives, Board, or essentially any group on the same page in minutes. Lastly, the structure lends itself for additional niching and business health assessment information coming in Chapters 5 and 6.

Another important element of Figure 4.1 is perspective. Are the segment allocations, or even the total market size, exactly right? Probably not. And as we mentioned before, that is all right as long as we feel they are close. Why? Because we're not so concerned with whether Segment 1 is really $405 Million or $390 Million instead of the $400 Million we show. What we are interested in is the fact that Segment 1 is roughly twice the size of Segments 2 and 3, and each of them are roughly twice the size of Segment 4. The relevance is important to understand. Suppose all six segments shown were equal in size? Or that Segment 1 was 90% of the entire market? That perspective is really important to have — and you would be surprised at how many companies don't.

Here are some of the strategic implications we'd likely pursue based on this tool:

- Does the result make sense to you?

- Were any of the resulting segment sizes different than you initially thought or expected? Why?

- Does this result challenge any pre-conceived notions prevalent in your organization or culture? Is there any work you will need to do to ease the group into the new understanding?

- Were the split and relative size of your segments a surprise to you?

- Have your efforts to this point been consistent with the size and split of your segments?

- What is your market share in each segment? In case you missed it, you actually have that information now: the total units for each segment is simply the denominator and your units the numerator, for a market share calculation.

- Is your share what you expected? If not, why? Are you higher or lower than you thought?

Our Favorite Anecdote Using This Tool

A talented executive was just promoted to President of a Business Unit within a $1 Billion subsidiary of a major Fortune 500 company. This company was well regarded for its strategic planning process and rigor. As luck of timing would have it, the annual strategic plan meeting was quickly coming. His BU was traditionally very profitable, but his dilemma was that revenue growth had stalled. As a result, this BU had become less exciting relative to its higher growth peers and was being increasingly seen as a "cash cow" legacy entity. He knew he needed to reverse that trend.

He began his effort by trying to take a fresh approach at sizing his market. Industry statistics and years of market leadership were helpful in understanding its overall size. Using the methods of this chapter, he was able to break the greater market down to meaningful segments that made sense to him and his team. He also intelligently included parts and aftermarket revenue streams as two of his four segments in his segmentation map.

At this point he made some market share calculations. He knew his company served their segments very well, but was a bit surprised to find exactly how well, as market shares were well above 60% — in all segments (by the way, note how easy it is to show market share with this tool)! His growth dilemma was pretty clear: his share was too high! His team was rightfully proud of the leadership position they had carved out. The problem was that they were content with that. Customers simply needed to have a second competitive source to keep pricing in line. Hence, there was little opportunity for growth by future share gain. His segmented market map looked something like Figure 4.3

With the market and segment situation presented in this way, the President began to ponder the problem. He involved his team. The number two player in the market was also a division of a Fortune 500 company. It didn't make sense that number two could survive on the scraps of his strong segment shares. He challenged

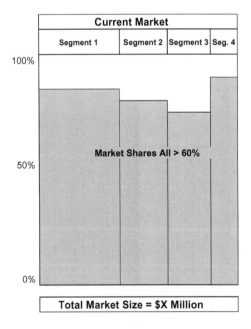

Figure 4.3: Market Segmentation for Business Unit.

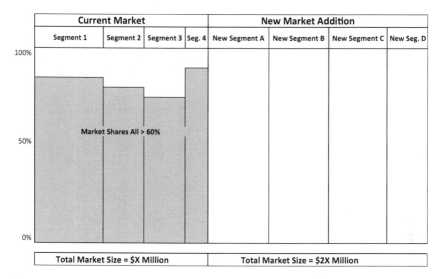

Figure 4.4: Expanded Opportunity Using the Market Segmentation Tool.

his team to find out where else his competitor was selling their product.

After further investigation by his team, he began to understand there was a completely different major market using similar products, and it was much larger than his. The situation was starting to make more sense. Once they sensed it was larger, they decided to size and segment it for better understanding. Using the tools in Chapters 3 and 4, they got their answer. Figure 4.4 shows the new market segmentation that resulted from their work. Note their estimate was that the new market was twice the size of theirs.

Including this new market space, the executive found himself at a combined market share of less than 30% with ample room to grow. With this new information, and using many of the ensuing tools in this book, he defined a set of new initiatives and activities to penetrate the previously unknown opportunity. His strategic plan meeting went well. Using the one-page output of Figure 4.4, he took his Board through the process, the newly defined market and segments, and the steps he planned to use to re-establish a growth trajectory for his business.

The Segment
Niching Tool

Strategy Question: *Now that my market is sized and segmented, how do I better understand segment niches?*

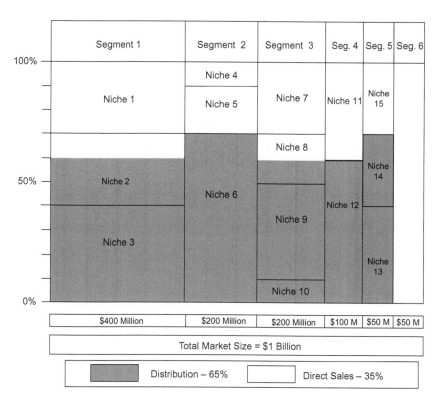

Figure 5.1: A Completed "Size, Segment and Niche" Effort.

Overview

The Segment Niching Tool gets to the next important level of detail in the understanding of an organization's market. The Market Segmentation Tool output from Chapter 4 serves as the starting point. We use a simple two-question approach, "Why they buy?" and "How they buy?," to help define segment niches in a timely and efficient fashion. Once niches are defined, we size those niches in much the same way that we sized the segments in Chapter 4. Once we understand our best niching categories and their size, we add a scale to the y-axis of the Segment Niching Tool output (Figure 4.1) and carve each segment column further into niches (shown by smaller rectangular sections), whose areas proportionately represents the size of that niche. By superimposing the "How they buy?" niching (by shading) over the "Why they buy?" niches (shown as rectangles), a market map begins to emerge in the form of Figure 5.1. Both the rigor of the two-question approach and the power of structuring the output in this simple one-page format provide the strategy team with valuable information in a very timely fashion.

Time to Complete the Tool

A first pass at niche additions can be completed easily in 2–3 hours. Confirmation and validation can be completed in 2–3 days, given internal and external expert availability.

Introduction

Continuing with our "size, segment, and niche" approach, niching segments is the next important step. A word of warning at this point: if you worked through Chapter 4, you can see how segmenting can be an area in which you could spend a lot of wasted time. Our advice there was to not overthink it; use your best judgement and go. Well, niching markets presents even more of a challenge. Niching is a potential time and resource sink; some would say it's unlike any other found in nature. You can spend days, weeks, and even months trying to niche out market segments. If you research this topic on the web you'll find numerous academic concepts, theories, and even statistical models. None, however, take you from theory to practical application. You can literally run circles around yourself logically — and many do. We certainly did, and have the strategy scars to show for it.

So how can we save you from that pain? We again are practical in our approach and have learned the hard way that we rarely have the time to engage in numerous attempts at being niche-clever, and therefore we end up making things way more difficult than they need to be. Our approach is simple and to the point, and as a result, we have gotten to the crux of our niches in record time (at least in our opinions).

Our niching criteria start with two, and only two, questions:

(1) Why they buy?

(2) How they buy?

When you think about it, these really get to three of our Four Ps. "Why they buy?" from the Product and Price perspective, and "How they buy?" (or how you go to market) as the Placement perspective. We niche by both questions — but only by those questions. The "Why they buy?" and "How they buy?" may, and probably will, have different answers for each segment. That is the power of this tool approach! You focus on the key questions for each segment rather than trying to find a niching technique that fits across all segments.

Lastly, while we like to niche by both questions, we oftentimes like to show the results of both niching exercises on one chart. By adding this information in the form developed in the Market Segmenting Tool, we convey in simple terms what many find difficult to capture and explain.

Let's look at Figure 5.2 in some detail to help explain the output for this tool. This reflects a completed niching exercise based

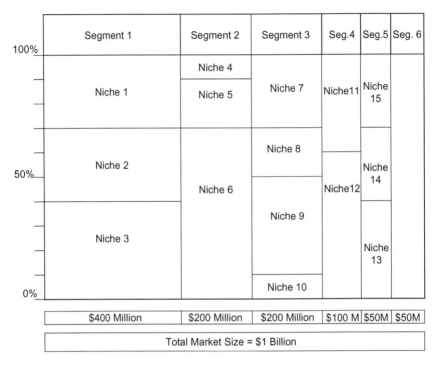

Figure 5.2: Niching on the "Why They Buy?" Question.

on the "Why they buy?" question. You will note we are starting with Figure 4.1 — the output for the Market Segmenting Tool. We add our niching results to arrive at Figure 5.2. We have niched out each segment where appropriate, sized each niche, and shown that niche information proportionately within each segment. For simplicity, we have labeled the niches from 1 to 15. We also add a simple percentage scale to the left Y-axis of the diagram. With this format, you can show niche size perspective within both the segment and overall market.

For example, look at Niche 3. How big is it? Well, just the visual area of the boxes gives you an immediate clue, but in 5 seconds, you can see it is 40% of a $400 Million segment, or $160 Million. And in 10 seconds, I conclude that Niche 3 alone is almost equal in size to Segments 4, 5, and 6 combined. This simple format provides you and your strategy team a "map" if you will, of your markets, segments, and niches. But we aren't finished yet.

We also need to niche out based on the second question, "How they buy?" This one is a bit easier because go-to market approaches are a bit more finite.

In thinking about the results for each of the two niching methods, we often like to superimpose both results on the same chart. This works especially well if you only have two or three channels to market. The process starts with Figure 5.2 as originally shown with defined "Why they buy?" Niches 1–15. To that we combine the "How they buy?" niching result. Figure 5.3 helps show this evolution (and this result is pretty typical).

As you can see, we now incorporate the results of both niching questions in one chart. The shading adds the extra dimension of the "How they buy?" results. In this case, roughly two-thirds of the segments are served by Distribution, and one-third by a Direct Sales force. You can also see that some niches are exclusively Distribution or Direct Sales, and some use both (i.e., Niches 2 and 8). You now have a powerful set of information in an easily digestible format to use in developing your strategic initiatives.

What You Will Need to Construct the Tool

- The total market broken into segments you feel properly reflect your business.

- Definition of niche criteria for each segment (this will be aided by our two questions).

- A method to define niche size within each segment.

- A team of internal and external experts to help you validate your assumptions.

- A simple spreadsheet software.

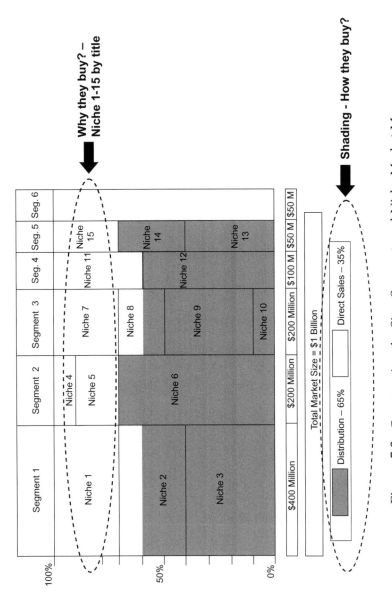

Figure 5.3: Constructing the Size, Segment, and Niche Market Map.

Where to Get the Information

Segmented market information — Use the output from Chapter 4 to begin this exercise. If you are starting here, recreate your current understanding in a format similar to Figure 4.1.

Definition of niche criteria — This obviously is the heart of the tool, as it is the way you save untold time and effort, or you save your marketing or sales groups hours of unintended frustration. We discipline ourselves to stay focused on the two niche questions: "How they buy?" and "Why they buy?"

How they buy? — As previously mentioned, this element is a bit easier to get a handle on. Figure 5.2 uses distribution and direct sales categories, and typically we'd see two or three go-to-market approaches in a segment. But, there are many options. Other "How they buy?" categories to consider in your niching exercise include retail sales, catalog sales, Internet sales, and telephone sales, among others that may be out there that are unique and relevant to your situation.

Why they buy? — This is the one ripe for bewilderment. Each segment is unique from the others; otherwise you wouldn't have chosen to categorize them differently. The "Why they buy?" question should be asked individually of each segment. Use this queue to help understand and define the main need being satisfied. For instance, in our automobile example, one of the segments defined is Light Trucks. Why do customers buy light trucks? Perhaps the reason is they need to move a lot of "stuff." That stuff may be physical objects, large families, or both. Hence, niches of pick-up trucks, mini-vans, and SUVs fall out.

As we mention, there are many ways to niche a segment, and you can take it multiple directions. We suggest not straying from the two core questions for each segment. There may be more than one good way to niche, too. Choose the best niching categories that fall out from your team's best efforts. Discipline yourself to this and we feel you will get to a "size, segment, and niche" framework that will allow you to move forward in a fraction of the time it would have otherwise.

Method to define the Niche size — If you don't have a feel for the sizes of your niches, or you feel estimates would not be accurate enough, there is an easy way to size them: use the Market Segmenting tool of Chapter 4. There we broke down the overall, already-defined market into segments. Here, you can simply use the same methodology to now break down the overall, already-defined segment into niches. Substitute "segment size" for "market size" in the two far-right columns, and substitute "niche size" for "general area or segment" in the four-column groups.

Team of internal and external experts — Similar to the segment definition and sizing effort, a trusted team of internal experts (usually for category definition and initial size estimates) and external experts (for validation of the category definition and size estimates) is needed. We don't want this to appear to be a huge group and effort. A group of 3–5 people invited for a 2- to 3-hour breakfast or lunch meeting can usually make great progress here — especially when you respect the rigor already imposed by the two-question approach.

Software — An adequate spreadsheet user can construct the charts in this chapter. We are by no means spreadsheet super-users, and we put the figures in this chapter together in less than 1 hour. There is also a software program called Mekko Graphics (mekkographics.com) that can be used to create the box-in-box graphics consistent with our market maps. Lastly, we have also built graphics like these out of presentation software (PowerPoint, etc.).

How to Construct the Tool

- Start with a representation of Figure 4.1, the output of the Market Segmentation Tool.

- For each market segment, choose niche categories based on the two-question "Why they buy?" and "How they buy?" approach.

- Size each segment niche using either the process in the Market Segmentation Tool or other method.

- Validate your sizing with internal and external experts.

- Add the segment niche information for the "Why they buy?" niching to Figure 4.1. Reflect the size of each niche by boxing out the area corresponding to the niche size in the appropriate segment column.

- Superimpose (if possible) the "How they buy?" niching results by adding shading, color, or some other contrasting means to the newly updated chart from the last step. This "Market Map" result should resemble Figure 5.3 in some way. If this isn't practical, develop a second chart based on Figure 4.1 and similarly add the "How they buy?" niche information there. You will then have two "Market Maps," one for each niche question.

Strategy Implications

This tool begins to bring real focus to the strategist. The knowledge of market size, identified and sized segments, and further sized and defined niches is very powerful. In fact, we could fill pages of potential strategy questions and ramifications. Here are some basic ones that we might suggest to get you started in understanding your particular situation.

- Does the "size, segment, and niche" result portrayed in your graphic make sense to you? Does it pass your test for reasonableness? If not, why?

- If this is your first pass at an effort like this, is the result surprising to you? Why? What does your answer tell you about your previous methods of characterizing your market?

- If you already had a strategic planning effort, how does this result differ from what you used in the past? What does this tell you about the systems and approaches you currently have in place? Are there areas you need to address?

- Are the niching categories so different from your current reporting structure that you will need to make significant changes to pursue these categories further?

- Looking at the niching results, are there any niches that surprise you in size or complexity (i.e., multiple channel overlaps?)

- Are the current initiatives you have in place consistent with the new picture of your market, segments, and the resulting characterization of the niches? If not, where are the inconsistencies?

Our Favorite Anecdote Using This Tool

Part 1 — A new leader was taking his team through his strategic planning methodology, which was proving to be more rigorous than what they were used to. The leader had been advised by his new team that he was wasting his time because their planning process was already very good. As a new leader and team outsider, his team recommended he default to their much more experienced thinking. Being new and knowing the Market Map tool was a good way for him to learn the markets objectively himself, he politely refused their suggestion and asked for their help in constructing it.

He actually had to start with the Market Sizing Tool (Chapter 3) because he got no response to how big their addressable market really was. Once that was completed, he moved on to the Market Segmenting Tool (Chapter 4) because again, there was no answer to the similar question as to how big each of the chosen addressable segments was. Once done there, they moved on to niching out the markets (Chapter 5). Each market segment had differing answers to the "Why they buy?" question — and the exercise actually challenged the status quo. But all agreed the new niches actually defined the business much better. Having only two paths to market, the "How they buy?" question was a relatively simple task.

The effort of sizing the market to totally niching it out took about 2–3 weeks to complete. The CEO put all the information in the suggested chart form. We have actually structured Figure 5.1 to conceptually reflect the output of their result. It was a bit startling for him. He studied the chart and then compared it back to the direction his team had been on just days before. Looking at Figure 5.1, we'll give you one guess as to which one of the six segments shown was the pre-existing choice for current and future company focus. It was Segment 5 — one of the two smallest.

Since the team really didn't have the perspective for definition of their segments or niches, this result was a total surprise for them. The size of their markets and niches gave them perspective on overall market share and segment share. The CEO pointed out their highest share, and market strength was in Segment 1, Niches 2 and 3. The team argued that the reason for the Segment 5 focus was its high growth rate. The CEO said that was a good observation — and asked what the relative growth rates for each six segments were. Again, he was met with silence; they had never done the exercise.

So the CEO took the team on the last effort, discussed in Chapter 6, to assess the business health of each segment toward constructing a finished Market Map. We'll conclude Part 2 of the story in Chapter 6.

The Market Map Tool

Strategy Question: Is there a simple yet comprehensive way to characterize the business health of my markets, segments, and niches?

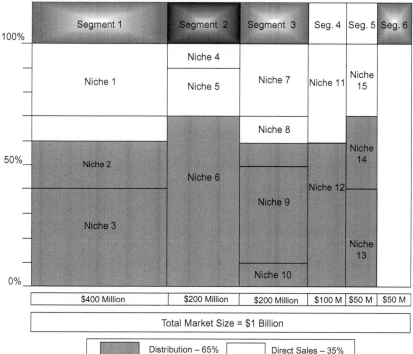

Figure 6.1: The Completed Market Map Tool.

Overview

It is important to understand the attractiveness of your market segments within the planning horizon being considered. This tool takes the user through ways to evaluate segments for attractiveness toward use in prioritizing their importance to product/service and channel actions. We build on the Market Segmentation Tool (Chapter 4) by assigning an attractiveness code to each segment column heading. We then rank and order the segments, with the one chosen most attractive positioned on the far left, and those next best ones located in decreasing ranked order to the right. When we add this detail to the Segment Niching Tool output from Chapter 5, we have a completed Market Map Tool, shown in Figure 6.1. The Market Map is among the most powerful visuals we know of for explaining overall market, segment, and niche and business health information in a simple one-page format.

Time to Complete the Tool

This tool should take 1–5 days depending on the availability of information you choose to build into your rating index.

Introduction

Understanding how strong your market segments will be during your planning horizon is extremely important. But how many companies out there have taken the time to forecast that? Certainly, the process of creating a strategic plan will help surface this need. Well, at least we think it would. But you would be surprised on how many organizations have put together strategic plans, or at least their versions of strategic plans, that treat this area superficially or gloss over it altogether.

Perhaps one reason is that they don't know where to find the information. Or how to use it. Or how to put it in proper perspective to arrive at a forward-looking forecast. You must spend time on understanding your environment, market, segments, and niches first. You must be able to put the situation into perspective and choose the right places to compete. But some argue that forecasts are simply that — forecasts. And yes, we hear arguments that with the volatility of business today, major geo-political events have the potential of rendering a forecast irrelevant. But that doesn't mean you shouldn't put a forecast together. Even if the worst case materializes, you at least need a baseline from which to navigate from.

So we springboard off the Market Segmentation Tool from Chapter 4. From this tool, our overall market has been broken into individual segments by size. The width of the column is the representative of the size of the segment, with the width of all segments totaling our overall market size estimate.

Our next goal is to somehow construct an "attractiveness metric" for each segment that is helpful to our business understanding. If you have been following our book in order, you can see we have already attempted to size, segment, and niche the overall market. At this point, we are looking purely at assessing the general health of the segment. Figure 6.2 shows a resulting attractiveness ranking as a simple segment growth rate range. There are many other elements that can go into this ranking. You should decide what metric, or combinations of metrics, makes sense for your situation. If you want to combine a growth rate and gross margin capture aspect to your metric, go for it. The point here is to rate the attractiveness of your segments in way that is meaningful to you.

Once this is done, we like to rank the overall attractiveness of the segments for the planning horizon. We reshape the chart by placing what we feel is the most attractive segment column to us on the far left, stacking the next bests in decreasing order to the right. Figure 6.2 captures both steps, as the segment attractiveness criteria have been added to the headings and the segments have been ranked 1−6 (Segment 1 most important far left to Segment 6 as least important far right). As mentioned previously, the combination of this work with the output of the Segment Niching Tool provides the one-page output of Figure 6.1.

(*Authors' Note: In our Market and Four P methodology, we stress knowing our markets before we start evaluating our products and services*

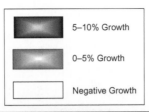

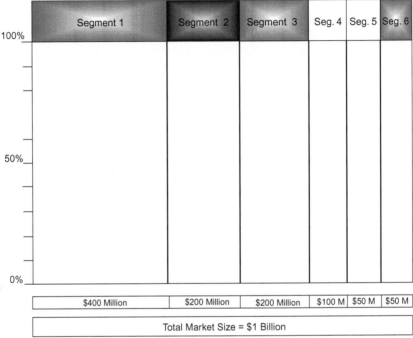

Figure 6.2: Assigning a "Business Health" Ranking to Segments.

*against them. Figure 6.1 provides this important information. Rest
assured we will be using the information generated in Chapters 3-6, and
the one-page output formats directly in the ensuing chapters.)*

What You Will Need to Construct the Tool

- A list of the market segments you have determined are relevant to your strategic plan.

- A way to evaluate the attractiveness of each chosen segment for your planning horizon.

- A final ranking of segments, based on the attractiveness chosen, for final graphing.

- If you want to complete the Market Map (Figure 6.1), you will need the output from Chapter 5.

- A simple spreadsheet program.

Where to Get the Information

List of relevant market segments — The Market Segmentation Tool (Chapter 4) is helpful in constructing this information. If you are starting the book here, you will need to list the segments you now follow. It would be helpful if you knew the overall size of each segment to add perspectives as shown in Figure 4.1 or Figure 6.2. If you do not have that, you can equally size columns for now.

A way to establish an "attractiveness metric" for each segment — The sources of information used in Chapter 3 (The Bottom-Up Market Sizing Tool) are also valuable in helping you to understand said expert's planning horizon thinking in each of their particular areas of expertise. We reference you back to Chapter 3 for further detail, but as a quick reminder those sources include:

- Macro-economic sources (US Government or Department of Commerce)

- Industry or Trade Associations

- Industry Experts

- Purchased Market Studies or Market Forecasts (note the cautions mentioned)

- Suppliers

- Segment or Group Sales Areas

- Competitors

In addition, since you are looking for specific segment information, you can use key players or industries within those segments to help you gain perspective. Additional areas we find helpful are:

- *Public Company segment or industry leaders* — Public companies are required to make various financial disclosures as part of their normal course of business. Reports such as Form 10-K or 10-Q, annual reports, etc. can provide insights as to how they are looking at the future for their respective industries. Examples range from Wells Fargo for banking and financial services, Caterpillar for mining and infrastructure construction, John Deere for agriculture, Pulte Group for residential construction, etc. Spending a few hours on the top two or three public company players in each of your chosen segments can be very enlightening.

- *Analysts covering these public companies and segments* — Many investor organizations (pension funds, index funds, etc.) have paid analysts that follow industries and individual public companies within them. They analyze the quarterly and annual reports and make on-site visits (at the companies and at their trade shows) to get a feel for them and for the industry in general (the analysts following a public company can be identified on the public company websites, usually somewhere in the "investor relations" section). The analysts provide forward-looking investment guidance on the industry and individual companies, resulting in stock price targets, and buy, sell, or hold recommendations for themselves or their clients. We have found this source and their work helpful in confirming and shaping our thoughts on projecting segment (and potentially niche) business health for our planning horizon.

Once you have the raw data, determine what metric you will use to assess your segments. Create an appropriate range within that metric and label them in some good, average, and poor category (again you see we simply used a growth rate in our examples).

A final ranking of your business segments — The appropriate leaders at your company will need to evaluate the attractiveness. This is important because further thinking will be influenced by the segments you judge as most attractive. Note the largest segment, or the segment scoring the highest attractiveness rating, may not be chosen as your most important segment. In our Figure 6.1 example, a case can be made that the largest Segment 1 with slower growth may still offer more business potential than a smaller Segment 2 with a higher growth rate — hence, we show it as the most attractive segment on the left of the chart.

Spreadsheet program — Excel works well initially. Depending on the number of segments and niches explored in Chapters 4–6, the spreadsheets may get a bit more complex. While we've had no problems with Excel, you may find a more sophisticated software more helpful. Again, we have also used Mekko Graphics (mekkographics.com) with some success for the box-in-box niching format.

How to Construct the Tool

- Identify the key segments relevant to your planning horizon.

- Create an "attractiveness metric" and use it to label each segment.

- Rank and prioritize each segment and list them in prioritized fashion.

- Create a simple spreadsheet chart in the form of Figure 4.1 or use the output from Figure 5.1 as constructed.

- Color code the heading of each segment column to indicate the attractiveness you assigned to it.

- Structure (or restructure if you are using the output of Chapter 4 or 5) the columns to reflect the chosen priority. The highest priority segment displayed on the far left, and the others in decreasing priority to the right.

Strategy Implications

We find we can spend a lot of time with this chart when completed, especially if it has the elements of Chapter 5 included. Again, the complete "Market Map" of Figure 6.1 is a representative example of such a chart. The clean and concise presentation of the business situation just naturally provokes questioning. You see the segment sizes and prioritization from left to right. You see the boxed "why they buy" niching in each section. Superimposed is the shaded "how they buy" niching. Hence, the entire market dynamic is there on one page. We could drone on with strategic questions based on an analysis like this, but here are some we'd naturally pursue:

- Does the market map created make sense to you?

- Are there surprises relative to the importance of the segments ranked prior to the exercise versus after the exercise? If so, why are they surprises? Did you have any blind spots?

- Did you find the assumptions behind your previous thinking valid or way off?

- (In the case of Figure 6.1) If our segments show higher growth rates, do our projected sales match those segment growth rates? Are our initial out-year forecasts higher or lower than the implied segment growth rates? If so, are we reflecting share growth or loss appropriately?

- Is the total market size as well as individual segment and niche sizes big enough to foster the growth we want?

- Conversely, are the segment sizes so large relative to our business that we need to niche further toward a more meaningful understanding of our situation? Do we need to redefine a large niche as a "market" and reapply our "segment and niche" process to it for further clarity?

- Is our go-to market strategy right? Do some segments and niches primarily use channels that we are weak in?

- What are our product/service strengths and weaknesses in the segments/niches on the left half (i.e., the most attractive segments) of Figure 6.1? How do we exploit the most attractive segments? (Upcoming chapters take this Market Map output and directly use it to help answer these questions.)

Our Favorite Anecdote Using This Tool

(If you are starting with this Chapter, flip back to Chapter 5 to get Part 1 of this story.)

Part 2 — The team got to work toward understanding and projecting the growth rates for each of their six segments. By using the techniques discussed in this chapter, they completed that task in roughly one week. It showed their chosen Segment 5 was not only the smallest, but it also had *negative* growth potential for their three-year planning horizon.

The new leader sat down with his team and reviewed his now complete Market Map (again representatively shown in Figure 6.1). With all the size, segment, niche, and growth potential shown in the Market Map Tool format, it was *immediately obvious* to his team they were on a very wrong path. The marketing and sales people had helped the CEO pull together the sizing data and growth projections he used, so they were satisfied with its accuracy. However, they had never really assembled the information in a structured way to help inform their longer-term thinking. Since they had no idea of their market segment sizes, let alone their niches, they were flying blind.

So how could this have happened? It seems at this time, Segment 5 was awash in government subsidies. This company (and actually many competitors) was caught up in that frenzy. Most of the company's major initiatives and spending were focused there. But they were not looking forward — they were managing through the rear-view mirror. They all knew the government subsidies were likely to be discontinued in year two of their planning horizon — lessening demand to almost zero — but never tied it back to a discussion on planning horizon, or whether there were other areas more fertile for growth. In fact, their planning horizon had always been just one year!

The new leader's only question to his team was how their self-described "very good" planning process could have led them in exactly the wrong direction: focusing on the smallest and most unattractive segment of their market. The new CEO didn't beat them up, but used it as a teaching point for the need to understand markets, segments, niches, and the growth potential of each. The team quickly understood that their focus need to be elsewhere — and also recognized that the new CEO might actually bring something to the table. Segment 5 was immediately abandoned. Segments 1–3 became the segments of interest and Niches 2, 3, and 6 their primary focus. The team then moved forward, using many of the upcoming tools in this book, to reshape their plan and resource focus, and positively impacted the company in very short order.

The Strategic Environmental Scan Tool

Strategy Question: How do I develop an effective plan and strategy in an environment that is highly uncertain, turbulent, and unpredictable?

Introduction

No organization exists in a vacuum. Every enterprise is subject to forces outside the strategist's control. Much as we might like to be able to predict, forecast, and/or control externalities, reality is that much of what affects a company is outside the strategist's domain. We've often heard managers complain that strategies and strategic planning don't work because "you can plan all you want, and them something happens that's outside your control or that you didn't plan for and wrecks everything."

This is the nature of planning and strategy. Stuff is going to happen, stuff that you don't expect. We're talking about planning for the future of the business here. No one can predict what's going to happen in the future, and a lot of what happens is outside of the organization. That's the essence of the planning problem: setting a purposeful program of action for a future that is unknown. If the executives had anticipated the event during the planning process, they would have planned for it and built it into the strategy. The things that threaten the strategy are always going to be the things that weren't in the forecast, the ones the strategist didn't think about and therefore didn't include in the plan.

Recognizing the limitations, managers hire consultants and analysts to generate studies, pore over data (maybe even "Big Data"), and develop accurate forecasts that will allow them to have better insight into the future. "If we can only figure out when the market's going to turn, or how the legislation's going to get written, or when that technological breakthrough will become cost competitive, we can develop a strategy and plan to take advantage of the future." This is the strategist's nirvana: having the insight into the future that will allow the development of plans and strategies that are proactive, anticipating the future, and allocating resources accordingly.

But nirvana's not going to happen anytime soon. Want proof? Think for a moment about the "Great Recession" of 2008–2009, arguably the most significant economic event of the last 50 or more years. Go back and look through the major business and economic articles that were being written in the first half of 2008, and see how many economists, prognosticators, and analysts were suggesting that the housing market in the United States was going to implode and take the economy down with it, resulting in a financial crisis and the deepest recession since the Depression of 1929. We did this exercise a while ago, and couldn't find too many people who were predicting the economic downturn. How about the Internet — how many people saw the effect the Internet would have on business and commercial activity in the 1990s and predicted the rise of Amazon? What about social media? How many people predicted the impact of Facebook and Twitter on the way we work and live? If the experts can't predict the major events, what chance do we have when the issues are specific to an industry or a geographic area?

Think about a company that, only a couple of decades ago, was arguably one of the most recognized brands in the world: Kodak. The little yellow box of Kodak film was at every cash register of every grocery, convenience, and drug store in the United States and could be found all over the world. Kodak was innovative. The company stayed innovative, developing the technology that allowed for fast in-store photo development ("1 hour photos!") and the single-use camera. Kodak was one of the most admired companies in the world and one of the most valuable, and effectively "owned" the photography market. In 1975, an engineer at Kodak named Steven Sasson developed the first digital camera (U.S. patent #4,131,919). But the executives at Kodak were afraid the technology would cannibalize existing film sales, so they effectively put digital photography on the shelf. While the company did make money from the patent, the patent expired in 2007; and in 2012, having never successfully transitioned to the digital market, Kodak filed for bankruptcy protection.

Get the point? A company that was the market leader, that had access to all of the market data, that had the technology, marketing power, infrastructure, and organization to dominate the industry couldn't see the future — even though it was their own people who made the future possible. If an organization so close to the market and with so many resources couldn't get the plan right, what chance does a small organization have?

We are going to have to live with the fact that we're imperfect prophets in a dynamic world; we're not going to see everything coming, and the effects of decisions half a world away can affect the future of our business. Unfortunately, for a long time, too many organizations have operated in a planning mode that can be thought of as "move the train down the track." In other words, we do our analysis, set the vision and mission, see what direction we need to go, and then commit resources toward moving along the path that we've established. This is a good exercise for managers; it forces us to think about larger issues than the day-to-day operations of the company. But it doesn't fit with the reality of the strategist's world.

We'd like to suggest an alternative image. Think about guiding a raft down a river. The guide has a lot of people in the boat with different skills; has an idea about where the trip will start and end; and, if the guide has floated the river before, may even have a sense of the twists, turns, rocks, deadfall obstructions, etc. But the guide can't control the wind or the weather or the current of the river, and has limited control over the people paddling the raft. The goal is to get the group from the put-in point to the take-out safely, so the guide has to navigate a dynamic environment, keep everyone working in the same direction, and try to get to the goal without running into the banks or the obstructions too many times. How does the guide operate in such a turbulent situation? By (a) realizing I've probably been here before (or in a situation like this before) so I do have experience that helps me figure out what's going on and what's likely to happen, and (b) assessing the situation in real time and making constant adjustments.

This is the way strategists have to think about strategic planning. The strategist is the guide for the raft; she or he has a lot of people (executives, managers, workers) counting on the strategist to provide direction, and to know how to handle the inevitable variations in conditions that will occur. Like the guide, the strategist has to know the various circumstances that can impact the journey and how those circumstances can affect the trip, which ones are most likely to arise, and how to commit resources to keep everyone moving in the same direction. Most important, though, is that the guide has to know the river — not as a static entity, like the railroad track. The guide has to know the nature of the river, understand how the river flows, how it works its way through the terrain, how weather impacts the river, and how the river will affect the trip.

In the same way, the strategist has to understand the nature of the organization's environment. What are the fundamental dimensions of the environment? How will the environment impact the organization? How will the environment likely change in the future? What elements will strengthen and which will diminish? How will those elements affect the firm's activities?

But we've already noted that the future is highly uncertain, very dynamic, and generally unknowable — at least when it comes to significant events. There is no possible way to get everything right, but it's still necessary to have a sense of the key issues that are going to affect the organization. How can the strategist still develop an effective strategic plan in light of the uncertainties surrounding the enterprise? By using a Strategic Environmental Scan (SES).

The Environments of Organizations

Before we talk specifically about the tool, a little perspective is useful. Every organization or business enterprise operates within an industry (yes, even the not-for-profit ones) that provides some product or service, so every organization is subject to industry forces; and one of the fundamental questions a strategist ought to be able to address is "how good will this industry be in the future?" Every industry operates within a larger economic environment that affects how well industries perform. Some industries move with the economy; when the economy is doing well, firms in the industry generally do well (for instance, construction, finance, and consumer durable goods). Other industries are counter-cyclical to the economy and do well when the economy is in a down cycle (such as fast food companies, discount retailers, and auto parts retailers), while others are somewhat immune to economic cycles (such as food producers, tobacco companies, and personal care products). However, as we've seen over the past few years, every organization and every industry are impacted in some way by the economy.

Finally, the economy is also affected by the larger social context. Trends in society (such as demographic changes; think aging baby boomers), politics (the regulatory climate, taxation), legal and ethical issues, psychographics (changing tastes and preferences), technology, and international events will affect how well the economy does, how well industries perform, and company performance. All of these issues are capable of impacting the organization at any given time, and the real challenge is to understand how these forces will affect organizations not only today but in the future in order to set a framework for planning. So every organization is nested in several environments: the industry environment, the economic environment, and the larger general environment. The strategist therefore has to consider multiple environments — plural, not singular — when developing the strategic plan. Visually, it looks like Figure 7.1.

A couple of things to note about this figure. First, notice that there is a "nesting" feature. The enterprise is "nested" within an industry that is "nested" within the economy that is "nested"

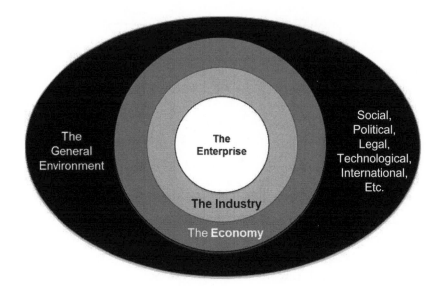

Figure 7.1: The Environments of Organizations.

within the general environment. So, there is generally a definite order to the level of impact a firm can expect, depending on the issue. Industry issues will be most immediate in effect, followed by economic issues and other general issues. While this may hold true for every issue, the general rule is the closer to the enterprise, the greater the impact.

Second, notice that there are boundary lines drawn around the various environments (industry, economy, and general) as well as around the enterprise. This is useful for understanding the different types of forces that are acting on the firm, but in reality, these are not hard lines; the boundaries are extremely permeable. Forces within industries can affect the economy and the general environment. Economic events can affect specific industries in different ways and can have differential effects on the general environment. Firms can affect entire industries, and as a result, they can influence the economy and general social forces, as Apple did with the introduction of the iPod (which transformed the music industry and the way we listen to music). For analytic purposes, we have to create categories, but in reality, the distinctions are not always clear. In fact, it may be the interrelationships among environmental forces that have the greatest impact on organizations, so not only does the strategist need to consider the various forces at work but the interactions among those forces as well.

The result, of course, is well beyond the ability of any human being to comprehend. Research indicates that the working memory for most people only allows them to keep 3 or 4 ideas in mind at once, while research on cognitive complexity suggests that most people use very few frames of reference when analyzing data. The problem the strategist faces is how to determine those issues that will significantly impact the organization and that need to be included in the strategy and plan, as well as which to ignore — when the volume of information exceeds the ability of the strategist to process all of the variables that need to be considered.

This is probably part of the reason that many organizations (or at least those who can afford to do so) hire consultants or analysts, or they pay thousands of dollars for industry, economic, and environmental analyses. There are large consulting organizations who generate billions of dollars in revenue each year, feeding strategists and senior managers with reams of information about probable future directions of the economy, industry forecasts, and environmental assessments. Companies with really deep pockets might even commission a specific study to gather what is perceived as essential strategic information and insights. Again, though, the problem is that the strategist will read the 200-page report on the future of the XYZ industry (with all the attendant charts, figures, and tables) and will still boil the report down to two or three issues that are seen as most relevant to the strategy. The executive has no choice; no one can possibly consider everything. In many cases, the reasons for the studies are (a) to confirm what the executive already intuitively knows, or (b) to provide cover for the executive in case the strategy goes bad (as in "According to the study, we needed to expand into that market to be successful"). So why are so many paying so much for what is often minimal strategic value? Isn't there an alternative that would be less expensive, easy to use, and would provide good information for strategic decision making?

Overview

To address this need, we have developed a tool that we call SES. The tool consists of a basic one-page framework along with a process to gather, assess, and organize the information so that the strategist can determine what issues deserve serious attention in the development of the strategy and plan, which issues need to be monitored, and which can be ignored (for the time being). The basic framework for the SES is shown in Figure 7.2.

We'll admit it — we're biased toward simplicity. Too many executives make strategy and business planning too complicated. In our view, if you can't get it onto a single sheet of paper in a way that everyone "gets it," it's too complex. If it is too complex, it's not understood. If it's not understood, we don't have to do anything with it. If we don't do anything, nothing happens. The result is the organization keeps doing things the same way because nobody has a clue what the leadership is talking about — and the strategy never gets developed, communicated, or executed. So the first thing to note about an SES is that is has to appear on a single sheet of paper.

Second, an SES incorporates all of the environments of the organization: industry, economic, general, and organizational, as well as including the issue of complementary products or services — those products and/or services which are complements for the company's products and services and which can affect the supply and demand for the things the firm provides. By limiting the available space, however, the SES forces executives to include only those 20% of the issues that will impact 80% of the firm's performance. In this way, the SES becomes a useful and usable tool for strategists and executives to focus attention on the issues and elements of the environments of the organization that are strategically important. By following the process for developing the SES, the strategist can perform the environmental scan and present the information in a way that is useful for planning purposes.

The SES is a combination of the elements that are found in the organization's environments (the general environment, the

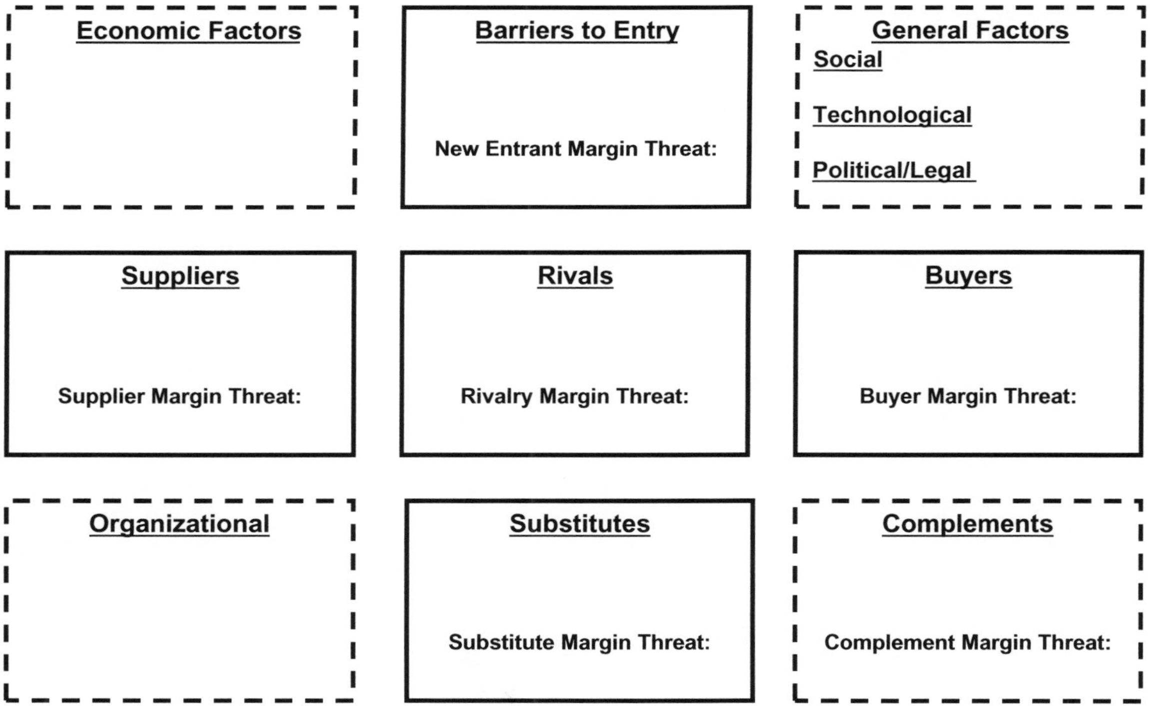

Figure 7.2: Strategic Environmental Scan: One-Page Framework. *Source:* Fairbanks and Buchko. Adapted from Porter (1979).

Economic Factors

General Factors
Social

Technological

Political/Legal

Barriers to Entry

New Entrant Margin Threat:

Suppliers

Supplier Margin Threat:

Rivals

Rivalry Margin Threat:

Buyers

Buyer Margin Threat:

Organizational

Substitutes

Substitute Margin Threat:

Complements

Complement Margin Threat:

economy, and key organizational issues) along with the major components of Dr. Michael Porter's (1979) Industry Analysis (Bargaining Power of Customers, Suppliers, Threat of Entry, Threat of Substitution, and Competitive Rivalry). Research has demonstrated that Porter's model of industry analysis remains the "gold standard" for strategically understanding how industry forces affect organizations, so we've incorporated his model into the SES. In addition, we also include the issue of complementary products and services, if there are any effects from goods or services that are necessary to the business but are not technically within the scope of the market or industry.

The key to successfully using the SES is FOCUS. The primary problem strategists face is too much information; there are too many issues to consider, and thus any single issue gets lost in the informational "noise" associated with traditional methods such as environmental analyses, market studies, industry assessments, and the like. The strategist has to concentrate on those few issues and elements of the environment that are going to have the greatest impact on the organization.

Time to Complete the Tool

1–2 weeks, depending on the amount of information gathering desired.

What You Will Need to Construct the Tool

- A method for gathering data from multiple input sources. This can be done via e-mail, survey, or online. Our preference is for use of online survey tools, as these are most efficient.

- A panel of stakeholders with knowledge of the business and industry and who are willing to spend 15–20 minutes responding to some simple questions.

- 2 or 3 meetings to compile and sort through the data by the individuals responsible for strategic planning.

Gathering Information

The first step in the process is to gather the information needed for the SES. What are the key issues that the strategist needs to consider when developing the plan? As we noted, there is far more information available than the strategist can comprehend, much of which is of marginal value. Some organizations will hire analysts or consultants to perform a systematic study of the industry, the market, or customers, etc., in order to get a general sense of the issues. These are generally expensive efforts and again, because the analyst or consultant tends to take a broad view of the environment, there will be an excessive amount of information, and a lot of the information will be of limited use in the planning process.

Our recommendation is that the strategist takes a more focused approach to gathering the information for the SES by asking those persons who are closest to the situation and have an understanding of the organization a very simple question: "What are the (pick a number — 3,4,5) issues that are going to have the biggest impact on our company's performance in the next (pick a time frame — 2,3,4,5) years?"

This very basic question should be asked of key employees and staff, customers, suppliers, bankers, clients, advisors — any individual with good knowledge of the organization and the organization's environment. The more information that is gathered during this process, the more material the strategist has with which to work and the more likely it is that key issues will be identified. When gathering information for an environmental scan, more is always better. Not only will this help identify and validate key issues, but the likelihood of finding an issue or idea that might spark a creative insight or new strategic opportunity is increased.

The number of respondents should be dictated by the strategist's knowledge of the situation, but when in doubt, more respondents are preferred. Since any individual respondent is limited by her or his frameworks and biases, increasing the number diminishes the chances that any one individual can overwhelm the model and force a single perspective on the analysis.

Key stakeholders ought to be invited to provide their views of the major issues that are going to be impacting the organization to create involvement, which can help later on with strategy execution.

The key issues can be obtained electronically via online survey techniques, from written responses, or through interviews by members of the strategic planning team or senior leadership. The point is to gather as many opinions as is feasible to provide for a more comprehensive scan of the environment. The quality of the SES is fundamentally determined by the information base; better information will inevitably result in a better scan.

Sorting the Information

All right, we have our data. We gathered input from 50, 75, 100 people, all of whom are familiar with the organization and the industry. We asked for their top three issues. As a result, we have somewhere between 50 and 150 issues that could impact the company. We therefore have a problem: we have about 45–145 issues too many. There's no possible way to develop a strategy that will address so many issues, so we need to condense the information.

That's the purpose of step 2 in the SES process: to narrow the information base by performing a sort of the data. The first way to do so is to group like items together. If three or four people say that "new technology will require changes to the product" in three or four different ways, these ways ought to be combined into a single issue, perhaps something like "technology-driven product changes." All of the issues should be sorted into similar groups or categories, and those groups should be given a single-issue designation to reduce the number of issues to be considered.

The second sort of the data is based upon the perceived impact of the issue on the future performance of the organization. While there's no right or wrong answers here, the group needs to talk through the issues and determine how the issue is likely to impact the organization, the magnitude of the impact, and the probability of occurrence. Think of the issues in a 2 by 2 matrix (Figure 7.3).

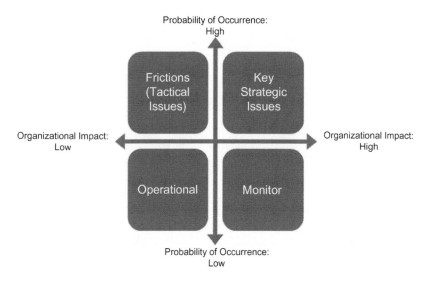

Figure 7.3: Issue Prioritization Matrix.

The focus of this second sort is to identify the items that are in the upper right quadrant, those that have a fairly high probability of occurrence and that have a significant impact on the organization. These items are those that are the Key Strategic Issues (KSIs), the issues that have to be addressed by the strategic plan. Issues that have a high probability but are low in impact need to be addressed through tactical plans, otherwise these issues can become frictions that jeopardize the strategy. Issues that are high impact but low probability need to be monitored to be sure that the probability of occurrence stays low, otherwise, these can become major issues. Issues that are low probability and low impact are operational activities but are not strategic in nature.

Having identified the KSIs, the final sort in the second phase of the process is to take the KSIs and allocate these among the nine categories on the SES, depending on the area to which the issue most belongs. For example, if the KSI is "social media will drive market awareness of our products," this item would most likely be listed as a Technological issue in the General Environment. If the issue is "Economic downturn will continue and will lead to sales declines," the issue would be listed under the Economic factors. If the issue is "Customers will have increased access to information via the Internet and will use this to put pressure on prices," this would be listed under "Buyers" as a Buyer Margin Threat. At the end of the sort, the strategist should know the Key Significant Issues and how those issues are aligned.

Forecast the Effects

The third step in the process takes the SES with the sorted data and forecasts the likely effects of these issues on the future performance of the organization. Will this issue have a positive or negative effect on the firm's revenues and profitability? If the issue will have a negative effect, then the issue is coded in red. If the issue will have a positive effect on performance, then the issue is coded in green. Finally, the strategist draws a conclusion about the overall effect of each of the nine categories of strategic environmental issues and codes the overall category as negative (red) or positive (green) by highlighting the outline of the box. This allows the strategist to see, at a glance, the issues that need to be addressed by the strategy and the business plan.

Testing the Model— Before closing out the analysis, the strategist needs to test the model. There are a series of questions that need to be considered based on the issues and the likely forecast effects:

- What are the likely effects of these issues on the firm's CURRENT strategy? How weak is the firm's current strategic position?

- Are there any issues that represent potential "game changers"? That is, do they threaten to invalidate the firm's current business model?

- What are customers going to want or demand that jeopardizes the current business model?

- What might competitors do to change the rules of engagement in the industry and jeopardize the current business model?

- What other issues threaten the viability of the current business model and need to be elevated in strategic importance?

Key Strategic Questions

Having completed the SES, the final step in the process is to establish the Key Strategic Questions that have to be answered by the strategy. In our experience, great strategies don't come from great analyses. Great strategies come from asking the right questions, questions that will drive the creative insights and innovative ideas that generate new business models. The purpose of the analysis is to lead the strategist to identify these questions. Thus the final element of the SES is the derivation of two or three questions that will enable the organization to break away from existing frames of thought and models and develop new insights that will generate new strategies for the enterprise.

Some of the questions that can arise from the SES include:

- What are the critical issues that will have the greatest impact on our firm's performance in the next few years?
- How is our organization positioned in light of these critical issues? Where are we vulnerable? Where are we well positioned?
- What can we leverage to take advantage of the changes and issues we anticipate?
- Are there any changes that are likely to jeopardize our existing business model?
- Are there any "game changers" that will fundamentally change the structure of the industry?
- How good a business will this be in the future?
- Are we likely to see new firms enter the business in coming years? What new capabilities would these firms bring to the business?
- If our business is affected by economic cycles, what is the economy likely to do in the future?
- What major trends are going to shift the nature of the business in coming years?

Our Favorite Anecdote Using This Tool

The SES in Action

The senior leadership of a medium-sized bank in a moderately sized metropolitan city in the southern United States was engaged in the process of developing a strategy for the bank. The bank had been around for many years, having been founded in the 1930s, and was reasonably successful in the market area. Assets were over $1 billion and the bank had several branches that covered the eastern part of the state.

The Great Recession, though, had negatively impacted the bank's operations. Profit margins were squeezed as interest rates dropped and larger national banks were making inroads into the region. In addition, the presence of Internet banks was affecting the industry, as more and more customers shifted to online banking as the preferred way of handling transactions. Add to that the increased regulatory requirements imposed by the Dodd-Frank bill, which increased the bank's costs of compliance. The executives realized they needed to rethink the business model and strategy for the bank.

As part of this process, the first thing the executives did was to engage in an SES. They involved everyone in the bank along with other key stakeholders: key customers, shareholders, employees, and vendors. They set up an online web survey and asked three basic questions:

1. What are the two biggest issues in the external environment (economic, social, political, technological) that are going to impact banking in our region the next 10–20 years?

2. What are the two biggest issues within the banking industry (customers, vendors, competitors, etc.) that are going to impact banking in our region in the next 10–20 years?

3. What are the two biggest issues within our bank that are going to impact our performance in the next 10 years?

The URL for the website was provided to each group separately so that the executives could monitor the differences in perceptions, so customers, shareholders, senior leaders in the bank, and staff employees' responses were recorded separately. The groups were given 1 week to respond and provide their thoughts. At the end of the survey period, all of the replies were compiled and reported verbatim to the senior executive team.

The senior executive team then sorted out the various replies, categorizing the responses based on the similarity of the thoughts expressed by the respondents. The team developed general headings to describe the various replies. For example, one group of replies was classified as "Regulatory Requirements," another was "Customer Requirements," and still others included topics such as "Federal Reserve Actions," "Capital Requirements," "Internet Banking," and many more.

Once the team had identified the thoughts and ideas provided by the key stakeholders, they then aligned the categories of responses based on the 9 dimensions of the SES. "Regulatory Requirements" and "Federal Reserve Actions" were included in the Political/Legal area of the general environment. "Customer Requirements" were analyzed and discussed in terms of the impacts on customer price sensitivity and leverage. "Capital Requirements" were identified as a Barrier to Entry for the industry, and "Internet Banking" was discussed both as a technological issue in the general environment as well as a form of increased competitive rivalry. The SES for the bank is shown in Figure 7.4.

The team then met and reviewed the SES. The discussion centered on identifying the priority issues, those that would likely have the biggest impact on the bank. The team concluded that the industry was likely to see increased competitive pressure in the future and increased customer pressure in retail banking in coming years, as the availability of online banking diminished customers' personal relationship with the bank. Regulatory requirements were viewed as significant but not strategic; instead, the executives spoke of regulations as "table stakes" that had to be addressed to operate in the industry, but they would not materially impact the bank's strategy (after all, no one picks a bank based on the fact that the bank has a better compliance department).

Commercial Banking – Strategic Environmental Scan

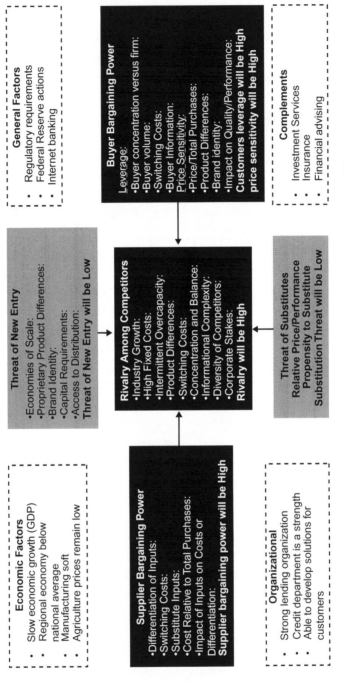

Figure 7.4: Commercial Banking — Strategic Environmental Scan.

At the same time, the executives realized that commercial banking — business loans, commercial real estate, governmental entities, etc. — was likely to continue to rely on personal relationships with bankers who knew and understood the business's needs. Large national banks with corporate offices located hundreds of miles away, with small branch offices, simply could not provide the level of customer intimacy and knowledge that would enable banks to properly price loans and develop ongoing relationships with customers. Similarly, the team also recognized that business customers were more reliant on the bank for day-to-day operations; retail customers may only visit a bank once a month, but business customers have constant ongoing interactions with their bank as part of normal financial operations. This would create an opportunity for the bank to position as a preferred partner of commercial customers, enabling the bank to fend off the impersonal, process-driven models of the larger national banks that were trying to enter the bank's market area.

As a result of the SES, the team decided to re-orient the bank as a commercial bank. Retail banking was expected to continue to be part of the firm's operations, but primarily as a source of funding for commercial banking activity. The bank invested in technology to improve the website and make online banking easier for retail (and commercial) customers to preserve the base, but it focused marketing and business development efforts on commercial banking activity. The result was that the bank came to dominate the region for small- and medium-sized business commercial banking activity and quickly carved out a position as the leading B2B bank in the market. The bank was able to leverage this presence to increase retail business by offering employees of business customers direct deposit of payroll, preferred rates on retail auto loans, and credit cards. The bank leveraged its knowledge of the business to enable better pricing of retail products due to the bank's greater familiarity with the commercial customer. By focusing on commercial activity, the bank more than doubled its assets within 5 years, increased profitability, and became the major bank in the region.

The executives noted that the SES was instrumental in making the decision to focus on commercial banking and also to de-emphasize retail banking. The CEO of the bank observed that once we looked at the situation in the banking environment, it became apparent to us pretty quickly that retail banking was going to be a tough market for us. There were too many negatives: big national competitors bidding down rates, customers who expected more and more free services, and a regulatory environment that was going to become more and more restrictive. Commercial customers, though, were still going to value personal relationships, and national banks couldn't provide the same level of service as a result. Add to that the fact that the big banks were going more and more to remote decision-makers with no knowledge of our market area, and we saw a chance to stake out a great position in the market.

While the SES did not "make" the decision for the senior executives, the result of the information and the discussion made it apparent to the strategy team that the bank needed to change focus. They admitted this was a difficult decision; after all, the bank had started out in the community years ago as a retail operation and had many customers in the market. Emotionally, many of the executives felt a personal connection to the community. The team knew that it had to maintain that regional presence. But the executives also recognized that the future of the bank was as a commercial banking entity; as more and more retail customers became less loyal to the bank, commercial customers would need more of the bank's expertise. By shifting the strategy and resources to commercial banking, the bank was able to grow and improve performance. Taking a good, hard, honest look at the environment convinced the executives that a re-orientation of the strategy was going to be necessary for future success.

Reference

Porter, M. E. (March–April 1979). How competitive forces shape strategy. *Harvard Business Review*, 57(2), 137–145.

The Product Volume Margin (PVM) Chart Tool

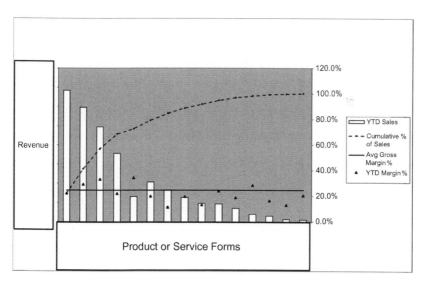

8

> **Strategy Question:** How do I assess the "business health" of my products or services?

Figure 8.1: A Typical Product Volume Margin Chart.

Overview

Our Product Volume Margin (PVM) tool is used to construct a picture of the Business Health of a company's products or services.

It is designed to provide a clear and concise "current state" business profitability picture as a function of the products or services it provides. Concurrently, the chart structure provides a means for quickly developing a deeper insight into strategic issues that may exist. The one-page summary, similar to Figure 8.1, is an especially powerful discussion output.

Time to Complete the Tool

One hour to two days pending available information.

Introduction

Now that we have a better understanding of our markets, segments, niches, and environment, we turn to the first P — our Product or Service offering. An understanding of the viability of our product or service is necessary. We have found a good way to discern this is to break down the product/service offering in two ways: *Business Health* and *Market or Competitive Health*. We like the PVM tool to tackle the Business Health question, and we address that in this chapter (the next chapter will deal with the Market or Competitive Health of the product or service via the Strategic Market Portfolio Matrix Tool).

The PVM analysis is among the most helpful tools in our arsenal, and the one we typically use first as we enter a new business situation. It provides a significant amount of perspective — both at the higher strategic level and at the actionable tactical ground level. We rarely find information presented in a PVM framework, and the answer to "why?", grounded in the nature of small- and medium-sized businesses.

Many companies we encounter simply have not had the time to pull information together in this way. We encounter a number of typical hindrances. Margin information may or may not exist, and if it does, it many times is either a closely guarded secret of the finance group or simply one of many outputs hastily prepared for the end-of-month report from an understaffed accounting group.

Salespeople, incented on top-line growth, drive revenue for those products/services that they are comfortable with, or those that will provide the biggest commission checks. Revenue reporting then tends to follow convenient sales group buckets (geography, salesperson, etc.) rather than a solid product/service breakdown. Engineers sometimes cling to and lobby for those products/ services that are high-tech, even if they are minimally profitable. Many companies also endure "legacy" ERP systems or financial reporting formats that may not optimally reflect the structure for today's business environment, but they are far more risky, resource-intensive or expensive to change (or to even upgrade to the latest version). Whatever the malady, the good news is that the PVM tool can easily and quickly cut through these constraints and provide a useful perspective.

What You Will Need to Construct the Tool

X-axis: A breakdown of your products or services. This is perhaps a less obvious, but *extremely important*, part of the analysis (and will be useful in many of the coming tools). This needs to be the first step, as the following financial data must follow the product forms chosen. We have found that this tool works best with 12–15 product or service entries. This forces those companies following only 2 – 4 product/service categories to take a deeper look and analyze the usually relevant next level of detail. It also forces those who may be following too many categories to logically combine them into more strategically-common buckets. We find that once the effort is started, organizations quickly hone in on what is most relevant to their circumstances.

Y-axis 1 (left side of chart): Revenues compiled for each product/ service category chosen above. Revenue is used as the primary comparison basis for a "Pareto" presentation of the product/ service categories. For purposes of discussion, we are using revenue in dollars.

Y-axis 2 (right side of chart): Profitability breakdowns for each product/service category chosen. Many companies track profitability in different ways depending on their company, industry, or marketplace environments. We have found Gross Margin percent (GM%) to be a good place to start, especially for product- or service-oriented businesses. GM% provides a basic indication of organic profitability and helps to isolate SG&A (sales, general, and administrative expense) impacts that may cloud an initial analysis. In a majority of cases, starting with GM% has provided an insightful baseline, and we will use this for discussion purposes.

Where to Get the Information

Many companies usually have business information that in some way financially tracks their products or services. Existing basic financial reports should initially provide some guidance for the tool. We find that companies will at minimum track revenues in this way. Usually some type of product- or service-based profitability information is kept as well. This is also a ready source of gross margin information and a quick way to construct the first pass at this chart. It may take some work to reconstruct revenues and margins from existing formats into the specific product/service forms if new categories are defined, but this work will pay dividends in your understanding for this (and forthcoming) tool.

Due to market fluctuations, commodity-based businesses may use different revenue and profit metrics (tons and $/ton, square feet and $/square foot, bushels and $/bushel, etc.). This can also be effectively used in this tool (i.e. tons for revenue and $/ton for GM).

If you are a smaller company or organization and have not quite developed the aforementioned sophistication, you might consider the following thought starters for potential product/service breakdowns:

- Manufacturing — new products, refurb products, service parts.
- Vocational (plumbing, HVAC) — routine tune-up, service calls, new construction.

- Medical services — wellness, office visits, emergency, surgical, specialty (cardiac, neurology, etc.).

- Web services — new projects, hosting fees, storage fees, maintenance fees, etc.

- Financial services — wealth management, tax services, audit services, etc.

- Sales services — in this instance, sales by geographic region may make sense.

- Food services — appetizer, main course, dessert, liquor/bar, to-go, etc.

Additionally, if you don't have a formal process for calculating or tracking Gross Margins or profitability, consider a simple process of allocating headcount and basic material costs against each revenue category chosen as a directional attempt at calculating a pseudo Gross Margin. Iterate until your allocations feel right. You can fine-tune if needed based on your first pass.

How to Construct the Tool

Any spreadsheet-based graphing software should be able to handle this simple chart. The checklist steps are as follows:

- Using a spreadsheet, create a column with the 12–15 line-item product/service categories chosen.

- Enter the corresponding revenue dollar (or revenue metric) and GM% (or profit metric chosen) in adjacent columns.

- Use the spreadsheet sort function to arrange the three columns based on revenue dollars (highest to lowest).

- Format a chart from the three resulting columns (i.e., product/service item, revenue dollars, and GM%). We like to represent the revenue dollars by bars and the GM% in point fashion.

- Optional — Engage the Pareto function for revenue dollars, which will add a line showing cumulative revenue dollar percentage to 100.

- Add for reference the "Average Gross Margin" (or average profit metric chosen) for the overall business as a horizontal line using the right-hand percent scale.

- The result should structurally look like Figure 8.1.

Key Strategic Questions

We find an accurate PVM chart is very powerful in its ability to elicit key strategic questions. No doubt you'll be able to dig right in once you see the result. Some of many questions we'd likely pursue are:

- Does this chart accurately reflect our business? (This may take a bit of reflection.)

- Are our revenues even across the board, or do we have one or two categories that dominate and a number of smaller tag along categories that may or may not make sense?

- Do your gross margins scale logically with revenues (i.e., Do your highest volume products reflect your highest gross margins?)? If not, why not? Does this make sense?

- Are those products/services that are individually "accretive" to average GM representative in some way of a distinctive competency? Or a favorable market segment? Can we leverage this?

- Are there individual product/service categories that appear outliers to the overall trend? Why?

- Given this picture of your business, do you believe your results are consistent with what you know about your industry or competitor's performance? Are you better or worse? Is this an issue?

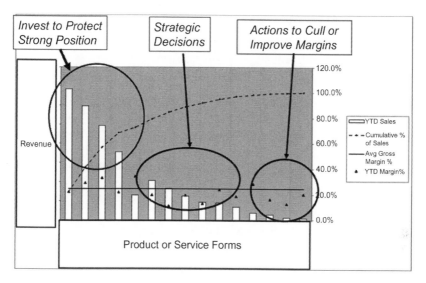

Figure 8.2: Strategic Implications of the PVM Tool.

You can also structure a series of strategic questions based on the chart shown in Figure 8.2, such as:

- Do you have solid plans in place to protect the 20% of the product or service forms that make up 80% of your gross profits?

- Are those lower revenue products/service forms that are individually "dilutive" to overall GM critical to your business?

- Are those lower revenue products/service forms that are individually "dilutive" to overall GM worth keeping, culling, or improving?

- What do we need to do with those products/service forms that are in-between the high and low performers?

Our Favorite Anecdote Using This Tool

A new CEO was brought into a manufacturing company due to poor performance. The formerly family-owned company never had a comprehensive strategic plan or effort. The company had underperformed at a time the anxious new owners were expecting timely top and bottom-line improvement. The new CEO found that each Board member, Vice President, and key functional expert in the company all thought they knew what was wrong — and thus had the obvious solution. As is often the case, none of their opinions were based on solid fact or common knowledge (since none existed), and recommended solutions largely entailed finger-pointing and calls for the other functional areas of the company to get their acts together.

The CEO, being intimately familiar with the tools in this book, traditionally used this tool as the first analysis step. In this case there were two reasons: (1) as a normal way to quickly familiarize himself with the business and (2) to provide an initial, factual base-line to begin the improvement effort. Having done many of these in his past, the initial results were so unusual that it didn't pass his first "Does it make sense?" question (i.e., they looked nothing like Figures 8.1 or 8.2). He had the numbers checked and re-charted — with no change. The initial chart is shown in Figure 8.3.

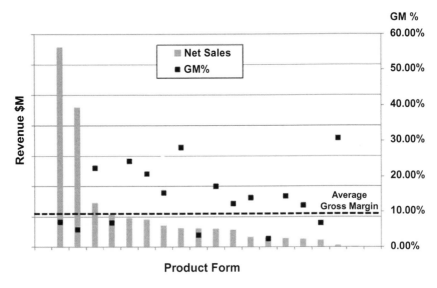

Figure 8.3: PVM Analysis of Manufacturing Company.

The strategic implications of this quick analysis were very revealing.

- The company had dangerously low average gross margins. After SG&A, overall profitability was very low.

- Two major product forms made up a majority of the revenue. They had dilutive GM% and were the significant drag on company profitability.

- The smaller volume product forms had much better and accretive GM%.

- The nature of this PVM analysis was significantly different than other, more traditional results.

As the numbers were confirmed to be accurate, the question turned to "what is driving the phenomena?" Within four weeks of joining the company, the CEO used this single analysis to call a special board meeting to review results toward getting all stakeholders on the same page. The simple presentation of the facts facilitated by the PVM chart served to: (1) illustrate the problem was company-wide, (2) show how, why, and where the issues were, and (3) provide a means to prioritize actions, given limited company resources. Within six weeks the team had figured out what was behind the poor performance, and, using additional tools shown in this book, they then developed a plan to improve product performance and profitability. Equally important — with newfound Board understanding of the situation, the team was actually allowed to execute rather than be constantly second-guessed from afar.

The Strategic Market Portfolio Matrix Tool

Strategy Question: *How do I assess the "market health" of my products or services?*

Introduction

This is a great question. Few, if any, organizations operate in a single market with a single product or service. Most companies offer a range of products or services to a range of markets with a range of customers and segments (see our earlier discussion of market mapping and segmentation in chapters 3 through 6). Yet the resources of any organization are scarce, limited, and finite (remember, that's the strategy problem!). So how does an executive determine where to invest resources — time, effort, and money — in order to provide the best chance of achieving superior overall firm performance?

All too often this is an emotional decision, based on how the manager "feels" about the product or service. Or it may be data-driven, but the data are difficult to acquire, sort through, and organize in a systematic way that will lead to good decisions. Or it might be influenced by which of the product or service managers make the best case or best presentation. We've been here; we've seen managers dump loads of data in favor of "but I think this is a service we ought to offer because it's our legacy." We've seen managers gather all kinds of market analyses and forecasts, then get stymied because the data are often conflicting or nebulous. And we've seen a really good, dynamic, extroverted Division President make such a great presentation that the Executive Office decided to give her more corporate budget dollars to invest in new capital and people. Three years later, the company sold the division due to poor financial performance.

A number of years ago, one of us, in our professional career, was running the company's annual strategic planning retreat. Each of the vice presidents of the company was asked to make a presentation about their functional area's future goals and plans. As the session wore on (a lot of strategic planning sessions are like elephants giving birth — it takes a long time, it's done at a high level, it's accompanied by a lot of noise, and when it's done there's not a whole lot to show for it), it became apparent that what was happening was that *each of the VPs was trying to show how her or his area of responsibility deserved more of the company's resources.* They were trying to justify why they ought to get a bigger slice of the budgetary pie. Marketing said, "after all, we generate the revenue dollars that keep the place going." Operations said, "we need to be able to reduce our costs to increase our profit margins." Finance and Accounting said, "we need to be able to lower the cost of capital." Human Resources said, "our single biggest cost is people, and we need to make sure we're getting the best from our talent," etc. Everyone's area was the most essential. Now the CEO had to decide how to allocate the budget when everyone said their area was most deserving. Who gets what, and why? This is a major problem for strategists.

Multiply this problem across multiple products or service lines. How does a bank allocate resources among commercial real-estate loans, hospitality loans, farm loans, corporate lines of credit, manufacturing loans, and many more? How does an auto manu-facturer allocate resources among economy cars, midsize cars, luxury cars, minivans, SUVs, and trucks? How does a hospital allocate resources among cardiac care, orthopedics, emergency room (ER) services, surgery, and the like? When decisions such as these can have such an impact on corporate performance, on strategic direction, and on people's lives, we don't think it's a good idea to let the emotions dominate. But we recognize that getting the necessary information can be expensive, time consuming, and difficult. So how do we provide managers with a quick, easy to use, data-based tool that allows them to allocate organization resources in an effective manner, and balance that with the need to optimize financial results?

In our view, the best way to get a strategic view of the problem — and therefore to get some strategic direction on the decision process — is to reduce the question to a simple figure that provides multiple insights, yet organizes the data in such a way as to provide strategic insight. The tool we use is the Strategic Market Portfolio Matrix (SMPM).

This isn't really a new tool. It's been around in various forms for a long time in business, going as far back as 1970 and the Boston Consulting Group's (BCG's) Product Portfolio Matrix: the classic 2 × 2 matrix with relative market share on the horizontal axis and market growth on the vertical axis (Boston Consulting Group, 1973). Business Units were placed into one of four quadrants on the matrix, depending on whether relative market share was high or low, and whether market position was high or low. The BCG also gave clever names to the four quadrants: high market share/high growth potential businesses were "Stars", high market share/low market growth businesses were "Cash Cows", low market share/high growth businesses were "Question Marks", and low market share/low growth businesses were "Dogs". The problem with the BCG matrix was with the products in the middle, the so-called "black hole" of the matrix. What should firms do with products or services that were on the borderlines?

To address this issue (and probably believing that a 3 × 3 matrix had to be more than twice as good as a 2 × 2 matrix; 9 boxes versus 4, right?), General Electric (GE), in collaboration with McKinsey Company, modified the BCG approach to incorporate more data than just relative market share and the growth rate (Springer, 1973). The planners at GE decided to examine business strength (how well-positioned a company was in the industry) and industry attractiveness (How good is the industry?). This was a positive advancement and benefit over the BCG model. The businesses in the middle remained problematic, but it opened up the decision process to a wider array of factors than just relative market share and relative market growth.

We should note, however, that there is a tendency for managers to presume that business strength is highly correlated with relative market share; after all, if we've got the biggest share, we must be the strongest, right (ask Sears or Macy's how well that market share leadership thing worked out for them)? And likewise, industry attractiveness seems to be highly correlated with growth rates (never mind the fact that Culver's and Subway entered a very mature, low-growth industry and were able to carve out a significant, profitable presence). There's more to the decision than just how big our market share is, how strong our competitive position is, how much the industry growth is, and how profitable the industry is. Managers need to consider a wide array of factors when making the decisions on how to strategically allocate resources across multiple product or services. But they also need to be able to simplify the information so they can make good decisions. That's why we developed our version of the matrix, the SMPM.

Overview

The tool consists of a one-page, 3 × 3 matrix along with a process to gather, assess, and organize the information so the strategist can determine how the various products and services of the business are positioned in the respective markets, how well each is performing, how much each contributes to overall firm performance, which products/services have potential for future performance, and what types of approaches might be appropriate for allocating resources. The basic framework for the SMPM is shown in Figure 9.1.

Like the GE matrix, the SMPM is a 3 × 3 or 9-cell matrix. On the horizontal axis is measured Market Attractiveness; the vertical axis measures Competitive Position. We'll have more to say about

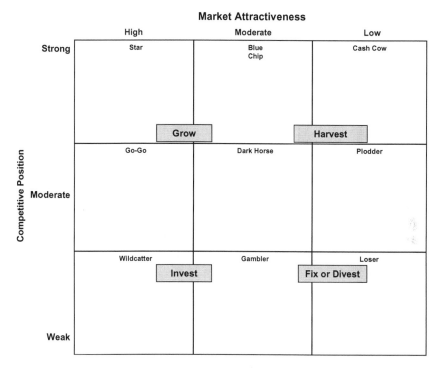

Figure 9.1: The Strategic Market Portfolio Matrix.

these in a bit, but for now, notice that these are scored from High to Low for Market Attractiveness and from Weak to Strong for Competitive Position.

Each of the cells has a descriptive name that indicates how businesses in these cells are likely to be regarded by the strategist. For example, firms that are High in Market Attractiveness and in a Strong Competitive position are the Stars, while those with High Market Attractiveness but a Weak Competitive Position are the Wildcatters. We'll discuss each of these after explaining how to develop the SMPM. In addition, notice that the four general regions of the SMPM have a generic strategic approach attached to the area. Those in the upper left (tending toward High/Strong) are Growth opportunities; those in the upper right (tending toward Low/Strong) are candidates for Harvesting; those in the lower left (toward the High/Weak) are likely investment contenders; and those in the lower right (Low/Weak) are targets for divestment.

Time to Complete the Tool

Two days to two weeks, depending on the amount of information available and the time required to gather the information.

What You Will Need to Construct the Tool

- A methodology for gathering data from knowledgeable sources on the various elements of Market Attractiveness and Competitive Position. This can be done online using web-based surveys, via e-mail, via paper, or other similar methods.

- A panel of individuals with knowledge of the various businesses.

- Information on the revenues and gross profit margins for each of the product or service groups (see the PVM Chart in Chapter 8).

- Additional data, such as size of the market, segments, and niches (from Market Sizing and the Market Map, see Chapters 3, 4, 5, and 6), industry profit margins, relative share of market, and market growth rates, which can be compiled and applied as available to enhance the analysis of the SMPM.

Where to Get the Information

For purposes of this process we presume that you have gathered any public information, such as forecasts and market analyses, that can be easily obtained from secondary data sources. This information should be distributed to the panel of individuals with knowledge of your firm's markets and your competitive position to read and digest. If your organization is like most others, you have these people resident inside the firm, but you can use selected suppliers/vendors and customers to provide additional insights.

You need to classify your products or services according to major market or industry group, using your own internal system. It is essential that you are able to clearly delineate the respective businesses in which your firm competes; try to avoid overlap where possible. Financial reporting records can be a useful way of doing this, since most firms tend to keep revenues and costs separated by major product or service area for accounting purposes.

Having identified your product and/or service markets, you are going to ask the panelists to rate each of the product/service-market areas on the two dimensions of Market Attractiveness and Competitive Position. They are to determine if the market is High, Moderate, or Low for the various dimensions of Market Attractiveness, and if the firm's position is Strong, Moderate, or Weak for the various dimensions of Competitive Position. Our preference, based on experience, is that you limit your panelists to only three possible ratings for simplicity, accuracy, and ease of assessment.

For *Market Attractiveness*, the dimensions to assess can include any or all of the following:

1. Market Growth/Potential — how much growth or opportunity will there be in the market in the future?

2. Market Accessibility — are the markets accessible, both geographically and in terms of available customers?

3. Barriers to Entry — markets with high barriers to entry are attractive if the firm is in those markets, but unattractive if barriers to entry are low.

4. Cost of Market Entry — markets with low costs are more attractive for new entry, but they are unattractive if it is easy for new firms to enter the market and erode profitability.

5. Level of Rivalry — is competition cutthroat or mild? Are there entrenched dominant firms that will fight to maintain their share, or is the industry fragmented?

6. Fit with Existing Competencies — how well does the market "fit" (in other words, value) your firm's current capabilities and value proposition?

7. Market Profitability — does the market provide above-average returns and profitability?

8. Market Size — how large is the market?

9. Market Stability — how stable or volatile will the market be in the future? Is there the potential for disruptive technologies to transform the market dynamics?

10. Market Risk — what is the overall level of market risk? Does the market behave in a predictable manner or is there a high degree of variability in market actions?

There are additional factors that firms may wish to consider, but these are our "Top Ten." Note that for the assessments, markets are rated as High (above average; better than other markets), Moderate (average; similar to other markets), or Low (below average; poorer than other markets). The relevant comparisons are those markets in which the firm currently competes; new potential markets can be evaluated using the same criteria, but since the firm does not currently have an established position in those markets, the scope of the analysis is one-dimensional and therefore limited.

For *Competitive Position*, the dimensions to assess can include any or all of the following:

1. Share of Market — the larger the share of market, the stronger a firm's competitive position.

2. Efficiency — to what extent is the firm's cost structure efficient relative to rivals? Is the firm the low-cost producer? Are there economies of scale?

3. Uniqueness — to what extent is the firm's value proposition different or distinct from its competitors'? Are there things the firm does better than rivals and for which customers will pay a premium price?

4. Alignment — to what extent are the activities of the firm's business model integrated and aligned with one another? Are the activities of the firm mutually reinforcing?

5. Value Network — to what extent does the firm have a position within a network (such as suppliers, information flows, and access to capital) that provides it with resources outside the firm's boundaries?

6. Agility/Speed — how quickly can the firm shift resources relative to competitors? How quickly can the firm initiate new actions?

7. Preemption — to what extent does the firm possess resources, such as talent, access to markets, capital, and intellectual property that act to lock out rivals?

Again, there may be additional factors that firms may wish to consider in determining the relative strength of the organization's competitive position, but these are our "Magnificent Seven." Notice that the evaluation of Strong (above average), Moderate (average), or Weak (below average) for this assessment is done by comparing the firm to its competitors in the market, while Market Attractiveness compares the markets relative to other markets.

These assessments can be distributed "cold" to the panel of executives, or can be shared after discussion among the group. The executives are instructed to consider each of the firm's markets and perform the Market Attractiveness evaluation. Likewise, the panelists are instructed to perform the competitive assessment for each of the firm's product or service-market areas. Table 9.1 shows how a Market Attractiveness assessment might appear; Table 9.2 provides an example of a Competitive Position assessment.

The values for these assessments can be scored as High = 9, Moderate = 4, and Low = 1. Transforming the assessments into a numeric score enables you to add up the values for the respective scores for the various dimensions of Market Attractiveness and Competitive Position and determine an overall average for that product or service area (as is shown in the sample tables 9.1 & 9.2).

Table 9.1: Sample Market Attractiveness Assessment.

	Service A	Service B	Service C
Market Growth Potential	H	M	L
Market Accessibility	H	H	L
Barriers to Entry	H	L	M
Cost of Market Entry	M	M	L
Level of Rivalry	L	H	M
Fit with Existing Competencies	H	H	H
Market Profitability	M	L	M
Market Size	M	H	M
Market Stability	H	L	H
Market Risk	M	M	L
Average	6.60	5.10	3.80

Directions: for each of the service areas listed indicate whether you believe the market is High (above average) Moderate (average), or Weak (below average) when compared to the others.

These scores can then be recorded and calculated for all of the panelists, resulting in a group average score for the Market Attractiveness and Competitive Position. (For purposes of this illustration, we'll use the averages calculated in Tables 9.1 and 9.2.)

How to Construct the Tool

Here's where the SMPM really shows its advantages relative to other portfolio matrices. Yes, the use of multidimensional scaling to assess Market Attractiveness and Competitive Position is an improvement over the BCG or GE models; but once we properly array the data, the SMPM becomes a strong strategic tool. To properly display the data on the matrix:

Table 9.2: Sample Competitive Position Assessment.

	Service A	Service B	Service C
Share of Market	H	M	L
Efficiency	H	H	L
Uniqueness	H	L	M
Alignment	M	L	L
Value Network	L	H	L
Agility/Speed	H	L	H
Preemption	M	L	L
	6.43	3.71	2.57

Directions: for each of the service areas listed, indicate whether you believe our firm's Competitive Position is High (above average) Moderate (average), or Weak (below average) when compared to our competitors.

1. Determine the *total revenues for each product or service relative to others in the firm's portfolio*. We generally do this by using the product or service with the highest revenue in the firm and scaling the others based upon the percentage relative to the revenue leader. Let's say that Service A generates US $4 million in annual revenue, Service B US $2.5 million, and Service C US $1 million. Service B has 62.5% of the revenue of Service A, and Service C is 25% as big as the revenues for Service A.

2. For each of these service areas, we are going to create three circles that represent the *relative size of the revenues*. This means that the diameter of the circle for Service B is going to be six-eighths of the diameter of Service A, and the diameter of the circle for Service C will be one-fourth the diameter of Service A.

3. Next, we are going to color-code each circle based upon the service area's gross margins from the Product Volume Margin (PVM) analysis (see Chapter 8). If the gross profit

margins are above some given standard (perhaps industry average, company average, hurdle rate, etc.) the circle will be coded in black. If the margins are at or near the standard, the circle is coded in white. If the margins are below standard, the circle is coded in gray (note we often use green, yellow, or red shading as well when possible).

4. Now the fun part. For each of our service areas, we will take the ratings from the Market Attractiveness and Competitive Position assessments and position the center point of the circle at the intersection of those values on the SMPM. Figure 9.2 shows how this would look visually for the example we've been using.

Notice what this chart tells the strategist. At a single glance, it is possible to discern the relative strength of the three service areas in the company's portfolio compared to one another. Service A is

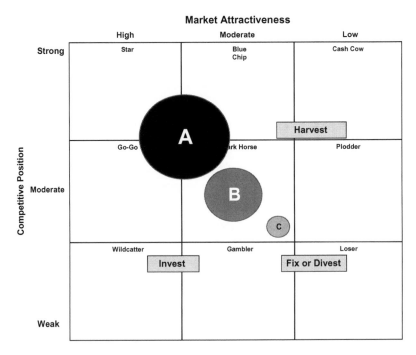

Figure 9.2: SMPM for the Example Firm.

clearly the star, with large revenues, above-average margins, and a relatively strong position in an attractive market. This suggests that the company ought to commit resources to grow the service area. Service B is the problem child, the Dark Horse; the market is somewhat attractive, but the competitive position is relatively weak and the margins are poor. The strategist may want to consider likely future directions of the market and competitor's likely moves; if the market is going to become more attractive and competitors weaker, the firm might want to invest to improve margins and improve the competitive position. However, if the market is going to erode or competitors are going to get stronger, Service B will become a likely candidate for divestment. Service C is probably the most challenging in this scenario; the margins are acceptable, but the revenues are small and the Market Attractiveness and Competitive Position are weak. Unless there are good indications of future market potential or opportunities to improve the competitive position, Service C probably should be divested, and the funds used to support growth of Service A.

Please note that we are being somewhat simplistic here; the issues surrounding the various markets, margins, positions, etc., are likely far more complex and will require more discussion and analysis before making a definitive decision. Nonetheless, the proper use of the SMPM does provide some direction for discussion, comparison for analysis, and leads the strategist to asking additional questions that can result in better strategic decisions and resource commitments.

We also want to mention various ways we've seen executives modify the SMPM chart process to enhance strategic decision-making. Two of the more notable examples came from a not-for-profit community service organization that provided multiple service lines to serve different populations. The CEO of the organization wanted to indicate which service lines provided the greatest margins to the organization, as well as the share of the population that was being served by the organization. She modified the chart by gathering data on the organization's share of service and then displayed this in a pie chart format. The SMPM for the organization is shown in Figure 9.3.

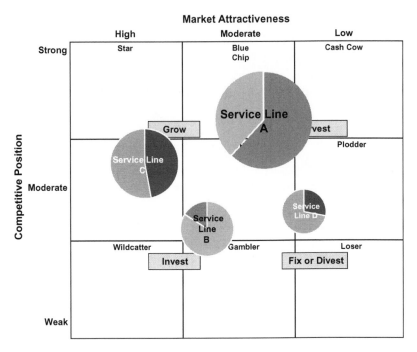

Figure 9.3: SMPM — Service Lines, Returns, and Share of Population.

Displaying the information in this format led to a discussion of ways to grow share of population for Service Line B (in white) or else to transfer the service to another community provider. It also stimulated conversation about how to grow margins on Service Line C (in gray), since the organization was a leader in providing the service in the community based on the share of population; the organization just wasn't very efficient at doing so. The team also had some difficult conversations about the future viability of Service Line D (the small gray circle), inasmuch as the amount of resources needed to improve the firm's position in a difficult service area was questionable.

Another manufacturing organization wanted to incorporate information about forecasted market growth into the decision process and to link complementary products together when discussing the firm's strategic resource allocations. One of the executives decided to use the border lines of the various circles to indicate market growth forecast. A double line would indicate forecasted growth of more than 7% per year, a solid line would indicate a growth forecast between 0% and 6%, and a dashed line would indicate a negative growth forecast. The firm also used common colors of the borders to show those products that were complementary to one another. The SMPM for this organization is shown in Figure 9.4.

In this example, the team noted that Product A (the large black circle) was clearly the star in the firm's product portfolio. Market growth was forecast at greater than 7% and margins were above average. Product B (in white) was in a market with solid growth forecasted, but the margins were below average; it was determined that there needed to be emphasis on improving costs to increase margins for this product. Product C (dark gray) was put into a holding pattern; margins weren't great, and the market was

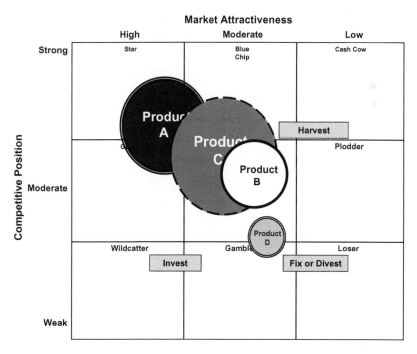

Figure 9.4: SMPM — Products, Margins, Forecasted Growth, and Product Complementarity.

expected to decline in the future. And Product D, while marginal in the firm's portfolio, had good margins and was complementary to the star Product A; thus, the team decided to continue to devote resources to preserving the performance of the product in order to protect and support Product A.

These are just two examples of ways in which firms can modify and use the SMPM to enhance strategic decision-making. Incorporating key information into the model improves the richness of the analysis and can lead to the development of key strategic questions that can enrich the strategy process.

Key Strategic Questions

Some of the strategic questions that can arise from the use of the SMPM include issues such as:

- What is the overall health of our portfolio? Do we have enough Stars, Cash Cows, Go-Gos, and Blue Chips to secure our future? What are we doing with our losers? How are we going to handle the Dark Horses or the Plodders?

- Which markets/products/services should we be concentrating our resources on for maximum benefit?

- Which products/services have the greatest potential for future growth?

- Are we allocating resources to the right products or services, in the right amount, to enhance the total portfolio?

- Should we be considering divesting or eliminating some of our products or services?

- Which products are underperformers and why? Is it an issue of market penetration, market attractiveness, competitive position, or margins? Based on this analysis, where should we be committing resources?

- Do we have enough products or services under development to enhance our future portfolio? Are our products or services "getting tired," or being harvested without significant growth opportunities available?

- Are there opportunities to leverage resources across products or services to improve competitive position or enhance margins?

- Do we have complementary products or services in our portfolio, and if so, are we linking these in our analysis? If not, should we be looking at adjacent markets to take advantage of complementarities?

- Will we be able to generate sufficient resources internally to support the overall growth and performance of our portfolio, or should we look externally for capital or funding?

Our Favorite Anecdote Using This Tool

The SMPM in Action

The Board and CEO of a community hospital in the Midwestern United States were engaged in a process of developing a strategy and plan for the enterprise. Like any hospital or healthcare organization, it provided a variety of healthcare services to the community. There were other larger urban hospitals within a reasonable distance from the community, though, that also provided multiple healthcare services. As part of the strategy process, the CFO of the hospital performed the PVM (gross margin) analysis from Chapter 8 to determine the profit margins of the various healthcare services the hospital provided. The CFO also provided the data on the total revenues generated by each service area. The Board and senior executive team used information gathered as part of the strategy process to rate the hospital's competitiveness in each service area, and the market attractiveness of each of the services. Using the techniques described, the SMPM for the hospital was developed. It is shown in Figure 9.5.

The size of the circles represented the total annual revenue from each service area for the hospital. The color of the circle indicated if the returns were well-above average (black), above average

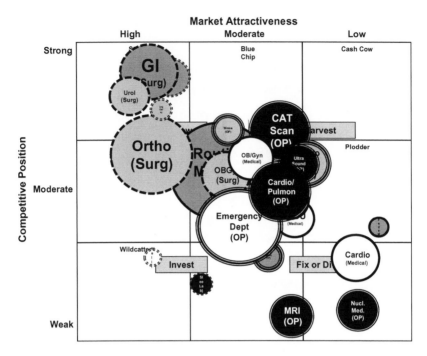

Figure 9.5: SMPM — Midwest Community Hospital.

(light gray), average (dark gray), and below average (white). In addition, the strategy team decided to code the circles by shading the border lines as surgical services (heavy dash), medical services (solid), independent outpatient services (light dash), and ancillary outpatient services (triple ring).

The Board and senior leadership team then engaged in a series of discussions regarding which services to keep and which to consider exiting. The conversation proved enlightening in several areas. One of the physician leaders on the team inquired why the hospital was getting below-average returns on cardiology, when other hospitals in his experience found this to be a very profitable area of service delivery. The Board challenged the CEO regarding whether or not the ER services were needed, since returns were so low. The CEO's answer was strategic: "It's the front door to the hospital. You see these areas where we make money? (Such as orthopedic surgery, urological surgery, and gastro-intestinal surgery.) More than half of all our patients come to those areas through the ER." The Board members challenged the CEO then to determine if perhaps ER services might be outsourced; while this would reduce revenues, it would also grow margins.

The conversation lasted for well over three hours, just based on the single, one-page output shown in Figure 9.5. Board members and staff were fully engaged during that time, and a new level of understanding and appreciation for the portfolio of services was achieved. The chart was incorporated into a presentation that was given to all hospital staff as well as key stakeholders in the community. The CEO remarked, "I knew we had something here when I presented this to our physicians, and one of the docs who is big in gastro-intestinal surgery came up to me right after and wondered why his circle was the wrong color (dark gray instead of black). We then had a ten-minute discussion on ways to reduce costs and improve efficiencies in GI surgery, all initiated by the doctor." A Board member remarked, "Until I saw this chart, I never really understood what businesses we were in. This helped me ask the right questions that will drive the right strategies and plans."

We have seen the power of the SMPM time and time again in our work with organizations. To be sure, some firms are frightened of the results; the analysis can lead to some difficult questions. Why are we in this business? Is this a market we really want to be in long-term? Would we be better off taking the resources from this service area and shifting them to another? These are often difficult conversations. But that is the purpose of the tools in this book — to give managers the information they need to make the right strategic decisions for the organization.

References

Boston Consulting Group (1973). The experience curve reviewed: IV. The growth share matrix or the product portfolio. *Perspectives No. 135.*

Springer, C. H. (1973). Strategic management in General Electric. *Operations Research,* 21(6) (November–December), 1177–1182.

The Customer Value Analysis Tool

> **Strategy Question:** *What do our customers really value in our products or services?*

Introduction

We've said it before; we'll say it again: strategy begins in the marketplace with a customer. All of the analyses, all of the tools, all of the models, and all of the planning sessions are useless unless we know how to position our products and/or services in the mind of the customer. Remember our definition of strategy? "An integrated set of actions and resource commitments that position an organization within the competitive environment so as to generate superior results over time." The purpose of the actions and resource commitments is to position an organization within the competitive environment. How do we define that position?

As we've noted earlier, the word "strategy" has a military background. The first recognized book on strategy, *The Art of War*, by the Chinese general Sun Tzu, dates to the 5th century B.C. and established the importance of strategy as a competitive practice for military success. Armies have long understood the importance of positioning on the battlefield: the importance of holding a superior position, of selectively applying force at the right place and time (position) to disrupt the enemy, how to deploy one's troops to take advantage of the landscape. Julius Caesar, Napoleon, Karl von Clausewitz, and countless military commanders have written extensively about the importance of understanding the structure of the battlefield and positioning.

Understanding positioning, though, comes from a thorough understanding of the terrain over which the armies are fighting. Where are the elevations? Where are there natural barriers? Which areas provide a defensible location? The ability of a general to determine the most advantageous position comes from having an in-depth grasp of the terrain.

In the military, armies compete for territory, for physical space. In business, firms compete for customers, for markets. Therefore, a fundamental understanding of the nature of a firm's customers and markets is essential to effective strategic decision-making, actions, and commitment of resources.

What we have seen all too frequently is the tendency of managers to oversimplify their understanding of the market. "Our customers don't care about anything except getting our products at a lower price." "Customers aren't really concerned about service quality; they just want to get the order on time." "Clients are only focused on one thing — can we deliver the project under budget?" While there is certainly power in the focus that comes from identifying critical value drivers and simplifying the firm's strategy, the danger in these analyses is the risk of missing some factors that could enable the firm to create a unique, differentiated value proposition.

Worse than that, managers can miss changes or disruptions in the market because they are focused on what they think customers want, rather than understanding what customers really value. It's all too easy to oversimplify the market and to miss the critical differences that enable some firms to succeed at the same time that rivals are declining. Firms can define their markets too narrowly and miss critical disruptions. Kodak thought they were in the film business; that customers wanted pictures printed on paper. As a result, Kodak developed an extensive technology and product line of films, chemicals, and photographic paper. But what the customer valued was the image, not the picture; the format didn't matter as long as the image was intact. As a result, Kodak imploded — even though the company developed the original technology for digital photography! Kodak made better films, cameras, and created technology for 1-hour developing, but what the market wanted was an image.

Consider the airlines for a moment. What is it customers want? Safe air travel at the lowest price, right? (Well, except for those who can afford Business Class or First Class.) If you talk to most airline executives, the focus is on safety, convenience of schedule, and fares. And there's certainly a good reason for this; as any air traveler knows, there's a reason most of the seats are in the Economy section. In their understanding of the market, the airlines' market research is clear — the above three factors are the ones that drive customer decision-making.

Until we look at Southwest Airlines. Southwest doesn't offer anything different than other airlines with respect to the three key demand drivers: they are safe, convenient, and have low fares. But Southwest has identified a feature of the market that the other airlines seem to have missed: the traveling experience. Southwest knows that, for many people, airlines are cattle cars; passengers are in uncomfortable seats, the space is small and cramped, the environment is not a pleasant one. Customers put up with it because there aren't many options for getting to the destination so quickly. But what if an airline could make the experience not quite so unpleasant? What if, by encouraging the gate agents, crews, and flight attendants to create positive interactions with passengers, there were a way to make the experience better? Would passengers choose the airline based on the quality of the air travel experience? The answer apparently is yes, as Southwest year after year generates a record of success in the industry.

Or think for a moment of Walt Disney World in Orlando, Florida. If a research firm was to conduct normal market research, they might ask something like: "Would you be willing to pay over $100 to stand in a line in 90-degree heat and humidity with your children for an hour for a 2-minute interaction with a costumed actor?" The sane answer is no, of course not; that's not very appealing to anyone. But as you read this, 100,000 people will have made the decision to do just that today. What does Disney understand that other theme parks or entertainment companies don't seem to get? What Disney knows is that people aren't paying for a vacation, or for the ride, or for the park, or for the hotel room; what they want and what they will pay for is the experience of happiness and the ensuing memories. And if Disney can deliver that experience and create happiness for a moment, people will pay a lot and endure a lot of inconvenience for that moment.

See where this is leading? The tendency of managers is to ask customer what they want and, based on customers' responses, to try and figure out how to respond accordingly. But customers don't always know what they want because they don't know what firms are capable of providing. Or customers may not really know what they want because what they want isn't something tangible but emotional, a feeling that they can't articulate. Or customers may not even be aware of the factors that are driving their decision because the knowledge is hidden or their behavior is based on habit.

Many of us have heard the stories. 3M created the QWIP machine technology to allow firms to transmit pages of paper instantaneously over telephone lines (okay, this was back in the early 1980s, so it does seem quaint). The paper was expensive and the process took a long time, but it worked (we know, because one of us used the early QWIP machine at the company where he worked). In trying to determine what the market potential might be, customers were asked, "would you be willing to pay $4.00 to send a page instantly over the telephone line, or would you continue to use the postal service?" — which at the time was charging 15 cents for a first-class stamp? Guess what customers said? "No, we'll continue using the postal service" — because they couldn't conceive of a need to send a page of paper instantly. Business practices and habits were oriented around the U.S. Postal Service for document delivery. Everyone was used to the process, and no one was thinking about how things might change if they could get the letter instantly. As a result, U.S. firms concluded that there was no market for facsimile technology, so they licensed the technology to Japanese firms. The result was the Japanese companies like Brother, Sharp, and others came to dominate the market for

Fax machines, which became fax-printers, 3-in-1 and 4-in-1 machines, etc. Similarly, when Fred Smith conceived the idea for Federal Express in a term paper for an economics class he wrote as a student at Yale, he supposedly was told by his professor that to get a grade the idea had to be "feasible." After all, why would anyone need a package delivered overnight? Ken Olsen, while CEO of Digital Equipment Corporation (DEC), was famous for telling his people, "there is absolutely no reason for anyone to have a computer in their home." Xerox told their researchers at their Palo Alto Research Center (PARC) that people had no need for a "mouse" to control a computer.

We could go on and on. The essential point is this: we're not very good at intuiting what it is that customers really want or value. Our own biases get in the way. Our own processes get in the way (we're afraid of anything that would disrupt our current business model). The data and analytics get in the way (we look at the numbers without understanding the reasoning behind the data). Emotions get in the way. Worse, customers often don't really know why they buy particular products or services. They may be unsure of their rationale. They may be afraid of looking foolish. Or they may be buying for emotional reasons which are notoriously hard to articulate, so they take the easy way out with "it's convenient," "the price was right," "I like the quality," and other seemingly logical reasons to justify their behavior. In some cases, it's a failure of imagination; because we have no experience with the potential product or service, we cannot imagine a need for the product. There's a great scene in the movie *Jobs* when Steve Jobs (played superbly by Ashton Kutcher) is trying to convince his friend and co-founder, Steve Wozniak, that the business has a future. Wozniak says, "nobody wants to buy a computer." Jobs' response is telling: "How does somebody know what they want if they've never even seen it?"

Yet we're convinced that if firms are going to develop really effective strategies, they need to accurately understand their markets and customers. It is absolutely essential to take the time to understand the customer's underlying value model, keeping in mind all the while that customers don't always really know their value model. Awareness of the value model enables the firm to develop an effective product and service offering. It gives firms a chance to align resources around those elements of the product or service that genuinely matter to the customer. It is the basis for effective market segmentation. It is the course of meaningful differentiation. It is the fundamental knowledge that underlies every strategic decision the firm will make.

But as we've noted, most firms don't have the time or resources to do in-depth market research or to hire the consultants to do it. Firms that have been around for long periods of time tend to get complacent, to believe that "we know what they want; our customers constantly tell us what they expect from us." Some firms believe that their past success is a validation of their market knowledge. Whatever the case, most organizations don't really think about or truly understand the customer's value model. To address this shortcoming — and to provide a sound foundation for strategic decision-making — we developed the Customer Value Analysis (CVA) tool.

Overview

The CVA tool consists of a survey/questionnaire and an analytic methodology for sorting and displaying the survey results. Unlike many techniques, the CVA does NOT begin with *a priori* product or service features and ask customers to rank their preferences. Such methods, we have found, are too susceptible to the organization's or researcher's biases. The goal of the CVA is to identify the CUSTOMER'S underlying value model, not to confirm or disconfirm managers' preconceived ideas regarding value.

The reason we call this the Customer VALUE Analysis is based on the definition of value: the relative worth, merit, or importance of something. In business and economics, we often use price or money as a proxy measure for value or worth. However, the use of the financial metric misses the essential nature of value.

Here's a silly but enlightening example of the difference between price and value. Have you ever had a mouse or mice in your home? If you have, you know how traumatic that can be (one of us has had the experience fairly recently). People are frightened and upset, food gets spoiled, you don't know where the vermin are coming from — it's just a total unpleasant experience. If you've ever had a mouse problem, what is it worth to you to eradicate the mouse from your house? How much would you be willing to pay to eliminate the source of anxiety? So you go to your local Wal-Mart store and there you find an 8-pack of Victor Original Mouse Traps, guaranteed to kill the mouse, for $2.55 (or maybe even less). Is this not the greatest value in economics? For roughly 32 cents, you can eliminate the pest and all of the related emotional and physical damage. Consider what it's WORTH to you to get rid of the mouse, and what the PRICE is to get rid of the mouse.

Value, then, is based on what the product or service is worth to the buyer. It includes not only the physical components of the product or service but the emotional ones as well (this is how it is possible to charge over $200 for a pair of denim jeans with about $55 of actual product cost). It is determined by the customer, not by the provider or seller. It can include not only the actual product or service, but also the sum total of the buyer's experience — from initial information search, to review, to comparisons, to dealing with the firm's representatives, to the actual purchase, delivery, use, and after-sale service and support. That's why it is more proper to use the term value chain rather than supply chain — because the purpose of the chain is to deliver real value to the end-use customer, not simply to supply a product or service.

Understanding the concept of value, then, is the first essential part of performing a CVA. The goal is to understand the customer's value model. Based on our experience, the two niching questions we asked in Chapter 5 are essential: (1) why does the customer decide to buy a particular product or service? and (2) how does the customer decide to buy a particular product or service? Note that the answers to these questions can be intertwined; sometimes the reason why a customer buys a particular product or service is because it is easy to do so. Similarly, in the process of determining which product or service to buy, a customer may discover new information that changes the decision model and introduces new reasons to prefer one product or service over another. Nonetheless, we will treat these as two separate concepts for analytic purposes.

First, why does the customer buy a particular product or service? We call these the Purchase Criteria. The criteria can vary widely, but they can be boiled down to one fundamental driver: the customer wants to solve a problem of some type, to alleviate some type of deficiency between what is (the current state) and what is desired (the future state). It doesn't matter if the customer is buying a pair of shoes, blue jeans, Big Mac sandwich, car, house, health care, hotel room, loan, machinery, investment advice, education — the fundamental driver is the discrepancy between the status quo and the intended, preferred future result.

The psychology behind this can likewise be simplified. People buy products or services for one of two reasons: to seek pleasure or to avoid pain (in either case, the intent is that the future state is better than the current or likely state). Behind this, though, there are countless specific reasons that the customer has for making a specific decision about a particular product or service. It is this cognitive process that organizations need to understand in order to properly identify customer-based value and identify the key purchase criteria.

Second, how does the customer purchase the product or service? We call this the Purchase Process. What is the process the customer goes through in deciding whether or not to buy a particular product or service? What features of the process are important at what times? For example, the reason grocery stores put chewing gum and similar small candy items, such as breath mints, at the cash register is because they know that these are "convenience" goods. Very, very few people think to themselves, "I need to stop at the grocery store on the way home and get a pack of chewing gum." If that's all they need, customers are far more likely to stop at a convenience store (why do you think they call them "convenience stores?"). But if the customer is at the grocery store getting a gallon of milk and a loaf of bread for dinner and sees the gum at the checkout counter, the hope is that the customer will think, "yeah, I could use a pack of gum" and toss it into the order — thereby increasing the average order size and transactional profit for the grocery store.

For other products or services, the customer will actively shop for the purchase; comparing prices, features, etc. (perhaps clothing, a home improvement feature, banking services such as a commercial loan, and many others). Other products or services will involve negotiation (homes, cars, business phone or computer systems, construction services). Still others may be due to availability (think Starbucks or McDonald's). The point is to understand the process by which the customer makes the purchase decision and how the purchase criteria may shift at different times during the purchase process.

Here's an essential point: any time there is a fundamental difference in either the Purchase Criteria (Why They Buy) or the Purchase Process (How They Buy), you have a different market segment. In fact, we would suggest that all market segmentation is based on differences in one or both of these areas; other forms of market classification (such as geography, product or service use, and customer type) are useful for identifying various sectors, but in terms of strategy, they are often artificial distinctions that have no real strategic value. Meaningful market segments are based on differences in Why or How customers buy products or services.

The CVA model is intended to be a quick guide to the process used in the identification of the customer's key Purchase Criteria and the key components of the customer's Purchase Process. Some models can be very simple; for example, Trigger Point: I'm hungry; Problem Definition: I need something to eat, and I don't want to take a lot of time or go out of my way; Information Search: What's close by? There's a Subway sandwich shop on the corner ahead; Analysis/Evaluation: That sounds good, I can get a sandwich made to order; and thus, the decision is made to pull into the shop. In this case, the key purchase criteria were food that was quick and convenient and that could be tailored to the customer's taste and preference. The key elements of the process were decision speed and the ease of getting the information.

Other models can be very complex, such as a decision regarding which physician to use for a procedure, which college to attend, which home to buy, which bank to use for the loan, which factory machinery to buy, and similar purchase decisions that individuals have to make. However, in every case, the basic process of the CVA model holds.

Time to Complete the Tool

One to four weeks, depending on the number of customers to be surveyed and the time required to gather the information. We recommend a variation of the 80/20 rule: since 20% of customers usually account for a majority of sales, firms should always survey half of the core customer base at a minimum, and roughly 5–10% of the remaining customer base. In highly fragmented markets, a survey of 30–60 random customers can be sufficient.

What You Will Need to Complete the Tool

- Agreement on the part of your customers to participate in the survey process.

- Key decision-makers willing to commit the time to talk with customers. Key members of the organization's strategic planning process should participate in some minimum number of survey interviews. If available, sales representatives can be a source of additional interviewers.

- The list of key questions for CVA (listed in the right-hand column of Figure 10.1).

- Capability to take comprehensive, accurate notes on the customer's responses.

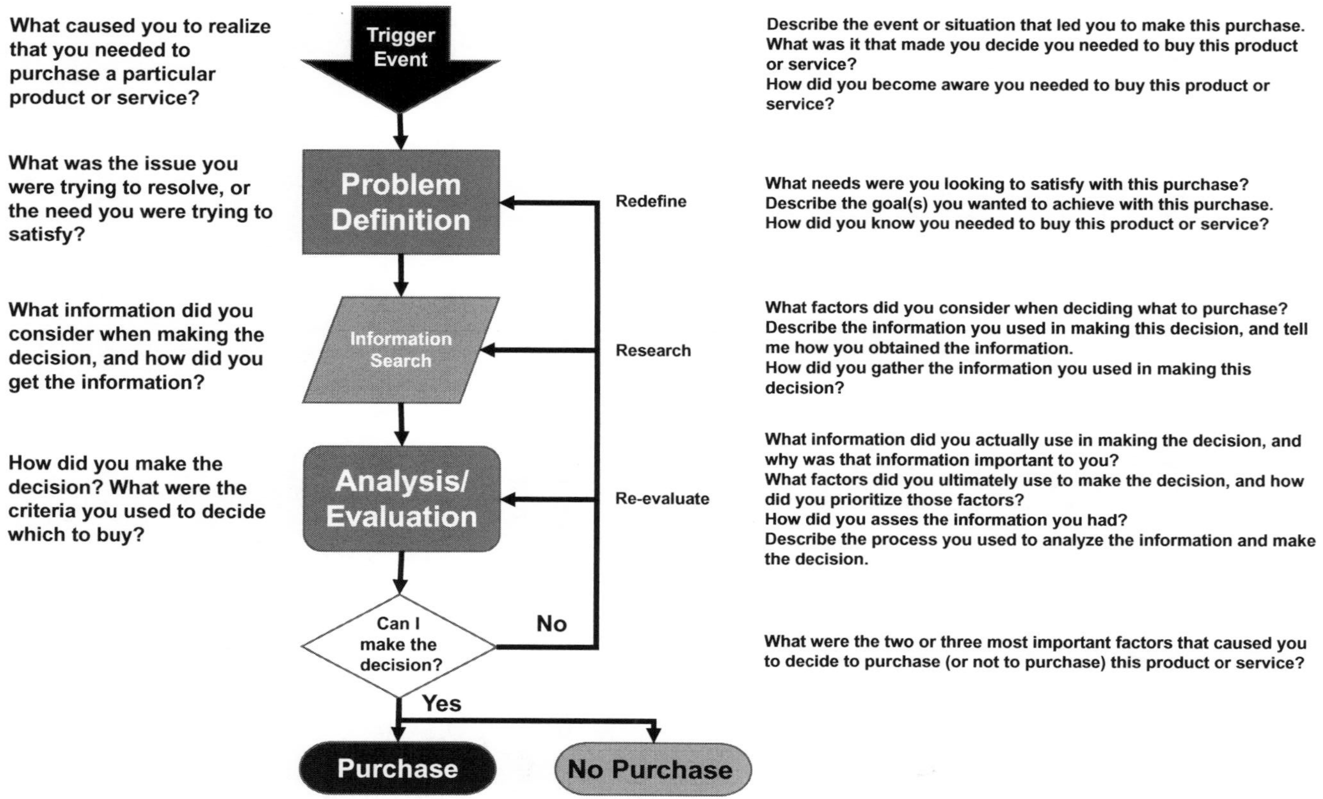

Figure 10.1: The CVA Model.

Top text blocks (right side in rotated view):

Describe the event or situation that led you to make this purchase.
What was it that made you decide you needed to buy this product or service?
How did you become aware you needed to buy this product or service?

What needs were you looking to satisfy with this purchase?
Describe the goal(s) you wanted to achieve with this purchase.
How did you know you needed to buy this product or service?

What factors did you consider when deciding what to purchase?
Describe the information you used in making this decision, and tell me how you obtained the information.
How did you gather the information you used in making this decision?

What information did you actually use in making the decision, and why was that information important to you?
What factors did you ultimately use to make the decision, and how did you prioritize those factors?
How did you asses the information you had?
Describe the process you used to analyze the information and make the decision.

What were the two or three most important factors that caused you to decide to purchase (or not to purchase) this product or service?

Flowchart labels:

Redefine

Research

Re-evaluate

Trigger Event

Problem Definition

Information Search

Analysis/ Evaluation

Can I make the decision?

No

Yes

No Purchase

Purchase

Bottom text blocks (left side in rotated view):

What caused you to realize that you needed to purchase a particular product or service?

What was the issue you were trying to resolve, or the need you were trying to satisfy?

What information did you consider when making the decision, and how did you get the information?

How did you make the decision? What were the criteria you used to decide which to buy?

Gathering Information

For purposes of this analysis, all persons involved in the strategy decision-making process should be involved in gathering the information from each customer. Once the number of customers to be interviewed has been determined, each person should commit to a minimum number of interviews. When possible, two or more individuals from the company should be involved in each interview to listen, take notes, and discuss the results.

Customers should be contacted and asked to participate in the interview process. Once their agreement has been secured, a time should be established for the interview. (*Note*: these interviews can last anywhere from 10 minutes to more than an hour, depending on the complexity of the decision process.)

The interviewers "walk" the customer through the semi-structured interview, using the Key Questions from the CVA as the guideline for the interview. Interviewers should probe as needed and encourage customers to "go deep" in providing a response. For example, if the customer says, "I looked at some sites on the Internet to get some preliminary information," follow-up questions can include "Which sites did you look at?" "How did you find those sites?" "What sites were particularly useful to you? Why?" "Which sites did you like?" "Which ones did you NOT like? Why?" "What other information would you have liked to have seen on the website?" The purpose is to gather as much detailed information as possible on the Purchase Process and the Purchase Criteria. Again, if the customer says, "One of my big issues in making the decision was the quality of the service," follow-up questions can include such items as "How do you define service quality?" "Which of the elements of service quality were most important to you?" "How important was quality — 50% more important? More? Less?"

Another technique that can be borrowed from Six-Sigma methods is the WHY question. That is, keep asking why and by the third or fourth why question, the interviewer will generally get at the underlying factors. For example, if the interviewee says, "Ease of Use is really important to me," and the interviewer respond with, "Why is Ease of Use important?" the customer might respond "My employees aren't very sophisticated, so the product has to be easy for them to use on the work site." The interviewer has now found out a problem the customer is trying to solve, without the customer necessarily articulating that fact. The customer has a problem when products are too complex or difficult for employees to use. This fact can be instrumental in setting strategy or in product design, innovation, and the like.

The interviewer will want to gather as much content *in the customers' own words* regarding the purchase process and criteria. Note the emphasis in this last point: the goal should be to use the customer's language as much as possible and avoid providing the interviewer's interpretation. To the extent that this is possible, the interviewer should listen to the customer, write down what was said verbatim, and avoid "priming" or interjecting bias into the interview process.

Arraying the Data

Each person or team of people who conduct the interviews should take the results of the interviews and organize the information using Table 10.1.

1. The verbatim statements from the customers are reviewed, discussed, and identified. The statements are then summarized as Purchase Criteria or Purchase Process factors. These are given a label or title that describes the criteria or factor that the customer is using in the value determination process.

2. Based on the customer's statements in the interview, the interviewer(s) assign a relative importance weight to the specific Criteria or Factor, indicating the relative weight of the individual Criteria or Factor in the decision process. For example, if the customer says, "Price is by far the most important criteria for me, almost twice as important as quality and delivery," then Price would get a weight of 50%

Table 10.1: Key Purchase Criteria/Purchase Process Factors.

Purchase Criteria	Importance	Customer Statement
Criteria Priority 1	Weight, from 0 to 100	Verbatim from the interview
Criteria Priority 2	Weight, from 0 to 100	Verbatim from the interview
Criteria Priority 3	Weight, from 0 to 100	Verbatim from the interview
Etc.	Must Total 100	
Purchase Process	Importance	Customer Statement
Process Factor 1	Weight, from 0 to 100	Verbatim from the interview
Process Factor 2	Weight, from 0 to 100	Verbatim from the interview
Process Factor 3	Weight, from 0 to 100	Verbatim from the interview
Etc.	Must total 100	

while Quality and Delivery would each receive a weight of 25. Or the customer may say, "I use the web site for preliminary information, but at the end of the day I'm going to listen far more to the sales representative," which might result in the website getting a weight of 20 or 30 while the salesperson's presentation might be weighted as 70 or 80.

Clearly, this is a subjective process. The key issue is to try and maintain relative weightings, not absolute weights. For example, if the customer says, "how well the product performs on the shop floor is hands-down my number one factor; anything else isn't even close," the weights should reflect that subjective assessment. But as we've noted previously, when making these assessments, it is far more important to try for accuracy rather than precision. There's no way to determine what the absolute weights are in the customer's mind; but if the interviewer(s) can get the right directional weights, the result will be effective.

3. The results from the individual table are combined into a master table (or spreadsheet) so that all of the interviewers can see the data. The results are then combined, and differences in wording or interpretation are resolved by the group. Once the team has identified a common set of Criteria and Factors, these are combined and average weights for each are established. Finally, the Criteria and Factors are ranked by average weight to determine the Key Purchase Criteria and Key Purchase Process Factors. An example is shown in Table 10.2.

4. Next, the key Purchase Criteria and Purchase Process Factors can be compared to identify logical clusters of buyers. For example, the company might sort firms on Price and Ease of Use, and find that customers fall into certain logical groupings. The size of the circle represents the size of the volume of sales to that customer group. An example is depicted in Figure 10.2.

   Figure 10.2 shows three distinct segments. Segment 1, highlighted in light gray, is buyers who are indifferent as to price and expect the service to be somewhat difficult to use. These might be buyers who are looking for a moderately priced product that has other features that may make the product more complex to use, but as long as those features are available, ease of use is not important. The black circle, the smallest segment, is the price buyers; as long as the product is cheap, they aren't too concerned with how easy it is to use. The dark gray circle group, the largest segment, expects products to be somewhat inexpensive but extremely easy to use.

5. Additional sorts can be created using differing combinations or Purchase Criteria and Purchase Process factors. The sorts can then be combined (or used in a three-dimensional space or figure; or various statistical techniques such as multiple regression or cluster analyses can be used, if necessary) to identify logical segments of customers who are similar based

Table 10.2: Example: Customer Value Analysis — Key Purchase Criteria/Purchase Process Factors.

Purchase Criteria	Importance	Customer Statement
Price (competitive)	35	"If price isn't comparable to other products, I'm not buying."
Quality — Durability	30	"It has to last a long time or we can't afford to buy it."
Quality — Reliability	20	"When I go to use it, it had better perform right the first time."
Service	15	"When it breaks, I expect someone to fix it fast."
	100	

Purchase Process	Importance	Customer Statement
Order Entry	50	"I want to be able to order it when I need it without a lot of hassle."
Information Availability	35	"I need to be able to get information about operation, pricing, etc., right away."
Customer Service Interaction	15	"When I call with a question, I expect an answer — fast and accurately!"
Etc.	100	

on Why and How They Buy. This allows the firm to identify the strategic market segments.

6. Additional research can (and should) be done with customers who are in the market but are NOT currently buying the firm's products or services. This can enable the firm to

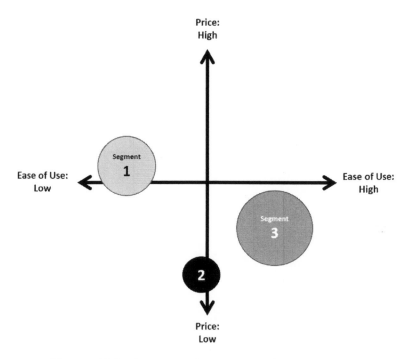

Figure 10.2: Customer Groups: Price by Ease of Use.

identify market segments that are available but are not part of the firm's strategic customer set.

7. Once the firm has generated sufficient data sorts and analyses, the firm should be able to generate individual CVAs for each of the major market segments. This enables managers to understand the customer's value model and the opportunities to position the firm's product and/or service offerings so as to align with the value model of the selected customers.

Key Strategic Questions

Some of the key strategic questions that should arise from the use of the CVA include such issues as:

- What are the key customer Purchase Criteria and Purchase Process Factors that we need to satisfy?

- What are the distinct strategic segments in our markets?

- Which of these segments do we currently align with? Which do we want to align with? What do we need to do and how should we commit our resources to insure our business model aligns with their value model?

- What can we offer customers that will enable them to better solve their fundamental problem that the customer hasn't thought of yet?

- How might the Purchase Criteria or Purchase Process change in the future? Do we have the resources available to address those changes?

- How can we get the customer the information they need at the right time in the process to influence them to consider our offering?

- Which segments are growing? Which are declining? Why?

- What problems does the customer have that we haven't thought about addressing?

- When should we be involved in the purchase process? With what information? How can we influence the customer's analysis and evaluation process?

- When customers DON'T buy our products or services, what are the factors that are knocking us out of the purchase decision?

Our Favorite Anecdote Using This Tool

The CVA in Action

The top leadership team of a transportation services company was engaged in the process of developing a strategy for the firm. Traditional market "segmentation" had divided the business by service line: (1) Household Goods Moving and Storage and (2) Logistics Services and Warehousing. Within these groups, the team had further segmented the market based on customer type. Within the Household Goods Moving group, there were Corporate customers and Retail (individual) customers. In Logistics Services, there were Transportation customers (those who wanted minimal handling of goods; single cross-docking of loads was sufficient) and Logistics customers (those who required Warehousing and Packaging services).

As part of the process of strategy development, the team was encouraged to think of the company as not being in the transportation business but rather being in the "stuff" business. That is, customers had "stuff" in one place, and they needed it in another place. Once the team had changed its view of the market, several things came to light:

1. There were, at a minimum, two distinct and significant segments of corporate customers. Some corporate customers wanted the lowest cost moves for their people, while others demanded accuracy, timeliness, and quality of service. For the first group, cost control and moving their executives as inexpensively as possible was important. For the second group, it was far more important that the employee's goods arrived on time, in perfect condition, and that the employee (and the employee's family) was treated well in the process.

2. The "low price" corporate segment generally used the Purchasing Department to make the buying decision. Since the purchasing buyers were rewarded based on the ability to save the company money, price was very important to them. The "quality" segment used the Human Resources department to make the purchasing decision. The HR department was more concerned with the attitudes of employees when moving employees and families to other locations. The Purchasing Process differed! The Purchasing Department buyers made extensive use of bid processes. The HR buyers set performance criteria, then negotiated terms, conditions, and pricing to get the best combination of results for the company.

3. "Retail" moving customers also had multiple segments. One group wanted to get the move done at the lowest price. A second group was primarily concerned with insuring that their goods were going to be treated well and that their items would arrive on time and in good condition. A third group was interested in being able to store certain goods and have easy access to those goods if necessary.

4. Logistics Service customers who were primarily interested in basic transportation services were price buyers, looking for the lowest rate per mile. However, certain goods that were time-sensitive had buyers who were far more concerned with the company's on-time record and delivery capability. These buyers were willing to pay a premium for the guaranteed delivery.

5. The team noticed that customers who had seasonal goods, such as lawn mowers, fertilizer, or grass seed, didn't have a demand for year-round transportation services, but during the season, transportation was critical to these buyers. As a result, the team developed a warehousing organization with flexible staffing capability to meet customer demand. This solved the customers' problem of having to hire their own seasonal workforce and enabled the company to charge a premium for the service; but by spreading out the work among multiple seasonal customers, the firm was able to increase operating efficiencies and grow the margins of the business.

6. As a result of the analysis, the team identified 12 distinct strategic market segments (instead of the 4 used initially). The team further determined that 3 of those segments did not align with the company's strategic positioning and, as a result, minimized resource commitments to those segments.

7. By treating the company as being in the "stuff" business and looking at solving the customers' problem (how do I get my stuff from point A to point B), the team was able to identify some new segments and market opportunities. A niche market was identified in moving motorcycles for people who

wanted to go on long trips or who wanted to attend major bike rallies, such as Daytona Beach or Sturgis. The team noted that there were customers who got caught when their existing transportation providers were not able to meet their peak demands; therefore, the company developed a brokerage business to move freight to meet short-term customer needs. Both the motorcycle business and the brokerage business had higher than average margins for the company, as the customers were not as price sensitive; they wanted their products delivered on time and in good condition and were willing to pay for the extra handling and transportation required.

By taking a fresh, strategic look at the company's markets, the firm was able to better align resources and actions to meet the customer segments' expectations. The management team was also able to identify new product and service offerings that provided superior margins. Certain segments that were identified as a poor fit or low margin activity were gradually diminished; the company stopped devoting resources to those markets and learned to say "No, we don't do that." By doing so, the company was able to maintain revenues while growing profit margins — all as a result of strategic market segmentation generated through an effective CVA model.

The Willingness to Pay (WTP) Ranking Tool

> **Strategy Question:** How do I understand my customers' "Willingness to Pay" for my products or services?

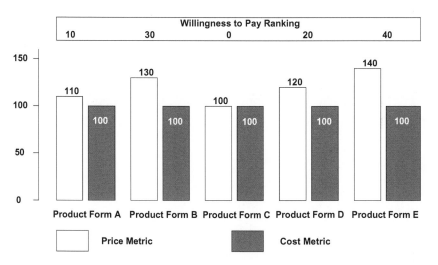

Figure 11.1: The WTP Ranking Tool.

Overview

This tool seeks to use very simple business cost and price information to provide perspective on customers' willingness to pay for the products or services you offer. The tool works equally well for those with modest financial rigor or those with a high-powered ERP system. The Willingness to Pay (WTP) Ranking Tool uses a simple process to ratio prices earned and costs (cost = 100) to arrive at a single figure of merit. This WTP Ranking, in the form of Figure 11.1, can be used (1) as an indicator of whether the value you provide is in line with the customer's payment, and (2) as a ranking for comparison purposes across the product/service lines you offer.

Time to Complete the Tool

This tool can be pulled together within 2–4 hours for a first pass, given appropriate cost knowledge.

Introduction

You likely offer a broad array of products or services to your customers. How do you really know if your customers are willing to pay for the *value* you provide? This question implies a need for a comparison between the price you are able to command in the marketplace, and the costs of supplying that product or service. Simple, right? All you need to do is send it to the Accounting group, have them crunch the numbers, and spit out a gross margin (GM) calculation, and then you have your answer. Well, maybe.

We default to the gross margin and gross margin percent calculation a lot in this book, and we believe it one of the best financial metrics (and the first we tend to use) for digging in and initially understanding product or service business health. We like gross margin because it is usually an apples-to-apples comparison across the product or service line, generally containing consistent assumptions across an organization's cost model. But in understanding value to our customers and their willingness to pay for that value, we sometimes need to peel back the onion a bit more and look beyond the gross margin calculation.

So why sully the reputation of a perfectly good financial ratio? Well, we use gross margin here as our starting point. But it is surprising how many companies define gross margin differently. No, not the formal, high-level definition of "Revenue minus Cost of Goods Sold (COGS)" — that remains rock solid. The concern is what cost line items each company includes in COGS for their gross margin calculation. It is not uncommon for organizations to define different combinations of line item costs for use in their GM computation. Some companies include engineering costs (or some portion of engineering costs) in gross margin, some do not. Some include supply chain personnel costs (or some portion of supply chain personnel costs) in gross margin, some do not. You get the idea. If any of these costs are not directly applied to COGS, they are usually included in a whole new grouping of line items called Sales, General, and Administrative (SG&A) expenses. Furthermore, many companies may also have additional corporate or "home office" costs charged to them. Where do they get placed in the cost structure, COGS, or SG&A? As mentioned previously, a company will typically have made those internal decisions and allocated these costs consistently across all the products or services in their cost model. But are they allocated correctly and in true proportions? Regardless, those assumptions get built into the high-level ERP code that generates the monthly financial reports. Sitting here right now, do you know where the "value added" costs you'd like your customers to pay for are slotted in your cost structure? The WTP answer in this case may, and many times does, lie beyond the gross margin line.

The question we have to contend with is which costs/expenses truly reflect the value we are supplying to our customers. Then we need to accurately capture them toward defining a figure of merit to understand and rank customer's willingness to pay for the value we supply. This is what the WTP Tool does. It defines a basic "Price Metric" and a "Cost Metric." The simple ratio of Price Metric divided by the Cost Metric yields a "WTP Ranking" that can be used for comparative insight across your product or service forms.

What You Will Need to Construct the Tool

- A "Price Metric" reflective of the price the customer has paid for, or the total revenues generated by your product or service.

- A "Cost Metric" reflective of the relevant costs defining the value you are providing to your customers.

- Availability of cost line items from which to construct the "Cost Metric." This will need to include both COGS and SG&A information.

Where to Get the Information

There are a couple of ways to approach this. If you have good costed "bills of material (BOM)," you will have Price and COGS line items defined by individual product or service form and you can take the "by individual unit" approach. The other approach is to rely on the formal financial statements where revenue, cost, and profitability of product or service forms are shown in aggregate dollar form. Where you may have a challenge is in defining any SG&A costs that are relevant to the particular product or service form. The good news is that if they are undefined, you should be able to estimate or capture them with assumptions based on your good judgement.

The Price Metric — The price metric is probably the easiest to calculate. It can be reflected by the price of a single product or service form (from the costed BOM), a compilation of product or service forms by way of a revenue figure, or some other appropriate representation of pricing or revenue intake.

The Cost Metric — The cost metric centers around the cost line items that truly define what you are offering to your customer. We start with gross margin and the line items that construct its calculation. You need to assess whether the costs defined there are inclusive of all the value you provide to the customer. If you find it is incomplete, you must further define those missing elements.

More often than not, there will be some element of SG&A that may need to be included. Tip-offs here are whether one product or service form takes significantly more time than others in key areas, such as:

- The outside sales group to sell

- The inside sales group to quote

- The estimating group to cost

- The engineering group to design.

Note those extra costs and add them to the appropriate product or service form to capture the relevant costs of the value being provided.

How to Construct the Tool

- Choose the product or service forms you need to evaluate.

- For each, calculate the "Price Metric" using either standard unit pricing or revenue data from your financial statements.

- Define your "Cost Metric":

  - Start with your standard gross margin.

  - Add any relevant SG&A line item costs to the COGS.

  - Sum those costs to define your cost metric.

- Calculate the WTP Ranking. The WTP Ranking is simply calculated by dividing the "Price Metric" by the "Cost Metric." To get the ranking, simply subtract 1.00 from the resulting ratio and use the remaining decimal as the WTP Ranking. (If you encounter a negative, show it as a negative WTP Ranking.) Additionally, since we are using cost as the denominator in our simple ratio, we are actually normalizing each calculation — so cost can be considered a baseline of 100 for each individual WTP Ranking. The result can be shown in graphical form similar to Figures 11.1, 11.3, or 11.4.

Let's provide an example to help illustrate the usefulness and construction of the tool. Consider a small company that builds homes. They have specialized in lower-priced "spec homes;" i.e. homes built to a common specification for sale to customers as is. In our example, each pre-designed spec home sells for $200,000. Let's assume the company owner has begun to venture into higher-priced and more customized home segments with the lure of higher profit. He created a second category offering, adding defined option packages to their spec homes. There are additional costs for salespeople, designers, and outside contractors implicit in the option packages. For our example, the average price for these houses is $400,000. Lastly, let's assume he stepped up to a third category and built a completely custom luxury home — for which he charged $2,000,000. The custom home, with infinitely more design complexity, necessitated even more added support.

Upon completion of the latter house, the owner asked to see the gross margins for each of the three categories of homes. In the case of the homebuilder, the term "sticks and bricks" typically describes the COGS for a house. The owner's outside accountant dutifully provided exactly what was asked for — the gross margin calculation for each home category. Choosing 10 spec homes, 5 spec plus option homes, and the single luxury home provided a common revenue dollar level from which to compare. Figure 11.2 shows gross margins of 18%, 23%, and 25% for the increasingly complex housing categories. The owner could pat himself on the back and conclude that his strategic venture into higher worth homes was a success. But he would be wrong.

Beyond the GM calculation, there are extra value-added costs that were not captured in the COGS. The five we cite in our example (costs to quote the projects, costs to engineer the projects, costs of outside contractors, costs to source the upscale materials, and legal costs to file extra permits for the extreme custom house) are reflective of typical costs categories that in many cases are not included in gross margin, but they are SG&A costs directly relevant to the value of the sale. Including these costs — in this case beyond the "sticks and bricks" tradition of gross margin for this industry — reveals a completely different story. Adding the

	Base Spec Homes (Quantity = 10)	Spec Home Plus Defined Option Packages (Quantity = 5)	Completely Custom Home (Quantity = 1)
PRICE METRIC — Revenue	$2,000,000	$2,000,000	$2,000,000
Cost of Goods Sold (Sticks and Bricks)	$1,640,000	$1,550,000	1,500,000
Gross Margin	$360,000	$450,000	$500,000
Gross Margin Percent	18%	23%	25%
Additional Content (Relevant SG&A Costs)			
Cost to Quote Projects	$0	$75,000	$80,000
Cost to Engineer Projects	$0	$50,000	$60,000
Costs of Outside Contractors	$0	$20,000	$20,000
Cost to Source Materials	$0	$0	$50,000
Legal Costs to File Extra Permits	$0	$0	$15,000
Cost of Extra Value Additions	$0	$145,000	$225,000
COST METRIC — Total Relevant Costs	$1,640,000	$1,695,000	$1,725,000
Price Metric/Cost Metric	1.22	1.18	1.16
WILLINGNESS TO PAY RANKING	22	18	16

Figure 11.2: WTP Ranking Example.

relevant costs for the five key line items not included in GM is critical to understanding the total value the homebuilder supplied to his customer. The total "Cost Metric" is shown in Figure 11.2 by adding the "COGS" and "Additional Content (Relevant SG&A Costs)."

The WTP Ranking is simply calculated by dividing the "Price Metric" by the "Cost Metric." To get the ranking for the spec home, we simply grab the decimal portion of the 1.22 result (i.e. 1.22 − 1.00) of 22 and use it as our WTP Ranking. In our example, you can see the WTP Ranking actually decreases from 22, 18, and 16, respectively, for the increasingly complex housing forms, exactly the opposite trend seen on the gross margin percent line. This result is shown in Figure 11.3.

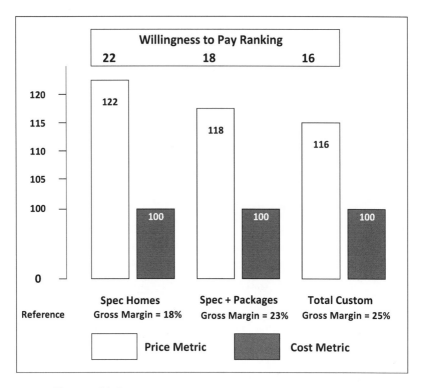

Figure 11.3: WTP Ranking for Homebuilder Example.

Key Strategic Questions

The homebuilding company's owner can ponder a number of strategic questions given this result. Some we might suggest if we were working with him:

- Does the difference between GM% and WTP make sense to you?

- Why do you think you are not getting paid equivalently for the higher two grades of homes?

- Why is the customer not willing to pay for the extra value you are providing them in your higher-end offerings?

  - Are you adding costs that your customer does not value? If so, why?

- Are your costs too high for those items that must be supplied — and hence your customers are not willing to pay above market price for them?

- If so, do you need to reduce process costs to meet the market need?

- Are you charging the correct price? Are you giving away value that your competitors aren't?

- Are you better suited to stay in the low-cost and low-value segment of the market where your cost model better suits your customer's WTP?

- Can you make up the 4- and 6-point gaps between your spec-plus and luxury offerings? Should you?

(Authors' Notes: Some of you more financially astute readers may be saying to yourself that we are simply approaching a calculation of "Operating Profit" (generally defined as Operating Profit = Revenue minus COGS minus SG&A costs), and you would be correct. But how many times have you seen a company calculate Operating Profit by product or service line? It is rare in our experience. Even If they do, have they taken the time to apply the SG&A costs properly across the product or service forms — or, more typically, just allocated them as a simple percentage of revenue? Note how our example would have changed if the $370K ($0 + $145K + $225K) cost of extra value additions had been averaged and allocated evenly at $123K across each of the three categories. If there are two or three line items over and above COGS that reflect and capture major differences in the overall cost of the value you provide, why go through all the work to allocate every SG&A line item to get an Operating Profit when you can apply the WTP tool to get that directional guidance you need? Remember we are practical in our approach and assume an organization's time and resources are limited. Don't get us wrong, if you can get to an OP number by product line, and the costs are truly allocated by effort, by all means use that!! But for all the others of us, this WTP Ranking tool can provide timely and efficient insight on whether the customer is indeed paying for the value you are providing.)

Our Favorite Anecdote Using This Tool

A new CEO in a manufacturing company was quickly working to understand the business health of his product lines. He used the Product Volume Margin (PVM) Tool from Chapter 8 as a logical start. As usual, the results from that tool were immediate, significant, and material. He now had a solid base of information to further help him diagnose issues and abnormalities.

He arranged the products in three groupings. The first was the top 30% of his product forms that contributed a significant portion of his revenue and gross margin. The second was the bottom 30% had the lowest gross margins and the lowest contributions to revenue. The third was that middle group (here 40%) of the product forms that had revenue and gross margin contributions between the outer two groups. Since he had a problem with the competency of his finance group at the time, he went to the financial reports himself to understand what comprised his gross margin calculations. He calculated and summed the revenues for each of the three groups, and similarly grouped and summed all the "cost of goods sold" line items for each of the three groups to get a composite COGS expense.

His representative gross margin for each of the three groups was:

- Top 30% — Average gross margin of 32%

- Middle 40% — Average gross margin of 22%

- Bottom 30% — Average gross margin of 15%.

The results seemed consistent and directionally what one would expect given the overall gross margin for the company. But as helpful as these tools are in giving the strategist a solid insight on what is going on, they are more about giving you a basis to ask the right strategy questions. In this case, while accurate, the results from the PVM chart alone didn't seem to accurately portray what he was feeling and hearing in the organization. In particular, when he talked to his Sales and Engineering groups, conversations would usually steer toward how much they hated that middle

40% of product forms. It seemed they spent most of their time dealing with them, rather than the other two groupings. The curious thing was the gross margins he calculated didn't seem to reflect the extra effort and angst he was hearing in the organization.

It seemed the one difference of that middle 40% was that the nature of the products was custom-engineering. The sales group worked with the customers and allowed them to throw any option into the mix they wanted. This forced the engineering group to practically engineer the entire product — just for a quote. Add to that Sales' desire to placate the customer when he wanted to make a change midway through Engineering's design process, and they had a perfect storm for the anxiety he was hearing.

He went back to his financial reports and dug a bit further. He called in his finance people and asked for better definition on some of the line items, especially how the engineering and sales efforts were allocated. He learned that his finance people got lazy somewhere down the line and simply decided it was too hard to track engineering's activities, so they just rolled them out of gross margin. They argued the sales costs were SG&A so the CEO shouldn't be concerned with them. And since the Bank didn't care and the auditors didn't seem to notice, the CEO was being unusually meticulous and wasting his time.

Well the CEO thought differently, especially when the CFO couldn't tell him which products were really making money and which ones weren't. He decided to create a WTP Ranking himself. Since he had already defined a "Price Metric" and the COGS part of the "Cost Metric" already, he started there. He queried his sales and engineering departments and simply allocated their expenses to the three groups of product forms based on their estimated percentage of time they spent on each. His shocking result is shown in Figure 11.4. The WTP Ranking for top and bottom product form categories remained in line with the gross margin calculation at 30 and 15 respectively. But the middle product forms deviated wildly, showing a −20 ranking against a gross margin of +22%. The costs (again the baseline for the calculation and denominator of the WTP ranking) were 20 points higher than the revenue they

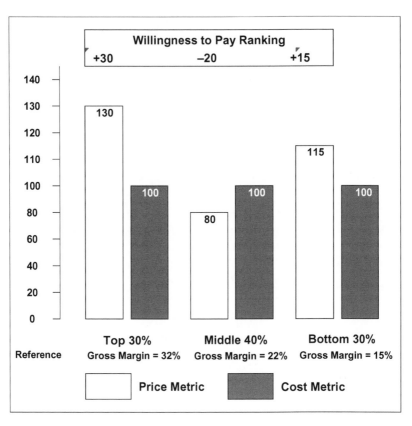

Figure 11.4: WTP for a Manufacturing Company.

were able to command for them. Furthermore, the WTP Ranking shows the middle product forms a full 50 points below the top category, and even 35 points below the bottom category of product forms. The company was losing significant money on the middle product category and all things being equal should have stopped making them immediately. In this case, the loosely defined financial reporting masked the situation the WTP analysis was able to uncover.

The CEO pulled his Sales and Engineering groups together and explained the situation. The conclusion that the customer simply didn't see value in, or pay for, the significant and detailed work they went through to prepare a quote was enlightening for them. The question was asked, and conversation shifted to what type of quote accuracy could be obtained for a 90%+ reduction in effort from both Sales and Engineering. Through a series of baseline bill of materials and "rules of thumb" guidelines, a new process was instituted with that 90% goal reduction in mind. After three months, they met their resource reduction goal and were within a few percentage points of the quote accuracy they had seen previously when they almost entirely engineered the special. This was deemed acceptable by the CEO.

The CEO shifted the freed-up resources toward strengthening and selling more of the top 30% product group. The WTP Ranking helped this company understand they were out of balance with their customer base and focused them to move to a place where their value add met the value the customer was willing to pay for.

The Product/Service Portfolio Matrix Tool

Strategy Question: *How do we determine and prioritize which products/services need action?*

Product Form	Segment 1	Segment 2	Segment 3	Segment 4	Segment 5	Segment 6
A	Price/Margin	Price/Margin	Price/Margin	Price/Margin	Price/Margin	X
B	X	X	X		X	X
C	Price/Margin			X		
D	X		X		X	X
E	X		X		X	X
F	Price/Margin	Price/Margin	Price/Margin		Price/Margin	
G	Price/Margin		Price/Margin		Price/Margin	
H	X				X	
I	X				X	
J	Price/Margin	Price/Margin	Price/Margin			
K		Price/Margin	Price/Margin			
L		Price/Margin	Price/Margin			
M	X		X		X	X
N		Price/Margin	Product			
O	Price/Margin	Price/Margin				
P	Product	Product		Product		
Q					Product	
R					X	
S	Product	Product			X	Product
T		Product		Product		
U	Price/Margin		Price/Margin			
V	X		X			
W	Product		Product			
X	X	Product	X	X	X	Product
Y	Price/Margin	Price/Margin	Price/Margin	Price/Margin		
Z	Price/Margin		Price/Margin	Price/Margin		
AA					Product	
BB	Price/Margin					
CC	Product	Product	Product			Product
DD						Product
EE						Product
FF						Product
GG			Product			

☐ No Deficiency

▨ One Deficiency — Product Performance OR Price/Margin

■ Two Deficiencies — Product Performance AND Price Margin

Figure 12.1: The Product/Service Portfolio Matrix Tool.

157

Overview

This very important tool is designed to provide a concise "current state" assessment of your product/service offerings in the areas of market competitiveness and price/cost position (the first two P's in our Market and Four P Tool approach). Three categories are used to rate each product/service:

1. No deficiency — competitive in both Product Performance and Price/Cost areas (color-coded white).

2. One deficiency — Product Performance *or* Price/Margin deficiency (color-coded gray).

3. Two deficiencies — Product Performance *and* Price/Margin deficiency (color-coded black).

When these product/service deficiencies are displayed relative to the most important market segments (ranked left to right in decreasing order of priority), the tool output serves as a strategic baseline from which to scope, frame, and define Product improvement and Price/Cost margin enhancement projects needed. The magnitude of deficiency and corrective actions necessarily provides insight on your current product/service positioning within and across market segment verticals.

Time to Complete the Tool

Two hours to two days pending availability of information.

Introduction

The previous chapters are all powerful and the tools are very useful individually. At this point, we begin to leverage those tools together and multiply their effectiveness. If you have been following the chronology of this book, you now have a pretty good baseline of information to work from. You know your market size, and you have segmented and niched it. You have established your priority for those segments and niches. You also have a good feel for the competitiveness — both performance and pricing — of your products and services.

This is a significant point for us. Referring back to our Market and Four P flowchart in Chapter 2, we are at a crucial juncture. This is where we begin to answer the questions implied in the Product and Price/Cost P's. What are the Product/Service improvement efforts we need to improve our position in our prioritized markets/segments/niches? What are the Price/Cost issues we need to focus on to improve our business health in our chosen markets/segments/niches?

The answers that result from this tool are important in framing key elements from part of our strategy definition, namely integrated activities and positioning within a competitive environment. This tool is where we begin defining those potential activities and their impact relative to positioning options.

Generally, an organization will position their offerings in one of three ways.

- Low Value–Low Cost. The organization aims to satisfy the basic need for customers whose only purchase criterion is the lowest price.

- Higher Value–Higher Cost. The organization provides extra value (better quality, more features, service, etc.) at a higher cost to a broader, differentiated market.

- Niche Focus–Focus on a very small category of customers to satisfy their particular needs. The product/service will typically demand a higher price, but one customers will pay for a unique solution to their problem.

For example, low-cost airlines like Allegiant Air in the United States or Ryanair in Europe provide basic, no-frills transportation. They focus on the vacation traveler, offer a limited number of flights to and from a limited set of destinations, and offer limited services and charge extra for them. In comparison, the higher value American Airlines or British Airways cater to a more diverse business and recreation clientele. They offer more flights to more locations and offer many more services (first class, in-flight entertainment, frequent flyer programs, etc.). Lastly, consider the niche traveler who cares only about convenience and the shortest travel time. Private executive jet services provide this niche service, but at a much higher price.

There should be numerous discussions that flow from the output of this tool. This is the point where positioning discussions and strategic direction starts to take shape. In some situations, the direction may be starkly clear. In others, there may likely be multiple directions to go. There are some tools coming that will help with sorting out the magnitudes and concrete actions you may need. But for now, we need to start by defining those potential activities that flow from potential strategic directions derived from this important tool.

What You Will Need to Construct the Tool

- *Columns* — A prioritized importance ranking of your market segments — either currently served or targeted for new penetration.

- *Rows* — A list of product/service forms — currently offered and/or targeted new offerings. List by line item each of the relevant product/service forms marketed into each segment.

- *Competitive Position* — An analysis of each line item chosen relative to product/service performance and price/cost positions within each market segment listed.

Where to Get the Information

Market segment attractiveness — If you have been working the tools in this book, the size, segment, and niche importance and prioritization conclusions from Chapters 4–6 will flow directly into this tool. If you are starting here and have yet to determine importance of segments, you will need to set a priority. Chapters 4, 5, and 6 will be helpful in this task. If prioritization has already occurred in your organization, use that breakdown.

A breakdown of your products/services — A good place to start is with the PVM chart of Chapter 8 — breaking down the 12–15 product/service forms you offer. For this exercise, however, it is usually appropriate to expand the product/service offering details. For example, the PVM chart may have broken the product forms into 2-, 4-, and 6-cylinder engines. Here it might be relevant to show the 2-cylinder engines further broken out into marine, motorcycle, or ATV applications. Similarly, service forms may have been defined as accounts receivable and accounts payable services. Here it might be relevant to further break down accounts payable processes into medical, dental, and veterinary clients.

Analysis of competitive position — Again, a good place to start is with prior tools. Those from Chapter 8 (PVM tool for business health of product/service forms) and Chapter 9 (Market Portfolio Matrix tool for market competitiveness of product/service forms) again easily flow into this tool. If those tools have yet to be used, you will need to consult your sales, marketing, technical, and finance people to get a sense for competitiveness.

How to Construct the Tool

This tool is easily constructed using any standard spreadsheet program. The checklist is as follows:

- For the columns — rank your most important market segments from left to right, with the most important segment placed on the far left. Place the next segments in descending order of importance to the right.

- Row line items — list each relevant product/service form, one per row. It is highly probable that during the growth of a company, one product/service form evolved to serve multiple segments. This is a great place to capture this aspect.

There may be slight product/service changes required to accomplish this. A question that commonly arises is whether to call each nuance a separate line item or combine them as a common line item serving multiple segments. You need to balance whether you call this a separate product/service or not. A guideline to consider: if a majority of the cost or technical performance is identical between segments, make it one line item and show it serving multiple segments. For example, if the aforementioned 2-cylinder engine is basically the same except for non-corrosive hoses in marine applications and specially sealed aluminum covers in ATV applications, consider them as one line item toward identifying whether the core engine itself is competitive in each segment.

- Individual matrix cells — start by placing an "X" in each line item cell where the product/service is sold into each segment.

- Leave blank the cells where the product/service does not play a part in a certain segment.

- For the cells with an "X," using the competitive information you've developed for each product/service, simply analyze and color code each box as follows:

  - White — product/service is performance and cost competitive

  - Gray — we have one deficiency — either a technical *Product* performance issue or a *Price/Margin* issue. Color the cell gray and replace the "x" label in the cell with the appropriate "Product" or "Price/Margin" to properly reflect the issue.

  - Black — we have both Product and Price/Margin issues. Color this cell black and replace the "x" with your assessment of the bigger development challenge — "Product" if the bigger task is product performance and "Price/Margin" if it is price/cost improvement.

The output should resemble Figure 12.1. (Note that outside of the black and white constraints of book publishing, we'd normally use green, yellow, and red color codes in place of the white, gray, and black shading.) Once complete with the first pass, analyze whether the results really represent your business. Freely make any tweaks in line items or segments that make the analysis accurate for your situation while maintaining the integrity of exercise.

Key Strategic Questions

We find a well-constructed Product Portfolio Matrix should help you put in perspective the magnitude of product/service work necessary. A few questions we'd likely pursue are:

- Can you get a general read on the health of your product/service portfolio (i.e. what is the mix of white "x", gray and black boxes)?

- How healthy (predominance of white "x" cells) is your product/service portfolio in your most important (farthest to the left) vertical segment? Your top three segments?

- Are most of your issues due to 1-deficiency (gray) or 2-deficiency (black) categories?

- Of the cells coded gray or black, are a majority of them due to Price/Margin? If so, is there something systemic going on? Can you be cost competitive?

- If you are focused on a low value—low price position, and most of your deficiencies are due to cost issues, do you need to reconsider your position?

- Similarly, if most gray or black cells are product/service performance related, why have you fallen so far behind your peers?

- If you are focused on the differentiated high value—high price position, and the majority of your issues are product performance related, are you capable of satisfying a broad market need with your market or product development expertise?

- If you are focused on a small, niche-sized vertical, are you competitive enough and commanding a high enough price to allow long-term survival?

- If most of your cells are colored white "x," are you significantly outperforming your competitors? You should be.

There are several strategic questions that can also be considered based on Figure 12.2, such as:

- Are there enough white "x" (and gray) areas for key product/service line items across vertical segments to suggest a competitive strength toward better leveraging this set of products/services across all segments?

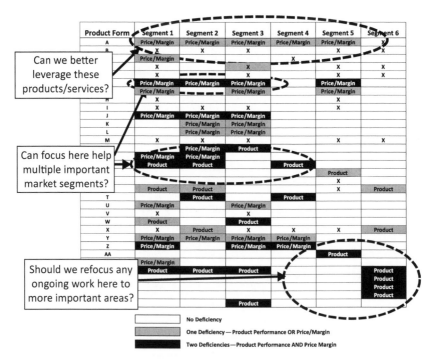

Figure 12.2: Strategic Questions from the Product Portfolio Matrix Tool.

- If improvement is needed, should we group improvement efforts to shore up one vertical segment at a time?

- Are there areas where one major improvement initiative could impact multiple vertical segments? (If so, these should be listed and strongly considered as potential product/service improvement or cost reduction initiatives for your strategic plan.)

- Are there ongoing initiatives whose resources may be better served elsewhere?

- Are there any vertical segments that are so far behind (predominance of black cells) that we should reassess our participation there?

- Are there any line items that are so uncompetitive that we should reassess our providing them in the future?

The position you take with your products or services is extremely important. We can get you far enough with this tool to help you understand and draw key insights on your position and disparities in your organization. If positioning appears to be critical to your immediate situation or survival, and this tool has surfaced major issues or discrepancies in your approach, you may need to pause here and consider a deeper dive into your situation. If so, we encourage you to dig deeper and pursue dedicated resources to this topic.

Potential Project Definition — At this key point, we refer back to the Market and Four P model. We in essence have started to gain visibility on the Product/Service improvement programs needed, as well as areas of Price/Cost problems that may need to be addressed. At this point it is critical to begin thinking about the general projects and activities implied by your analysis of the finished matrix. Tasks we would encourage next:

- Prepare a list of *all* improvement activities implied by the finished matrix. Note that this should include new product/

service improvement programs, product/service cost reduction programs, or product/service pricing programs.

- Based on the matrix (and previous knowledge from the preceding tools), place a "first pass" priority on each potential program (it can be as simple as high, medium, and low priority).

- For all the "high priority" programs, rank them in order of currently perceived importance.

This listing of potential programs will be very important. If you are like most of us, the full list of projects will demand many more resources than a typical company will have to work them. In fact, just scoping them for further action (what is the spec, what resources will be needed, what are likely returns, etc.) will likely be daunting. So, prioritizing the top projects as suggested for a next step of evaluation will be critical.

This is also a good time to start thinking about "integrating activities." How can we ensure we are doing the right things? How can we structure efforts to benefit us in a number of different areas? We offer tools to help with this next stage of strategy definition in the ensuing chapters.

Our Favorite Anecdote Using This Tool

(Authors' note — In a sense we've been setting you up. We hope you are already seeing that these tools are very powerful individually. However, the tools are also designed to build upon each other in a pretty unique way. This anecdote actually illustrates such a case and shows the power of these tools to help frame the strategic situation for a company to begin structuring the integrated activities necessary to fully defining their strategy).

A company with a new CEO (previously referenced in some preceding anecdotes) was developing his first strategic plan for his Board. The CEO, being familiar with many of the tools in this book, had completed the Market Map (Figure 6.1), which we re-introduce in Figure 12.3 from our work in Chapters 3–6. Here is a quick summary of the conclusions the company derived from the Market Map tool if you are joining us here.

Initially, the company had no perspective on the size of their overall market, nor the size of their segments and niches. Nor had they thought about the business health of each market segment they served. Due to industry hysteria at the time, all the company resources were being funneled to Segment 5. The completed Market Map Tool resulted in definition of the overall size of the market (Chapter 3), and the segment sizes shown proportionately to the overall market by the width of the columns (Chapter 4). Niches were also carved out (Chapter 5). The business health and importance ranking of each segment via a 3-year forward looking assessment was established and shown by color code at the top of the column (Chapter 6). The information was immediately helpful to the CEO and the team. With the most important segments to be pursued evaluated, chosen, and ranked left to right, it was obvious that the company's blind focus on Segment 5 at the expense of other segments was misguided.

This sets the stage for the Product Portfolio Matrix analysis.

The PPM shown in Figure 12.1 is actually also a representation of the situation this CEO faced when the Product Portfolio Matrix was completed for Manufacturing Company A. The Market Map and Product Portfolio Matrix results are shown side by side again in Figure 12.3 for reference. Note that segments 1–6 are identical in both tools. And as directed in both tools, they are presented in the exact same rank order, with the chosen most important "segment 1" placed to the far left and those in decreasing importance to the right. Using these two coordinated tool outputs was very powerful for the CEO and his executive team.

Reviewing the results, the team concluded Segment 5 was in pretty good shape on both product and price/margin fronts (due to the resource focus from the past few years). Having now sized and prioritized their market and segment on a go-forward basis, they also saw there were significant issues in Segments 1–3, which were now deemed the highest three priorities. While there were some big product issues in Segments 1–3, the price/margin issue

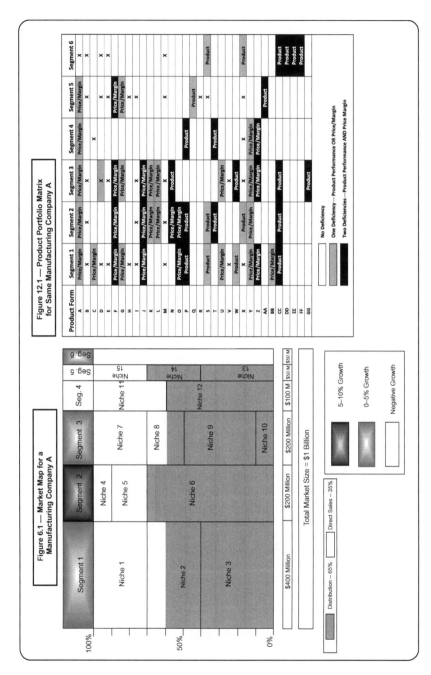

Figure 12.3: Market Map and Product Portfolio Matrix for Manufacturing Company A.

was even more prevalent. And in looking at the product/service line items (as suggested in Figure 12.2), there were areas where one project could benefit two or three segments.

The CEO had already spent 1 day on preparing the Product Volume Margin Tool from Chapter 8 to get a better feel for his price/margin situation. Conclusions from that tool were immediate and showed the margin issues were far more production cost related than they were pricing.

As a result, the list of potential product/service improvement and cost reduction initiatives were defined for the products/ services in all segments as per the PPM tool construction methodology. There were enough projects to keep the company busy for well over 15 years (especially at the company's current rate of product development). So, some type of logical prioritization needed to take place.

Per the PPM tool, the list of all projects defined was first scaled down to only those in Segments 1–3, and then further sorted on a scale of 1–10 based on currently perceived importance. The number of high importance projects still overwhelmed the company's bandwidth, and functional bickering was starting to enter the process (Ops wanting the tolerance relief they'd been complaining about for years, Engineering wanting to work the latest high-tech angle, Finance demanding margin improvement, Sales simply wanting the best specs and lowest price, etc.).

The CEO had enough information to start moving the ship. He now knew his market and segment sizes, business health, and hence segment priority. He now had vision to the product and cost strengths and weaknesses within each of those prioritized segments. He had a sense of the many projects needed to begin addressing those most important areas. But he also observed he had minimal resources, saw he needed to make progress on multiple business-issue fronts, and knew he needed to act now.

(Authors' note — This would actually be a great place to stop for a case study, wouldn't it? What would you do in this case? Do you shore up an individual segment? Or cross segments with efforts? What internal arguments would you anticipate? Superimpose this to your business

situation. Do you have this type of knowledge to shape a direction? How would you move in your organization?

Remember with the tools shown so far, the CEO can, and in this case, DID, go from a state of no business knowledge or structure (and blindly focusing on Segment 5 due to market hysteria) to a solid understanding of markets and product/services and an ability to begin shaping direction — in roughly 1 month!*)*

The CEO made his call. He decided first he needed to focus on the products/services horizontally across the prioritized Segments 1–3 rather than shoring up any individual vertical segment (and vertical Segment 5 work was immediately stopped). He gauged he only had resources for, and hence chose, two projects to move forward. Each addressed one of the two major production areas, so he could integrate activities and make needed operational improvement/cost reduction progress in each under the guise of the product development program. Knowing he would use the upcoming tools in this book, he mandated three requirements for each new product project:

(1) The product technical specification would be market based, but with functional input;

(2) The Gross Margin of the new product would be at least 500 basis points higher than the existing product it was replacing; and

(3) The project had to be completed in 12 months or less (well under 50% of the current development time).

(Authors' note — By the way, with the help of upcoming tools, all three requirements were met or bettered by the company!)

13

The Poor Man's Quality Function Deployment (QFD) Tool

> **Strategy Question:** How do I get the right product/service specification defined in timely fashion?

Rank Order	Feature	Requirements	Metric	Project Status	Best Competitor	Competitive Status
1						
2						
3						
4						
5						
6						
7						
8						

Exceeds Metric   Meets Metric   Below Metric

Figure 13.1: Example of the Poor Man's QFD Tool.

Overview

This tool provides a powerful way to define a specification for a product or service development project, especially when there is no prioritization clarity for the desired improvements. For each feature, a requirement and metric are developed by a multi-functional team considering market and business needs. Those line item feature/requirement pairs are then "forced ranked" against each other. Compromises in each line item metric, if necessary, are then made respecting the rank order chosen, with lower ranked metrics yielding to those of higher rank. The resulting prioritized line item list of features (with their associated requirements and metrics) defines the overall project specification and is used to manage the development project. The tool output chart also serves as an excellent one-page project management summary. It highlights overall specification development status by showing the status of each line item feature against both its defined project metric and that of the best competition (these comparisons color-coded "white fill" — exceeds, gray — meets, and black — below metric).

Time to Complete the Tool

- First pass — One to two days for directional guidance.
- Final pass — Likely two to four weeks to bring in all functional groups to (1) assess proper feature/requirement ranking and (2) negotiate project metrics based on that prioritization.

Introduction

You have decided you need to take on a major project in your organization. Perhaps there are many projects queued up (perhaps even through the Product/Service Portfolio Analysis process of Chapter 12) that need to be evaluated. How do we develop the project scope and specification? Everybody wants everything!

Quality Function Deployment has emerged as a sophisticated process to develop comprehensive specifications for new products/services. It is a powerful and at many times complex process of comparing the interactions and impacts of numerous features against others. A prioritization of features and setting of project metrics becomes the output of this approach.

There are numerous sources of information on QFD in the business literature, and the term "house of quality" is very helpful in highlighting "interactions" within specification elements (for instance, in an automotive application — where QFD is extensively used — the weight of additional metal to improve crash safety will likely negatively interact with a specification to improve fuel efficiency). While a powerful approach, the problem with QFD for most of us is the cost and time required. It is great for Fortune 100 companies trying to sort out the right spec for automobiles, consumer electronics, or even the right flavor for a cup of coffee. They can spend millions of dollars and many months on QFDs, searching for the right combination of attributes to define a project specification. The process works. Most of us, however, don't have the resource luxuries of a Fortune 100 company.

Identifying and correctly specifying the performance features, requirements, and metrics for a new product or service is critical to the success of that product development effort. And doing it in timely fashion is equally critical.

We are fond of the work by Reinertson and Smith in their books on new product development. They suggest the time taken to develop a specification may actually equal that of the ensuing development project itself. They call this the "fuzzy front end" where precious time (we're talking years in some cases) to market is wasted. This is why so many companies are late to market with new offerings. Think of the time to market advantages one could leverage if they could come up with a way to develop the right specification, for the right product needs, in short order.

We developed this tool for just this purpose. And we have been successfully using it for many years. It is a hybrid, or what we call a Poor Man's QFD. It carries a significant amount of the rigor relative to defining market and organizational needs — but it does so in a fraction of the time or cost of a typical QFD. It calls upon the project team experts to work the problems and evaluate trade-offs between attributes that commonly occur in development projects. A resulting forced ranking is used to drive the project. By keeping the list of line items limited to 10 or less, it provides a way to home in and stay focused on the most important market and/or organizational needs.

(Authors' Note — for those of you somewhat familiar with QFDs, you'll notice all the QFD areas — or "rooms" as they are often called — are included in this tool.)

Here is the power of the Poor Man's QFD approach. In a standard QFD, if you consider a starting set of 20 customer needs, 20 target goals, and 5 competitors, you have hundreds and hundreds of computations and assessments to complete — and hundreds more when next level deployments are considered. Most of us do not have the time or resources for this (although a consultant would love to bill the hours to do this for you). We have found empirically that in almost all situations (especially using tools like the Product Portfolio Analysis from Chapter 12), the team understands whether they have a cost or performance issue and know the key few technical areas that need to be improved. Ordering them effectively is more often the problem. Force ranking the project feature/requirement line items significantly reduces the time and cost to a winning specification.

What You Will Need to Construct the Tool

- A firm understanding of the deficiency of the product or service in the marketplace.

- Knowledge of competitor's corresponding level of performance of said areas.

- A firm understanding of the price/cost position of the product or service in the marketplace.

- Knowledge of competitors' corresponding price/cost position in the marketplace.

- An understanding of the internal issues for producing that product/service.

- A compiled listing of all desired features needed to improve the product or service.

- A method (team/committee and process) to consider all potential improvement areas and force rank these features for importance.

- A method (team/committee and process) to investigate the numerous metric trade-off scenarios implied by the feature prioritization and determine final feature metrics for each line item.

Where to Get the Information

Product or Service Performance Competitiveness

This one is fairly obvious. Sources can include competitive comparisons of marketing materials, technical competitive product analyses, and feedback from salespeople or customers upon losing an order. This is probably the most important input if your major issue is product or service related. You will need to know where you stand competitively, especially when feature and metric improvements are being defined and negotiated.

Product or Service Cost Competitiveness

This one is also obvious. However, it is critical that this be taken seriously — and be accurate. It is easy for a salesperson to say, "...we got beat by 20% on price..." in the sting of losing a deal. Making sure the pricing comparisons, quote comparisons, terms and conditions, etc. are apples to apples is important. Setting the right cost reduction target is typically emotional organizationally. Accuracy is important because the need for a 6.4% cost reduction, vs. a generically stated 20% cost reduction, may make the difference between a project moving forward and the product being shelved (due to the magnitude of effort) for the next better opportunity.

Internal Costs or Issues Are Critical Also

What major internal issues do you face with this product or service? What are the top three warranty issues? Are scrap and rework costs high in a particular production area? Is the product so complicated that it takes our internal sales group or engineering weeks to prepare a quote? Can any of these problem areas be attacked concurrently through this development project? You get the idea. In our experience, it is not uncommon for a line item or two to come from this category. Even costs outside the Gross Margin calculation, especially SG&A, also contribute positively.

(Authors' note — this is yet another way to integrate activities; attacking an office or SG&A problem by legitimately tying it to a development project can affect office change while also contributing to the necessary product/service competitiveness.)

A Listing of Potential Features to be Addressed

From the above three steps, collate a list of the potential features that you want to consider for your project. We also recommend that you keep them in the general categories you used above. This will aid in the sorting process(es).

Sorting Methodology

There are numerous sorting methods that can be used. We like the "Forced Ranking" approach and will use it further as we discuss this tool. However, there are other sorting tools that may be appropriate for your individual circumstance. These methods include "Decision Matrices" or "Paired Comparison Evaluations" or even paired "Conjoint Analysis." Each technique has the same basic objective: prioritizing attributes that are currently unranked or initially seem of equal importance (i.e., "everything is a number 1 priority").

There are ample explanations of each approach online through numerous sources, so we'll briefly introduce them but won't go into significant depth here. Generally, the "paired approaches" take all the attributes, compare them one pair at a time against each other, with the total times each attribute was chosen over the others scored, totaled, and used to produce a rank. "Decision Matrices" take a matrix approach to helping force the ranking. For example, criteria for buying a new house might be the number of bedrooms, number of bathrooms, new kitchen, school system, and nice neighborhood, and they may be weighted 5, 4, 3, 2, 1, respectively. Each house visited is judged by these criteria (say 3 if it exceeds the desire, 2 if it meets, and 1 if it doesn't meet). Four bedrooms when you want three would rate a 3. This rating times a weighting of 5 provides a score of 3 × 5 or 15. One bathroom when you want two would rate a 1, and against a weighting of 4 would provide 4 × 1 or 4 points to the total. The total of scores for all five attributes provides guidance as to the best ranking.

Agreement on Rank Order of Features/Requirements/Metrics

Here is where the rubber meets the road. This is the heart of this tool, and it is the most time-consuming. We are recommending a Two-Stage Approach. Stage 1 considers prioritizing Feature/Requirement pairs. Stage 2 uses trade-offs in the Stage 1 rankings to define metrics for each Feature/Requirement line item.

- *Stage 1 — Feature and Requirement Priority Setting.* List each major Feature category of action, and then list the initial Requirement you feel is needed. A *Feature* should be considered in terms of the general need (cost reduction, performance enhancement, functionality improvement, etc.). Consider the *Requirement* as a directional indication of where the Feature needs to go. Some Feature/Requirement pairing examples are given in Table 13.1.

- *Stage 2 — Metric Setting Using Trade-offs.* This information comes from the aforementioned sections (competitive comparisons and current performance status) and will be used as a starting point for the team-based trade-off process. We cover this step in detail later in this chapter.

Table 13.1: Examples of Feature and Requirement Definition.

Feature (General)	Requirement (Directional Statement)
Margin Enhancement	Be accretive to company gross margin
Functionality	Web site accepts credit card payments
Performance	Improve efficiency to meet new government standards
Performance	Customer wait times reduced by at least 50%
Pricing	Fall within 2% of Brands X and Y
Quotation Response Time	Quotations times at least meeting competitor's turnaround
Operations Capacity	Must scale up to meet market projections
On-Time Delivery	Must be best in the marketplace
Warranty	Must significantly reduce failure rates in area X
Functionality	Configurator must have mobile application capability
Technology	Get market protection from competitors copying designs
Performance	Functionality improvement for element Y
Timing	Product must be included in next customer catalog

- *Final Decision Maker* — You may face a situation where the trade-offs are defined, but you are deadlocked as to a decision. Here is where the leader gets paid the big bucks: to make the decision if needed. In fact, the leader (CEO, etc.) may look at all of your hard work and still want to mandate a number one or adjust the rank order of some Feature/ Requirement line items, and that is okay. You can rest assured you provided her or him with the best possible information from which to make that determination.

How to Construct the Tool

The construction of this tool, as with many others, is easily done with a simple spreadsheet program. Here is the suggested checklist of steps.

- *Fashion the Basic Tool Format* — Create a spreadsheet in the form shown in Figure 13.1. Show columns with headings left to right as follows: (1) Rank Order, (2) Feature, (3) Requirement, (4) Metric, (5) Project Status (against the line item metric), (6) Best Competitor (for that particular feature), and (7) Competitive Status (your metric against that of the best competitor). Create 10–20 line items to be used to capture the chosen attributes for the project (these will eventually be narrowed to no more than 10, but there is some negotiating to come, and the extra lines will help as you triangulate in on the final version).

- *Complete the Stage 1 Feature/Benefit sort* — Take the individual line items compiled from the Feature/Requirements list. By whatever sorting method you choose, determine which is most important. If there are 20 items, you must rank them 1 to 20. No ties (and don't say you don't understand our situation — we assure you we've been there; but if everything is number 1, or three items tie for number 2, you will have difficulty moving forward).

  We like the "forced ranking" process here because we see great value in the multi-functional, team-based working discussions. The discussions are rich with challenges, and both the Feature/Requirement definition and prioritization seem to always become tighter. For example, in one instance, a multi-functional team was going at it. The debate was whether product performance or cost reduction should be prioritized as number 1. When the thinking started to evolve, the question became, "was it cost reduction regardless of performance, or could they actually get some extra pricing (i.e., margin enhancement) if performance was there, so should product performance actually be first?" They concluded performance first, cost reduction second (with metrics to be tempered by the anticipated pricing offset). You owe it to yourself to really know what you are driving toward.

Choose the top 8 to 10 Feature/Requirement pairings and list them in prioritized rank order into the line items of the tool. (Note at this stage we do see tendencies to combine features to get them on the list — i.e., we'll tuck number 14 in with number 6. This may be appropriate. We'd suggest more often though, at this stage, it is not. Don't cheat the process. Guard against diluting the tough efforts you just put in.)

- *Complete the Stage 2 Trade-offs and Metric Setting* — Now that you have Features and Requirements rank ordered, it is time to begin setting and negotiating metrics. There are a number of ways to begin. Here is a good way to start:

  - Take line items ranked 1–5 and insert your "wish-list" performance metric in the cell.

  - For guidance purposes, fill in the last two tool columns for line items 1–5 — who the best competitor is and what their performance level relative to your metric is. Color-code the appropriate cell in the Competitive Status column: "white fill" if your spec is meaningfully (i.e., market will perceive it to be) better than that competitor, gray if essentially equivalent, and black if meaningfully lower. Note you are not necessarily aiming for all "exceeds metric" (see the anecdote), but you don't want to develop an all-black spec that will be uncompetitive in the intended market segment when launched.

  - Then fill in metric levels for Features/Requirement line items 6–10. *Do not* include "wish-list" goals that conflict with lines 1–5. Rather, be mindful of reduced goals here reflective of necessary compromises to achieve the higher priority metrics of line items 1–5, as they will likely supersede.

- Similarly fill in and color code the last two columns for line items 6–10.

- Begin defining and negotiating metrics. Pull your team together. Start with line item 1. Answer the question: can we meet metric 1 and still hit 2, 3, 4, 5, etc. If yes, fantastic! If not, what specification compromises would be needed in 2, 3, 4, 5, etc. Once done, ask the same question for metric 2 (or the restated 2) next on the list. Be sure the team knows that this is now a trade-off exercise. You will take a number of passes at this stage, and you will send your teams back numerous times to evaluate potential trade-offs. You will send your sales/marketing teams to validate various combinations of assumed performance and pricing. You will send your technical teams to evaluate elements of performance enhancements in various combinations. Your operations folks will be challenged with estimating production feasibility and costs, given scenarios of design changes and volume increases. The triangulation of this process is powerful, and the result more often than not yields a cross-functional win.

(Authors' note — the reason we include three columns — feature, requirement, and metric — is for exactly this point in the process: guidance in the trade-offs. For example, in one case a number 1 line item was defined as: feature — margin enhancement, requirement — accretive to average gross margin (>20%), and the "wish-list" metric was ambitiously set at 24% gross margin. The number 2 line item was: feature — performance enhancement, requirement — better than competitor X, and the metric was a minimum of 10% improvement. As the project work began, the team could get the performance improvement needed, but could only get to 22% gross margin as a result. The

team used the guidance from the line 1 "requirement" of being accretive to gross margin (i.e., >20%). While they didn't hit the 24%, they saw they met the intent of the line item (the CFO was still happy) and quickly agreed to continue moving forward without losing precious time to market.)

- Be sure your metric is specific and measurable. You will be tracking progress against it using the Poor Man's QFD Tool.

- Add the resulting metrics to the appropriate line item box in the "metric" column.

- *Resource Estimation* — With the overall specification as defined, what are the resource and financial payback criteria? Issues should not be a surprise, or at least minimized, given the team-based involvement in the feature/requirement/metric development process. Nonetheless, you should check this box off as part of your normal best-practice.

- *Finish the Tool to Serve as a Project Management Summary Format* — Leave the previously completed color coding for the far-right Competitive Status column. As you begin working the project, insert the current performance for each "metric" line item in the "Project Status" column. At this point color-code that status box as to whether you are "white fill" — meaningfully exceeding the metric, gray — meeting the metric, or black — meaningfully missing the metric (note: outside of the grayscale publishing constraints, we'd default to green, yellow, and red color coding). This one-page summary is likely all you'll need to do a project read-out. It shows the ranking of features and requirements, the associated negotiated metrics, whether you're on track, and whether something has changed in the competitive landscape to jeopardize the current project. Once the group understands the information therein, it is almost a management by exception process. Changes in ratings from "white fill" to gray or gray to black can be highlighted. The appearance of a black box in the top five prioritized line items is usually a stopper and a topic for discussion.

Table 13.2 represents a real Poor Man's QFD Tool output in a manufacturing company. This company had a severe capacity constraint. Note how the features/requirements/metrics address that major need and still remain integrated (i.e., all contributing to the core constraint problem). This snapshot, taken in the middle of the development process, shows also how the tool deliverable can be used as a robust one-page management update. Note this project appears to be on track for a very successful result; four of the top five features are significantly ahead of their competition, and all five are exceeding their project metric. Combined with the fact that there are no black boxes here, you have a big winner. *We'd take this result every time*!

Key Strategic Questions

Here are some questions we'd likely pursue if we were consulting with you:

- Have we successfully constructed a winning market specification?

- Were all functional groups able to participate equally in the ranking and specification setting? If not, why not? Are they all on board?

- Will the resulting specification put us in a positive position relative to our best competitors?

- Have we been able to address appropriate internal issues toward integrating activities?

- Have we "watered down" what we really need on our new product/service offering? If so, are we asking too much from one project?

- Can we accomplish more than just the stated features/ requirements/metric if we leverage the project team efforts?

Table 13.2: Poor Man's QFD for a Production Constrained Situation.

Rank Order	Feature	Requirements	Metric	Project Status	Best Competitor	Competitive Status
1	Meet Market Demand	Increase throughput in manufacturing	Wish List = 1 unit/day (2 shifts) Current State = 1 unit/4 days (8 shifts)	1 unit/1.25 days	Competitor A	1 unit/2 days
2	Performance Improvement	Feature 1 and 2 must exceed competition by 3%	1) Improve Feature 1 by 7% 2) Improve Feature 2 by 8%	1) +7.4% 2) +8.3%	Competitor A	1) +3.4% 2) +3.3%
3	Manufacturing Flexibility	Design allows for outsourcing back-up if necessary	Manufacturing 100% Outsourceable 1) Programs for cut parts 2) Fixture back ups 3) Harmonize 75% of purchased parts	1) Laser models OK 2) Drawings done 3) 80% of content	Competitor B	Has extra capacity but not currently able to outsource
4	Gross Margin Expansion	Improve Gross Margin from dilutive to accretive	500 bps Increase	+740 bps	Internal	Meeting with no price increase
5	Industry Unique Features	As major parts of product are being redesigned, add new, industry unique features within those changes with zero cost increase	Minimum of 3 new features	1) New XXXX 2) New YYYY 3) Enhanced AAAA 4) Redesigned BBBB	Industry - All Competitors	1) Unique 2) Unique 3) Unique 4) Unique
6	Future Design Expandability	DFMA processes designed to anticipate potential product changes	1) Potential added width of 1.5 feet 2) Potential added length of 5 feet 3) Potential HP increase of 10% 4) Potential new materials	1) Open ended fixture 2) Open ended fixture 3) Envelope design OK 4) Only 2 of 3 covered	Industry	1) Industry can do 2) Industry can do 3) We will lead 4) Sales Trade Off
7	Performance Improvement	Feature Z equivalence	Equal or lower than 1,500	1,600	Competitor C	1,550
8	Product Styling	Incorporate key Brand styling elements	Maintain JJJ and KKK colors and room for lables 12 and 14	Met	Internal	Brand ID Held

Exceeds Metric	Meets Metric	Below Metric

184   Performance-Based Strategy

- If we show "below metric — black" in the "project status" or "competitive status" columns upon initial work, is there a path toward actually meeting the project objectives?

- If we show all "exceeds metric — white fill" in the project status columns, can we advance the metrics further toward an even more competitive (perhaps even disruptive) offering?

Our Favorite Anecdote Using This Tool

A private company with ongoing struggles in developing new products hired an outsider (rare for this promote-from-within company) to head its new product development engineering group. On his second day, his Director called him into a meeting and presented him with a specification for his first new product, a piece of electro-mechanical rotating equipment. The project as specified from marketing had just been approved by the executive team, but he wanted input from the new manager anyway. It was a smaller version of a product currently well behind schedule in its development process.

The new manager read the spec, made a few calculations, rechecked his work, and knew he was in trouble. The specification, with a very aggressive timeline, called for a device that was 103% efficient.

Wondering how such a specification was even defined, he sought out and introduced himself to his marketing peer (promoted in from the sales force) who developed the specification for this, as well as the floundering sister product. The marketing manager explained his spec generating process with pride. Shown was a spreadsheet with the current product compared on the basis of numerous attributes to a broad range of competitors (of which most were *not* direct application equivalents). For each attribute, he chose the best performance of all these competitors, and then raised that level by a random percentage improvement to come up with his metrics for each feature. All feature metrics were called out as mandatory.

(Authors' Note: The marketing manager fell into what we call the "sports car — dump truck" trap. In this analogy, both are vehicles, but serve much different applications. If one wanted to specify higher speed as an attribute, the sports car's 0–60 mph speed of 4.0 seconds (as opposed to the dump truck's 18 seconds) would be improved to say 3.5 seconds. On increased hauling capacity, the sports car may handle a set of golf clubs but the dump truck may do 25 tons, so a spec of 28 tons might be chosen. Hence the collective vehicle spec would be 0–60 mph speed of 3.5 seconds and hauling capacity of 28 tons. Sounds ridiculous, right? But it happens all the time.)

Back to our story: the new engineering manager explained the fallacy of setting a specification this way and told the marketing manager this particular specification stipulated exceeding 100% of theoretical efficiency. The marketing manager, not comprehending what that engineering fact even meant, informed the engineering manager that marketing's only job was to set a spec that the sales group could sell. Based on his field experience, he knew he could have sold the specified product. Furthermore, he didn't have time to analyze the output implications or prioritize which attributes were the most important. It was engineering's job to figure all that out — and, by the way, they weren't doing a very good job of it lately because the current, larger version of the product was over one year behind schedule.

The engineering manager began sorting out his dilemma. He brought the development team together and got an earful. It seemed that the specification was cast in concrete. As often happens, somewhere in past company history, enough conflict arose that one group, in this case marketing, was given the role as judge and jury for the specification. The manufacturing and product engineers just rolled their eyes when cross-functional cooperation was mentioned — in fact, the marketing people didn't even attend the product development meetings.

The engineering manager created the "Poor Man's QFD" structure and began populating it with the line item features from the larger product specification. The development team helped with their perception of the rank order of each feature and requirement.

Then they filled in the current metrics and status of each line item. There were red (i.e., "missing metric") boxes on almost every "project status" metric. When prompted, the team addressed the interactions and had numerous options and ideas to improve those top five feature metrics they felt were most important to product success. All they needed were compromises in some of the bottom five feature metrics.

The engineering manager then completed the tool by adding the last two columns, "best competitor" and "best competitor status," for each line item metric for those *similar* competitive products. The final picture was telling. Working the interactions in the Poor Man's QFD tool, compromises produced "exceeds competitor" metric status for the top six ranked feature/requirement pairings. The suggested new Poor Man's QFD interaction-based product would be the equivalent of a marketplace home run. However, it still did not meet marketing's lofty metric levels, and hence the product was considered unacceptable and stalled. (Interestingly enough, the feature/requirement that was the biggest stopper for the team, ranked 10th out of 10 in importance.)

The new engineering manager called a meeting with the project team, his director, the marketing team, and their director. He then took them all through the forced ranking process and got agreement that the team's rank order of features and requirements made sense. Then, introducing the new Poor Man's QFD output tool (similar to Table 13.2) as a foil, he inquired why the implied product — which the team was ready to deliver on — was considered so unacceptable.

Epilogue: The team was given permission to execute to the revised specification. The resulting product was completed in timely fashion and indeed was very well-received by customers. Permission was also given to use the Poor Man's QFD tool toward a more relevant and market-based specification on the new, smaller product initially given to the engineering manager. The Poor Man's QFD tool was also quickly incorporated into the new product regimen for this company.

The Process Improvement Guidance Tool

14

Strategy Question: How should we approach our internal cost reduction/value enhancement efforts?

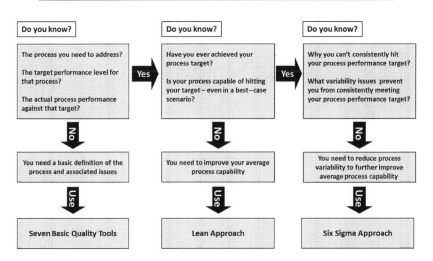

Figure 14.1: The Process Improvement Guidance Tool.

Overview

There are many approaches in business literature addressing process improvement toward better efficiency and/or lower cost. It is important to understand when they should be properly applied.

The Process Improvement Guidance Tool, shown in Figure 14.1, is designed to help the time-challenged user understand what process improvement approaches are appropriate, given the "current state" understanding and maturity of the process to be improved. To further assist the user, we also discuss the elements and techniques within each of the process improvement approaches we recommend, which, in order of least to most sophistication, are:

- *Seven Basic Tools of Quality* — the simple first step to be used when you are sizing up a new cost reduction/value enhancement or process improvement effort and you're not sure what you are dealing with.

- *Lean Approach (also referred to as the Lean Manufacturing Approach)* — to be used when you understand the process basics and are trying to improve it by eliminating "process waste" toward bettering its mean or average performance (assembly line throughput, inventory levels, time to process quotes, improving order processing time, etc.).

- *Six-Sigma Approach* — to be used to further improve process performance, usually by attacking variability around the "process average or mean" due to more complex issues or interactions from multiple sources. This approach is statistically based and the most rigorous of the three.

Time to Complete the Tool

A direction from this tool can be discerned in 15 minutes to 8 hours based on the knowledge and definition of the process "current state."

Introduction

You have identified a need for cost reduction. (Perhaps you see a significant indication of cost issues from the output of your Product Portfolio Analysis from Chapter 12.) So now what? Well, we see two approaches — internal and external — that we believe are relevant. Both contribute to our Price/Cost P from our Market and Four P approach. We will discuss outsourcing potential in Chapter 15. This chapter deals with those areas that must be tackled internally. For internal cost reduction issues, the main question we usually get is "Where do we start?"

There are a myriad of relevant and powerful cost reduction/value enhancement approaches in industry today. Information on these is ubiquitous and you may even have some experience using some of them. We do not intend a rigorous study of each here, but we do need to discuss them in enough detail to help you understand which approach may be relevant to you given your organization and problem nature. You would not try to fix a fine Swiss watch with a hammer, and choosing the wrong approach for your particular situation could have an equally detrimental result for you and your organization.

We believe three basic approaches can be used to define the broad spectrum of process condition you will likely face. The first we reference are the *Seven Basic Tools of Quality*. Prominent players such as Dr. W. Edwards Deming and Kaoru Ishikawa are often mentioned in the definition and evolution of this 1950s post-war Japan approach. The second we reference is the *Lean Manufacturing Approach*. Some trace Lean all the way back to Henry Ford in the early 1900s, while others cite its coming to prominence via Toyota much later in the 20th century. The third approach we reference is *Six Sigma*, who many attribute to Motorola and their critical 1980s challenge to improve their quality and reduce their costs. While these tools evolved from the manufacturing environment, they quickly found their way into improving processes in service, non-profit, and every other area where improvement is needed. They are truly universal in application.

We have yet to see a resource that helps the time-challenged leader sort through the alternatives to match the proper approach to their organization and respective needs. We provide Figures 14.2 and 14.3 to help you gain some perspective and narrow your

Seven Basic Quality Tools Approach	Lean Approch	Six-Sigma Approach
Basic — Understand the Process	*Intermediate — Eliminate Waste/Improve Process Mean*	*Advanced — Use Statistics to Reduce Process Variability*
Flow Chart	Five S (Sort, Set in order, Shine, Standardize, Sustain)	Six-sigma measurements (DPMO, PPM, sigma level)
Histograms	Value Stream Map — Assess process step Value/Non-Value Addd	Process Capability (Cp, Cpk, Pp, Ppk)
Run Charts	TAKT time — Customer required pace or rate of process	Gage R&R (Measurement Repeatability & Reproduceability)
Pareto Charts	Just in Time (JIT) — proper labor/materials exactly when needed	FMEA — Failure Mode Effects Analysis (Product and Process)
Check Sheets	Kanban (Scheduling) — Physical signal/prompt to reorder	Confidence Intervals — Hypothesis testing
Scatter Charts	Total Productive Maintenance (TPM) — Machine/system up-time	Attribute versus Continous responses
Cause and Effect (Ishikawa) Diagram	Single Minute Exchange of Dies (SMED) — Changeover time	Linear and Multiple regression and correlation
	Theory of Constraints (TOC) — Process Bottlenecks	ANOVA — Analysis of variance
	Poka-Yoke — Error proofing/defect prevention	DOE — Design of Experiments
	Visual Management — Easy visual cues to highlight abnormality	Response Surface Methodology
	Kaizen — Continuous improvement efforts	Control charts and charting

Figure 14.2: Techniques Associated with Three Process Improvement Approaches.

	Seven Basic Quality Tools		Intermediate — Lean Approach		Advanced — Six Sigma	
	Start	**Output**	**Input**	**Output**	**Input**	**Output**
Manufacturing	We are not hitting our productivity target of 10 units per hour. We don't have a clue why.	We are performing at 4 units per hour. Of our five production lines, Line C appears to be the bottleneck at 4 units per hour. Fishbone diagrams suggest three potential reasons.	We must improve productivity of Line C to 10 units per hour	We can get Line C to 10 units if everything is perfect. Variability is hurting us. We are improved but averaging 8 units +/– units per hour	What are the causes of variability? We need to improve the process to consistently meet 10 units per hour	Line C improved to a mean of 12.5 units per hour with a +/–3 sigma range of 2 units. Hence, Line C in control and meets customer need 99.7% of the time
Office	We are getting complaints on our order processing times being way too long. This issue suddenly came out of left field. Fix it!	It appears our customers expect us to respond in 24 hours. It is taking us 5 days. The order confirmation process has 15 steps and only 4 of them are <6 hours.	We must improve our order confirmation to <24 hours.	Our value Stream Map has identified nine non-value added steps that were eliminated.The remaining six have all been reduced to an averageof 4 hours. However, with only 2 shifts per day we are still missing our goal.	What do we need to do to further reduce process step averages and variability to our 16-hour operation?	Six-sigma regression analysis shows that 80% of the 16-hour processing time is queued behind other business operations in the ERP. Special code is being developed to run in off hours. Response times will be reduced to 5 overnight hours and all previous day order will be electronically confirmed at 8 am the next day.

Figure 14.3: Examples of the Progressive Use of the Three Approaches.

search, especially if these process improvement approaches are new to you.

Figure 14.2 is an overview of the three approaches, and the most common techniques within them.

1. The Seven Basic Quality Tools are graphical in nature, well described in a simple web search, and are capable of being constructed at any level in your organization. As you can tell from prior chapters, we are big fans of the Pareto Chart.

2. The Lean Approach is intermediate in complexity and focuses on elimination of process waste in its many forms (money, efficiency, time, inventory, wait times, delivery times, etc.). Included in the Lean Approach column are common techniques listed with the basic waste stream they address.

3. The most complex Six-Sigma Approach is based on the fact that many processes fall into the statistical category of a normal distribution (or a "bell curve"). Hence, the analytical tools statisticians use in analyzing normal distributions can similarly be applied to improving business processes. The statistical mean and standard deviation calculations (standard deviation being represented by the Greek letter sigma) then become important process predictors. Formally trained practitioners called black belts or green belts are almost always used to properly apply the statistical techniques.

Figure 14.3 is also very important to understand. It is very common to see all three approaches being used to solve the same problem as the outputs prove to be progressively more complex. The point here is that *each approach has a time and place within the spectrum of improvement effort*. Choosing the right approach is important (check out the anecdote at the end of this chapter). Figure 14.3 shows examples of a starting point, as well as how the outputs of one approach can feed into and become starting points for the next level approach. You can see how a Seven Basic

Quality Tool problem definition can lead to a need for the Lean approach and further to a Six-Sigma approach as process complexity further dictates.

As a leader, use these charts to help inform your thinking as you broach your internal cost reduction issues and corrective actions.

Our Favorite Anecdote Using This Tool

It is important as a leader to truthfully answer the questions in the Process Improvement Guideline Matrix. And it is critical that the leader focuses the effort on the right approach and techniques. Starting at the wrong place can and likely will lead to wasted time and undue frustration for your organization. Consider this true story.

A new CEO from a very large Fortune 500 background took over a smaller-cap company with numerous subsidiaries. Her charge from the Board was to outperform the industry average the company had historically been executing at.

She came in with a predisposed bias based on her large company experience. To address costs, she likewise mandated the company immediately apply Six Sigma at all subsidiary business units (which ranged from $25 to $100 million in revenue). The best people in each subsidiary were tapped for participation. An outside consulting firm was hired to train these people as champions, green belts and black belts (black and green belts being designations for trained full-time and part-time Six-Sigma practitioners within a company). The graduating black belts, now charged with full-time process improvement, were pushed back into the organization with high expectations. The CEO made commitments to the Board relative to the number of completed programs and resulting cost reduction dollars for each subsidiary.

Unfortunately, the business unit subsidiaries were not prepared for the rigor the Six-Sigma approach demanded. Many of the processes targeted for cost reduction improvement were poorly understood. The infrastructure wasn't capable of providing the level of detail required. While good, the quality systems were equally unable to support the effort. The black belts were demanding data to three decimal places to calculate p-values while the organization was still trying to figure out what measurement method to use. One business unit president characterized the situation perfectly: "the belts, trained to be Superman and Superwoman, were trying to be more powerful than a locomotive — while the business units were so immature they were saying, 'look at the choo-choo'."

Projects began to stall at the early stages of the Six-Sigma process. Frustration began to show in the new belts. Equal frustration rose from those others in the organizations assigned to the project teams. Dates began to slip. Pressure from the CEO to the business unit presidents ratcheted up. Tensions further rose as cumulative savings further slipped. Belts (the most talented people in the organization) started to leave. After about 12 months, the program lost all credibility in the business units, and it was chalked up by employees to be yet another useless initiative pushed by a corporate group that simply was out of touch with the reality at the subsidiary level.

They were exactly right. And it was sad because the thinking was sound in that a structured cost reduction effort was needed across the board — but the wrong approach was mandated. They should have started with the Seven Basic Quality Tool or a Lean approach to better understand the key areas of focus. The CEO eventually recognized her mistake, but she lost a significant amount of time and credibility, making the following course correction even more difficult to a now very skeptical employee base.

The Strategic Outsourcing Matrix Tool

> **Strategy Question:** Are we properly outsourcing key elements of our cost structure?

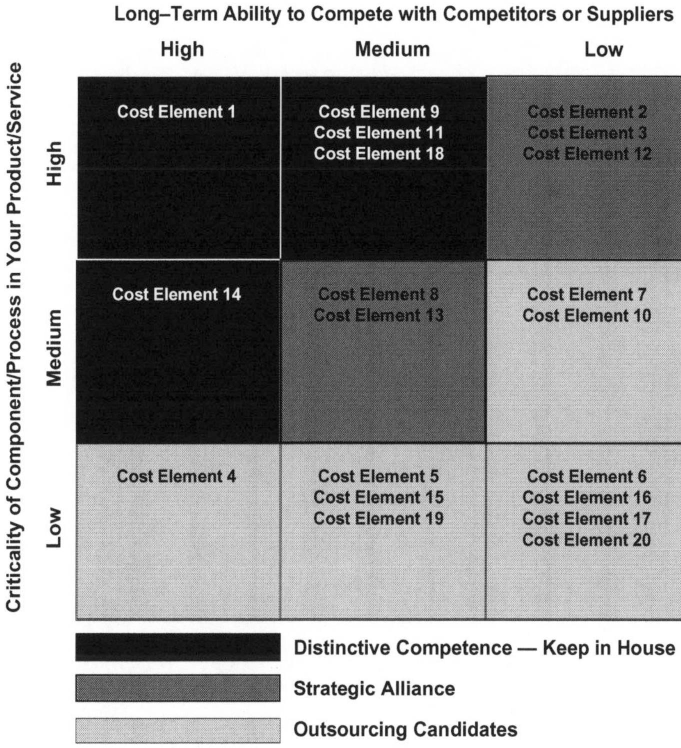

Long–Term Ability to Compete with Competitors or Suppliers

	High	Medium	Low
High	Cost Element 1	Cost Element 9 Cost Element 11 Cost Element 18	Cost Element 2 Cost Element 3 Cost Element 12
Medium	Cost Element 14	Cost Element 8 Cost Element 13	Cost Element 7 Cost Element 10
Low	Cost Element 4	Cost Element 5 Cost Element 15 Cost Element 19	Cost Element 6 Cost Element 16 Cost Element 17 Cost Element 20

Criticality of Component/Process in Your Product/Service

■ Distinctive Competence — Keep in House

■ Strategic Alliance

■ Outsourcing Candidates

Figure 15.1: A Typical Strategic Outsourcing Matrix.

Overview

The Strategic Outsourcing Matrix helps organizations better understand whether those key elements that comprise their cost structure are candidates for outsourcing. It uses two important criteria: (1) the ability of the organization to be cost-competitive in providing each particular cost element and (2) the criticality of that particular cost element to the function of the product or service supplied.

When placed within the matrix, the tool helps to identify those cost elements that are potentially out of place and candidates for strategic action in three categories:

1. "Distinctive Competencies" — those activities that are ranked both critical to success and cost-competitive that must remain and be nurtured in house.

2. "Strategic Alliances" — those activities critical to success but beyond the company's ability to do cost competitively themselves.

3. "Outsourcing candidates" — those items neither critical to success nor internally cost-competitive that should be considered for outsourcing through normal supply chain management.

The output from the tool, contrasted with the organization's "current state," provides a mechanism for discussion, definition of potential action areas, and a means to arrive at consensus for plan initiatives.

Time to Complete the Tool

Directional Pass: 2–4 hours, given available and reasonably structured cost information.

Final Planning Pass: At most 5 days, primarily to schedule and involve added functional groups (production, supply chain, financial, and technical) if needed to properly place all items within the matrix.

Introduction

Pricing issues can also be directly linked to the cost position of the product/service. Many companies can easily identify the fact they have a cost problem. The question most struggle with is where to start the improvement effort. Do we move directly to internal labor costs? Do we move to material, operations, or service costs? Do we just start with the highest cost element? We actually find the best place to start is to take a step back and assess whether the elements of our cost structure are being sourced in the right way.

The question of whether to "in-house" or "outsource" various elements of your product/service delivery is one every company has to wrestle with. A helpful way to better understand your situation is to employ an "outsourcing matrix." The theoretical business literature is again ubiquitous with outsourcing matrix examples. One can see theoretical approaches from a 2 × 2 (4-box) all the way to a 4 × 4 (16 box) matrices, but as you can tell we prefer a 9-box approach (adapted from Quinn & Hilmer, 1994).

The problem for us again is they are theoretical in nature. We are practical here and believe the best way to arrive at a quick, accurate result with buy-in is to directly involve your workforce (see this chapter's anecdote). Most of them will not be MBA's. Many of them will not be degreed. But all of them are smart, effective, and wise to their work environment. Engaging them with theoretical sorting criteria like the "proprietary nature of X," "cost per transaction," or "strategic vulnerability" is a sure way to lose them at the outset. You absolutely don't want that because outsourcing is among the most emotional subjects that can be discussed, and an initial bad reaction will never go away. Better to get them positively involved at first in a simple and straightforward way.

After years of experience (and numerous mistakes), and for just this purpose, we have adapted and evolved the theory to the pragmatic tool shown in Figure 15.1. It resonates with employees and works because it uses (1) easily understood competency and criticality metrics and (2) three basic result categories that are easy to comprehend. Hence, the intent of the analysis is quickly digested, and the eventual results are similarly presented in a simple and powerful format. We know that it works because we've seen it in action — many times. We hope it is equally successful for you.

What You Will Need to Construct the Tool

- *A definition of cost elements for analysis*: You will need a way to meaningfully break down the relevant cost elements of your products or services. This will be unique to each reader's situation, but with a little thought we find an actionable grouping will surface.

- *X-axis*: A perspective on the costs of you supplying each cost element and the equivalent prices of obtaining the same product/service from other internal sources or external suppliers.

- *Y-axis*: A perspective on what cost elements are technically critical to the success of your product or service, and those that are not.

- *Cross-Functional Agreement*: Properly constructing this tool for action will many times entail working through cross-functional opinions. While a first pass can likely be completed by a supply chain/value enhancement professional or relevant responsible team in a short time, cross-functional opinion on the above will likely be necessary (and valuable) to move forward on coordinated action plans. Depending on your situation, you may want to plan on this step.

Where to Get the Information

Cost elements — The items to be plotted will need to come from a breakdown of critical "value add" elements within your production process. A "Value Stream Map" that identifies the key production steps in a product or service, if developed, may be helpful here. Another thought is to use currently defined cost centers within the production process, if that accurately represents the flow of your production/delivery process.

Costs — This tool will require you to have/acquire reasonably accurate information on costs. In many cases, material and labor costs will need to be allocated and totaled to properly compare that cost element against the other internal sources or external market prices for the same cost element.

Technical competency rating — Key elements to the performance of your product or service should come from your engineering (internal experts) and sales/marketing (external perspective experts) personnel. Some conclusions are obvious. Some are not. Laptop computer companies do not necessarily specialize in the circuit boards and memory but they are obviously key to their product offering — so a Strategic Alliance with those suppliers certainly makes sense.

Group meetings (Cross-Functional Agreement) — In situations where the cost element, actual cost, or technical competency information are not readily available, or would be prohibitively expensive to acquire, we have found many times that you can arrive at a surprisingly robust result by pulling together key personnel (related technical personnel, hourly production supervisors, etc.) and working through the exercise in a group meeting. The result may be a bit more qualitative than quantitative, but oftentimes it is directionally accurate enough to detect important areas of concern or to provide enough insight to focus limited resources on information-gathering efforts in those key, newly identified areas.

If this approach is taken, be prepared for some lively discussion when trying to plot the individual component/process within the matrix. (See this chapter's anecdote for and idea of how to engage your team in this exeresis.) The resulting plot points for each cost element will usually morph in position during the discussions, but a collective and more actionable output will likely result.

How to Construct the Tool

The chart format is relatively simple. A 9-Box matrix that can be populated with text entries is all that is needed. A simple Excel spreadsheet or Word matrix will work. We prefer to use an Excel spreadsheet to incorporate the color/shading aspect. Here is the checklist:

- List each chosen cost element or cost center that pertains to delivery of your product or service.
- Rank (high, medium, or low) each cost element identified in terms of:
  - Long-term ability to be cost-competitive with competitors or suppliers
  - Criticality of this component/process in your product or service
- Plot each cost element in the appropriate box within the matrix.
- Optional — add the color/shading components for each of the three categories. The suggested categories shown in Figure 15.1 are ones we typically use as thought-starters, and they can certainly be adjusted to your individual circumstances.
- The result should resemble Figure 15.1 with your individual cost element labels therein.

Key Strategic Questions

We find a reasonably well thought-out Strategic Outsourcing Matrix will quickly provide a means for many probing questions. Here are some of many questions we'd likely pursue:

- Does this chart accurately reflect your situation? If not what needs to be adjusted?

- Does the tool output differ significantly from your current state? If so, where? And why?

- Is your philosophical approach to supplying your product/ service in need of revision?

- Are your rated Distinctive Competencies really competencies?

  - Could others easily duplicate them with investment?

  - Do your competitors already have a significant enough lead in this area that recovery efforts to be "best in class" will be prohibitively expensive?

- Are we properly using Strategic Alliances?

  - Do we have confidentiality agreements with those alliances already in place?

  - Are the alliances we have in place working?

- Are we properly committed to outsourcing?

Comparing the tool output to your current state, you can also structure a series of strategic questions, implied from the chart shown in Figure 15.2, such as:

- Are any of the changes suggested critical to short-term survival of the company? Longer-term survival of the company?

- Do we need to consider moving any items from an "in-house" to an alliance or outsourced category? Similarly, do we need to move any items the other way?

- How much will we need to invest in our Distinctive Competencies to keep our desired cost and technology position best in class?

  - Will this be prohibitive to the business over the next few years?

  - Do we have the capability to scale up these key areas for future growth?

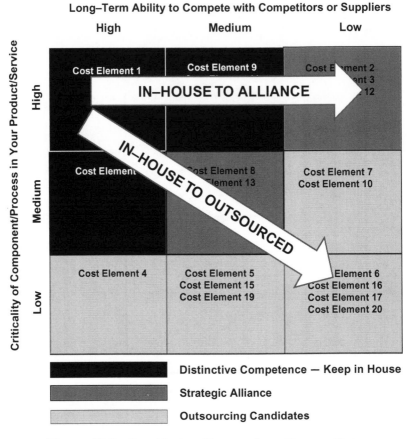

Figure 15.2: Considering Changes from Current State.

- Is the pace of technical change in critical components of your product structure (electronics, material technology, etc.) so high that it makes sense to ally with a leader in that area?

- Could such a strategic alliance bring needed technology immediately back to your product/service?

- How much gross margin benefit might we see in particular key component/process elements if we acted on shifts implied in the matrix? Is it minimal enough to just move on? Is it significant enough to warrant further definition?

- How many of the changes deemed actionable in the tool output could the organization realistically take on in the next year? Three years?

Our Favorite Anecdote Using This Tool

A CEO entering a new assignment wanted to get a feel for his operations team and their culture. Needing to address numerous cost issues identified using other tools in this book, and having less than perfect standard cost/financial data to reference, the Strategic Outsourcing Matrix was chosen as the tool to begin this process.

The CEO decided to use the tool to first define the current state of the business. With help from the operations executive, the CEO broke the company into 18 different cost elements for evaluation. They included processes for metal cutting, fabrication, welding of major components, and assembly of systems.

Invited to a meeting were the key stakeholders of each major cost center comprising these processes, including supply chain buyers for key components, technical product experts, plant supervisors, the only costing expert from accounting, as well as members of the leadership team (a total of about 25 people). Upon entering the meeting, each participant received a pad with 18 Post-It notes.

The new CEO explained the need to get a feel for the company and the true product value add that their manufacturing efforts contributed. He also asked the participants, many seeing the CEO for the first time, for the benefit of the doubt in using this exercise to help bring him up to speed. And after explaining the choice of the 18 categories to represent the business, asked all to take the first Post-It note and write the first category on it. The CEO then introduced an enlarged 9-box Strategic Outsourcing Matrix (without the three designated colored categories at this point) taped to the wall, and the group was simply asked to put their note in the box that represented their opinion of the criticality and competitiveness criteria. The exercise was then repeated for the remaining 17 categories.

The exercise was very telling for the CEO and all present. The participants on average ranked all 18 categories in the High/High upper left box of the matrix. The CEO was pleased with the pride and passion of the company in their wanting to be the best, but he was more concerned that this mindset significantly hindered progress and prevented pursuit of more cost-effective external solutions.

The CEO took the opportunity to challenge the group on each of the 18 elements towards a more realistic placement within the matrix. First, with a magic marker, he carved out the three categories on the 9-box wall posting and described the concept of "in-sourcing," "strategic alliance," and "outsourcing." He then engaged his team. The conversations mirrored the following example on the hydraulic cylinder category, which was chosen first as a teaching example for the group.

This company historically always made its own hydraulic cylinders (machining and assembly) for its products. The CEO asked how many cylinders the company made. After some quick discussion, the group determined annual production quantities were about 8,000 per year. The CEO asked the group if they thought they could be as cost-competitive as those large outside suppliers making 800,000-plus cylinders a year. After some help from the cost accountant and purchasing folks, a perspective emerged between "estimated" internal and external costs (again, this company's costing system was unsophisticated, but meaningful directional conclusions could be discerned). Begrudgingly, the production group answered probably not. That moved the x-axis plot point from "high" to "low" on the cost-competitiveness axis. The CEO then questioned what was critical or proprietary about the company's design versus all the others. The technical people argued one or two points, which the purchasing people countered were now commonly available at external suppliers. After lively discussion, the group agreed that lifting cylinders were not unique or critical enough to the product function to suffer the cost penalty being paid. That again moved the ranking from "high" to "low" on the criticality scale. Having moved from the high/high to low/ low box in the tool, the hydraulic cylinder item then became a candidate for potential outsourcing. Figure 15.3 shows the final result of this meeting in which, upon helpful group scrutiny, *initial placement of all 18 categories* actually changed.

The resulting tool output provided unified functional agreement and strong guidance for potential company action. With 2 hours of prep time (for the CEO and VP — Ops to define the 18 categories), the meeting took 6 hours from beginning to end, with a working lunch thrown in.

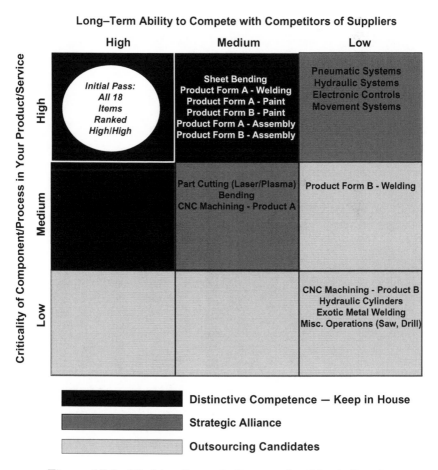

Long–Term Ability to Compete with Competitors of Suppliers

	High	Medium	Low
Criticality of Component/Process in Your Product/Service — High	Initial Pass: All 18 Items Ranked High/High	Sheet Bending Product Form A - Welding Product Form A - Paint Product Form B - Paint Product Form A - Assembly Product Form B - Assembly	Pneumatic Systems Hydraulic Systems Electronic Controls Movement Systems
Medium		Part Cutting (Laser/Plasma) Bending CNC Machining - Product A	Product Form B - Welding
Low			CNC Machining - Product B Hydraulic Cylinders Exotic Metal Welding Misc. Operations (Saw, Drill)

■ Distinctive Competence — Keep in House

▨ Strategic Alliance

▨ Outsourcing Candidates

Figure 15.3: Working Strategic Outsourcing Matrix Result.

Epilogue: Two items were chosen, based on numerous company criteria and resource availability at the time, for immediate outsourcing action (the hydraulic cylinders' cost element was one of them). Within 1 year, all actions defined were implemented to solid company gains. No jobs were eliminated as manpower was shifted to other areas. Additionally, one "distinctive competency" area was chosen for further improvement towards bettering the shown cost and technical competitiveness — and this investment insight and action ultimately paid the biggest dividend for the company!

Reference

Quinn, J. B., & Hilmer, F. G. (1994). Strategic outsourcing. *MIT Sloan Management Review*, Summer 1994. Retrieved from http://sloanreview.mit.edu/article/strategic-outsourcing

The Critical to Customer Mindset Tool: Where Are We Causing You Pain?

Strategy Question: How can we enhance our reputation with our customers in the most effective and efficient manner?

Overview

The previous tools in this book have dealt with significant and major strategic "go-to market" initiatives dealing with our Product, Price (cost), and Placement (channel) from our Market and Four P approach. But once those are in order or being addressed, it is critical to realize there is an equally vital element to consider: how well you service and support your customer. Your reputation here is important, too. The processes that touch customers need to be constantly monitored for effectiveness. This is another tool that is embarrassingly simple, yet too often neglected. Ask your customer where you are causing them pain — and then get busy eliminating it by fixing the issue!

Introduction

It is commonplace for a company to lose touch with their customer from time to time. It seems internal needs have a way of sucking customer-facing groups away from the reason they exist: the customers! People are so busy managing the processes, delivering the service, and developing the product that they lack the time or resources to interact with the actual customers. They then end up working internal issues rather than solving customer problems (this can especially befall a company working on its first strategic plan).

A. G. Lafley, former CEO of Proctor and Gamble, said that there are two "Moments of Truth" when dealing with a customer: when the customer DECIDES to use your product or service and when the customer actually USES the product or service. We agree. But we would suggest that the "Moments of Truth" are, more often than not, perpetually at work. Every interaction the customer has with your organization — from your website to your customer service desk to your sales force to your service personnel — is an ongoing Moment of Truth, because the customer is constantly evaluating the decision to do business with your organization. How does your business treat the customer? Does your company really care about the customer's needs? Is your company responsive? How does your firm handle the inevitable "oops" moments? In the marketplace, customers are always making an evaluation: should I continue to do business with this organization?

Do you have "The List?" Most of us do. We don't necessarily write it down or save it on a hard drive somewhere, but we carry it with us all the time. It's The List of Companies I'll Never Do Business with Again (Unless I Have No Other Alternative) — or, if you like acronyms, CINDBWA. We certainly will admit to having our own lists. The thing to keep in mind about The List is that *at one time, you did do business with the company. You purchased the firm's products or services. You made a DECISION and actually USED the organization's products or services. The company passed the "Moment of Truth test." But the business is still on your List.* We can all think of stores we'll never visit again, products we'll never buy again, services we'll never use again. Not because the providers didn't pass the "Moment of Truth" test, but because they failed the Customer Mindset test — they managed to convince the customer that remaining in the relationship wasn't worth the customer's time, energy, and effort.

Some companies we've come across have a complete disconnect. Their vision of what a customer needs is totally different from the customer's perspective. We've seen this time and time again. And, as you would expect, the less-sophisticated the company, the higher the probability this is a problem.

We are fond of the television commercial a few years ago in which a company president is handing out plane tickets to his team. He says we've lost touch with our customers, and we need to reverse that immediately by going back into the field. They asked him where he was going and he replies, "to visit the long-time customer that just fired us." That will certainly be a difficult meeting! So how do you keep tabs on how your company is doing relative to customer expectations? The answer is simple: just ask.

What You Will Need to Construct the Tool

- A list of responses from customers on service process satisfaction

- Prioritization and selection of the most critical process areas to improve

- The Critical to Customer (CTC) target metric for that process area

- A process improvement approach to work the problem.

Where to Get the Information

List of responses on service satisfaction — This need not be complicated. You need to talk to your customers. If your organization is very sophisticated and already tracking multiple customer service metrics, you pretty much have a decent handle on what your customers expect. You probably use web-enabled customer service surveys to further your understanding here. If this is you, we salute and congratulate you for being well ahead of the curve. Keep up the great work.

However, if you are like a majority of us, you haven't really dug into this to that extent. In fact, we have found in situations where a business is doing its first serious strategic planning, it probably has not done a thoughtful job in understanding what customers really expect. For those of us in that boat, we offer a simple way to find out. Simply pick the top customers by group (distributors, end-users, etc.) and schedule a personal visit with only one question: "Where are we causing you pain?"

Be ready for the onslaught of answers. When you ask customers this very simple question, they will unload. You're going to hear everything from the major issues ("Your salespeople have no clue how to deal with our buyers," "Your products are way too dated," "Your service delivery takes too long," and more) to the nitpicking ("I can't find stuff on your website," "Your Accounts Receivable people lack people skills"). Don't try to explain, don't try to justify why this happens, don't try to debate with the customer. Just note what the customers say. Period. Whether you think the customer is right or wrong at this point is immaterial; they're the customer, you're not. It's the customer's view that matters. Simply tabulate them and bring them back for evaluation.

We actually prefer that the organization leaders, hopefully the President or CEO and other members of the top management team, go out and ask this question personally. It gives the senior executives the perspective direct from the customer's mouth. Nothing is more beneficial than firsthand information; it's unedited and unfiltered. If you ask your salespeople to do this, or your distributors, you can expect some filtering will occur. After all, the sales rep or the distributor don't want to look bad; they don't want negative information to reflect poorly on them. But the very question you're asking — "Where are we causing you pain?" — is designed to get negative information. The problems are what you want to hear, so beware of the filtering tendency. Also, face-to-face conversation can allow the leadership to probe for understanding: "When you say that our delivery times are too long, what do you mean? What are your process requirements? How are we causing you problems in your processes by our long lead times?" This allows your organization to get a level of understanding FROM THE CUSTOMER'S PERSPECTIVE — which is the only perspective that matters at this point.

Prioritized list of processes needing attention — Look at the answers from each respondent. Read them over and look for the common themes or ideas. What is the customer saying? What is the issue that is causing the pain? This needs some attention, as often the pain that the customer is feeling isn't the cause of the pain. It's like a runner with pain in the foot; the feeling is "my foot hurts," but the cause might be that the shoes are old and worn so the gait is wrong, the runner needs an orthotic to support the arch, or maybe the shoe is just tied too tight. Your purpose here is to identify the things your organization is doing that may be the CAUSE of the pain. Group the answers in whatever fashion makes sense. Look for similarities and sort the results with a goal of choosing the most common complaint area to begin improvement efforts.

The Critical to Customer (CTC) metric — along with the query of asking where we cause the customer pain, ask them what it is that they need. That is, what would eliminate the pain for the customer? Have the customer tell you, in their own words, what would constitute a successful resolution of the situation — what, in their mind, would be "painless." And be sure to get them to be realistic. Everyone would "want" a result tomorrow, but what do they realistically "need" to be competitive? Compile the resulting "need" responses correlating to the chosen process to determine a realistic CTC target metric.

Process improvement approach to work the problem — You need to next diagnose what the current state of the process is. We refer the reader to Chapter 14 and the Process Improvement Guidance Matrix. There is ample guidance and detail for starting a process improvement task there. If you have yet to see Chapter 14, this quick diagnostic summary might help.

- Start with the *Seven Basic Quality Tools* if you had no idea this was a customer expectation — and you don't know where your performance levels are relative to your customer's CTC expectation (see anecdote). In our experience, we've found this to be the starting point in the majority of cases.

- Start with *Lean* concepts if you are already monitoring and improving a metric for the chosen problem but can't seem to get to the desired CTC level.

- Dig into *Six-Sigma* approaches if you can intermittently hit the CTC level defined, but variability keeps you from consistently meeting or exceeding it.

How to Construct the Tool

There is no real sophisticated construction process necessary here. Take the issues that customers are raising and then see which issues get mentioned most frequently. Look at the things you're doing that are CAUSING the pain. Count the number of times the issue gets mentioned by customers. How many customers have identified this as an issue? What do your largest customers say are the biggest pain points? Then prioritize the issues by frequency (which ones get mentioned most often) and by customer (which customers mention the issue). You'll find out very quickly which items are the priority "pain points." Then identify the Critical to Customer requirement that will define success in addressing the pain.

Strategy Implications

Again, the strategy implications here relate to how well you can improve those processes of customer importance you deem appropriate to fix. We'd suggest that if the list is substantial, you have a pretty big effort to satisfy your customer base and they are probably not happy with you (you may be on the verge of being fired yourselves). A process improvement effort may be one element of a larger program you might want to consider putting in place.

Some questions to consider in using the information from the CTC Mindset Tool:

- Where are we consistently causing pain to multiple customers? Are these customers experiencing the pain in the same way?

- What are some common causes of multiple pain points? Can we identify something in our processes that would address multiple CTC pain issues?

- Why do customers say this is a pain point? What is it about our customer's business activity that we don't understand?

- How can we encourage our customers to help us address their pain, and how can we demonstrate our success so that they recognize our efforts to make their lives easier?

Our Favorite Anecdote Using This Tool

A company's Dealer network had been complaining for months that their "Engineer to Order" (or ETO non-standard) quotation process had become a liability. Lead times were "way too long" and it was costing them business. The company had responded back with the sentiment that they were sick of excuses and for the Dealers to get their sales up. Order volumes continued to drop. Upon joining the organization, the new General Manager went to visit the top Dealers to get a feel for their opinions of her new company. The simple question of "Where are we causing you pain?" had never been asked of them before, and the bombardment of answers was intimidating for the new leader. She organized the answers from her visits and chose the top issue to address. It indeed was the timeliness of quotations.

She called a few of the Dealer principals she had just met to delve further into the problem. She found that competitors were responding in 7 days to customer inquiries, and the company needed to be at least that good, and preferably less. She knew she had to respond and called together her sales leaders to find out more. The sales leaders didn't even recognize this as a metric worthy of tracking. When asked what their response time was, she was met with deafening silence.

So, she turned to the *Seven Basic Quality Tools* to begin understanding the problem.

- The company fortunately had data as to when an inquiry came in and when it was answered. A *histogram* was prepared of the last 180 days to define current state. The result was an average response of 7 days. However, the range around that average was 0 to 51 days.

- A *Check sheet* was constructed as to the nature of the types of quotes. It turned out that the 7-day average was aided significantly as the data base included standard product quotes that were easily answered in 1 day. Therefore, the true response rate was much worse than 7 days.

- A *Cause and Effect/Fishbone/Ishikawa Diagram* was constructed, and a list of 10 potential defect reasons codes for the process was created.

- The 10 reason codes were applied to each of the entries in the histogram, and a *Pareto Chart* was constructed to see which of the 10 accounted for the highest percentage of the miss. The issue appeared to be multi-functional.

She then turned to *Lean* principles for the next step.

- A *Process Map* was constructed to ensure each step was accounted for. The surprising result was that almost every function in the organization felt the need to approve the request in some way. Outside sales needed to take and submit the request, inside sales needed to validate the request, engineering needed to validate the design was configurable, accounting needed to validate the costs, finance needed to approve the gross margin, manufacturing needed to approve they could make it, purchasing needed to approve they could buy the components, and on and on.

- Hence, a *Value Stream Map* was created to identify the *value add* and *non-value add* elements (and departments).

- The waste issue in this case involved the *poor process design* and *waiting categories*.

The company then began addressing the biggest contributors to longer cycle time. Figure 16.1 shows their progress. Within months the company had reduced the average response time to under the target set at 5.5 days (versus the customer-stated need of 7 days) and reduced the range from 0−51 days to 0−20 days. With Continuous Improvement tasks, the average eventually was worked down to under 2 days and a range of 0−7 days, which indeed proved to be a competitive advantage for them. Furthermore, a step was inserted into the process to alert Dealers if they were going to exceed 7 days, which the Dealers found acceptable and even beneficial, as their customers got the correct impression when informed that the Dealer was on top of the situation and looking out for them.

The company found numerous process and non-process reasons for their variability. One more interesting reason caused the noteworthy blip in the center of the chart (where the average shot up to over 8 days for that month). Well, it seems the month was November, and all the Customer Service personnel were also deer hunters, and they all scheduled vacation for opening day of the season. Well, in the real world, events like this play into results — regardless of all the textbook theory you throw at a problem. You will note that the company learned and didn't repeat that scheduling mistake in future years.

Both Dealers and end-users began commenting on how much more reliable the company was in addressing their special ETO quotations. It should be noted that with the organization's more

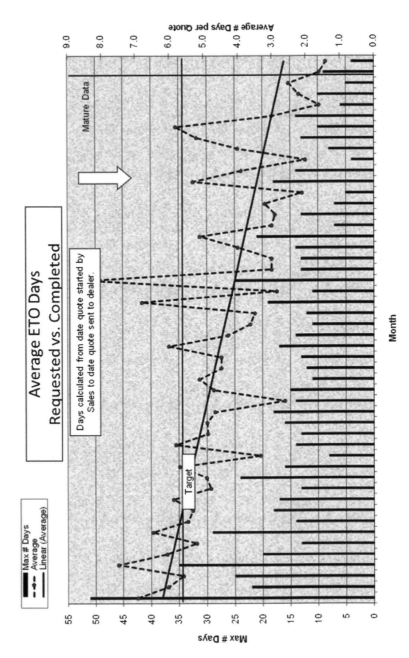

Figure 16.1: CTC Process Improvement Example.

efficient process, they were also able to quote more opportunities. The average number of quotes in the final 12 months of Figure 16.1 was roughly 50% higher than the first 12 months. With more quotes being processed in a much timelier fashion, end-user orders improved significantly.

Within 6 months of establishing ETO quotations as an important continuous improvement effort, the company then graduated on to tackle the second highest rated Critical to Customer process for improvement.

(Authors' note: It isn't unusual in our experience for channel partners to remember that "outlier" experience to use as a complaint or justification on how poorly someone is doing. In this case, the outside sales group kept getting pounded about that time it took 50 days to get a quote back. The outlier became the generalization with which to paint the company as horrible. With the one-page process summary chart shown in Figure 16.1, the sales group had an easy counter to diffuse that potential argument and to reset customer memory.)

The Brand Perception Tool

Strategy Question: *How do we effectively communicate our brand to our customers and our market?*

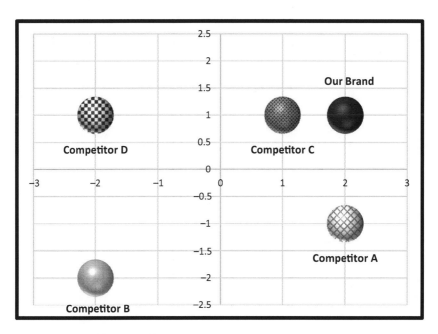

Figure 17.1: The Brand Perception Chart.

Introduction

You've done your analyses, you have the basic elements of your strategy in place. You've sized your markets, you know the customer's value drivers. You've determined the optimal position to hold in the market. You've been reducing your costs and improving your margins, and you have analyzed your channel to insure you're efficient in reaching the market. In our Market and Four P approach, you've successfully covered the first three P's (Product/Service, Price, and Placement). But what about the fourth P — Promotion? Do your CUSTOMERS understand your competitive position?

Ah, yes; herein lies the problem. You can do all of the analyses, develop all of the charts, make all the right decisions, and still miss the mark, because the customer does not share your wonderful strategic insights. In the customer's mind, you are still not on-target; you're not addressing the customer's perceived needs better than the competition. And at the end of the day, it is the customer who decides whether or not your strategy is successful — not you. It's a decision customers make every time they decide to purchase your product or service, and it's based on their perception — not yours.

We've seen plenty of organizations with sound strategies and good analyses come up short in the market because they do not understand this simple idea. To paraphrase that overused political phrase, "It's the customer, stupid!" Remember? "Strategy begins in the marketplace with a customer." We must have said this thousands of times to managers, employees, students, and clients. They all nod their heads in agreement and indicate that they "get it." But sales still slump and market shares decline.

So how do you understand customers' perception of your position? By analyzing their brand perceptions. But this begs the question, what is brand? We've seen the definitions in the marketing textbooks and websites — "The marketing practice of creating a name, symbol or design that identifies and differentiates a product from other products." "The process involved in creating a unique name and image for a product in the consumers' mind, mainly through advertising campaigns with a consistent theme." These may be great for a class on marketing principles. But these definitions of a brand do not capture the essence of a brand from a strategic perspective. The best definition we've ever heard for a brand came from the Vice-President of Strategic Planning for a major

U.S. manufacturing company. He said, "Your brand is a promise of an experience."

There it is. In a world where products and services can be remarkably similar, where differentiation is harder to achieve in the basic goods and activities, and where foreign competitors can knock off your ideas and copy your intellectual property with seeming impunity, less and less of your brand is associated with the things you make or the things you do. Customers today want an EXPERIENCE, defined as the sum total of the customer's entire interaction with your organization. Today the customer experience may begin with your website, or with an initial phone call (is your website customer friendly? Do you have a person to answer the phone or is the customer directed to a call center or automated system?). It may begin when a potential buyer has a conversation with a current customer (do you know what your current customers are saying about their experience?). It can extend throughout the entire purchase decision, and on into after-sale service and support. It's the whole total interaction that a customer has with your organization and with your products and services.

Think for a moment about the power of the customer experience. For many people, all we need to do is say "Walt Disney World" and immediately the phrase evokes wonderful memories of family vacations, attractions, etc. Coca-Cola doesn't sell flavored sugar water, they sell an experience ("Have a Coke and a smile"). Apple doesn't sell computers or cell phones, they sell images, lifestyles, interactions, creativity. Even industrial products are based on experiences. Caterpillar sells worldwide dealer service and support, not just the machines. Hospitals compete based on the patient experience, and they are measured and ranked based on both outcomes and the quality of that experience.

Once you begin to think of your brand in the broad sense to include the entire customer experience, you begin to see your brand in a whole new way. In effect, your brand becomes the essence of your strategy at the point of strategic contact: touching the customer. Whatever you may think of as your market position or your strategy or your competitive advantage or your distinctive competence, unless these views are held by the customer, your strategy will be ineffective. That's the purpose of brand projects such as advertising, website development, communications, training programs, and all of the related activities: to make sure that the customer understands your competitive advantage and that your strategy is effectively understood by the customer.

So how do you determine where to allocate your promotional resources to the various projects and activities in developing your brand? By determining how your brand compares with competitors on the dimensions that matter to the customer experience. You need to do a Brand Perception Analysis.

Overview

The Brand Perception Tool provides a method for analyzing how your brand compares with that of your competitors on the multiple dimensions that affect the customer experience. It allows you to look at your strategic positioning from the perspective of the customer. This is done by a simple set of comparisons and short customer surveys or interactions that enable you to quickly gather information and sort it in a meaningful way. Customers are asked to give their perceptions of your firm and competitor firms using multiple dimensions of the customer experience. These dimensions are then ranked to determine which matter most to the customer in the buying decision process. This enables you to prioritize those elements of your brand experience that truly matter to customers and to identify those areas where your firm has a competitive advantage or disadvantage relative to competitors. This analysis helps to determine how to shape the company's message and brand communication projects to derive maximum strategic benefit.

Time to Complete the Tool

The time it takes to complete this tool varies as a function of the ability to gather the necessary input data from customers. Once you have a sufficient number of data points, the actual analysis takes less than 1–2 hours, depending on the number of comparisons you make.

Guidelines

The factor that will determine the effectiveness of the Brand Perception Analysis is the cooperation of your customers. Since the analysis is based on customer perceptions, you will need to determine the simplest and easiest way to get the input from your customers. Assuming you've done your market and segment analysis, you should have some preliminary sense of the elements that are important to the customer experience. If so, you can create your survey pretty easily. If not, you will need to ask customers to identify the factors they consider when deciding why and how to purchase your product or service. Assuming you already have some sense of the factors that matter, you can easily use technology to create a simple online survey to gather the information. Alternatively, you can send out a paper survey or create a simple spreadsheet that customers can fill out to provide you with the needed information. You will need to consider your relations with your customers; the more data you can gather, the better the analysis will be.

However, the survey needs to be as short as possible. Don't waste time asking customers questions to which you already know the answer. For example, one survey we saw actually asked customers "Is price important to you when buying our service?" Now, unless you are selling medical services (no one generally tries to shop for the lowest price for their surgery so they can impress their friends by telling them how cheap their surgery was), can you think of a product or service you buy for which price is NOT a consideration? Granted, if you are already a billionaire or just won the lottery, there may be some products or services for which price is not a consideration, but these are pretty rare. Instead, the right question is "HOW important is price when you are considering buying our product or service?" Make sure you are asking intelligent questions that will get you the information you need!

What You Will Need to Complete the Tool

- Information regarding the key factors involved in the decision to purchase your firm's products or services. There should be no more than 7–10 factors; the fewer the better.

- A structured set of questions to ask customers about the customer experience with your product, service, and/or organization.

- A methodology of distributing the survey to customers in a manner that will enable them to complete the survey in less than 10 minutes.

- A simple spreadsheet or other method of compiling the data.

- A spreadsheet or process that will enable you to quickly generate two-dimensional (or even three-dimensional) graphs of the data.

How to Get the Information

We're going to assume that you have identified the 7–10 factors from your market and segment analysis that are important elements of customers' purchase decisions and purchase processes. (If you are starting the book here, note Chapters 3–13 are helpful in discerning market and segment drivers as well as product or service health issues in the marketplace — and in defining improvements you may need to better your product or service position.) Remember to ask, "What is the job customers will be hiring us to do?" "Why will they buy?" "How will they buy?" and "What is the experience that customers want?" when determining your key criteria. For example, when deciding which college to attend, key questions can include "What will the degree cost?" "What is the quality of education I will receive?" "What is the campus life like at the college?" "What are my chances of getting a job after graduation from this college?" "What information can I get ahead of time from the college's web site?", and a host of others. Your challenge is to identify as many of the significant factors ahead of time as you can.

Given your firm's intended strategic positioning, you would then identify the few factors or elements that could potentially be important to customers and/or buyers. For each of these factors, you are going to ask a very simple question with a very simple response set. The question is "How well does our organization compare to competitors on [this factor]?" The response set is "Worse Than Competitors," "About the Same as Competitors," and "Better than Competitors." You will then identify three or four of your key competitors and ask the same question for each organization. You can see what we've tried to do here: eliminate all of the survey/statistical/research method noise that can make it difficult for customers to provide you with an answer and that can make analysis problematic. Firms are either "Worse Than," the "Same As," or "Better Than" competitors.

Following this, you will ask a second question: "How important is [this factor] to you when deciding which firm's products or services to buy?" The possible responses for this question are "Somewhat Important," "Important," or "Very Important." Again, we're going to keep this simple for ease of customer response. (Some people have asked why there's no "Not Important" response. The answer is simple: if it isn't important, you shouldn't be asking the customer about this factor anyway.)

You can either set this survey up in an online format using one of the many available online survey tools, call customers and gather the information yourself from them in the course of a phone call, or mail a simple survey form that asks customers to check a box and return it to you. Experience says phone calls will get you the highest response rate, online surveys are second, and mailed surveys are worst. Your goal should be to gather as many surveys as you can from your customers. We've seen one client set up a survey on an iPad at the checkout area and ask customers to take the survey while paying for their services. However you choose to engage your customers, it should take no more than 10 minutes to complete the process.

How to Construct the Tool and Analyze the Information

1. Determine Which Factors Are Most Important. The first step in the analysis is to determine the factors on which you will develop your Brand Perception Chart. (In effect, you will begin with the second response set.) If the customer response is that the factor is "Somewhat Important," assign a value of 1 to the answer. "Important" gets a value of 3 and "Very Important" a value of 6. Sum the individual responses and calculate the average important score for the factor. Then rank the factors from the most important factor (with the highest average score) to the least important factor (with the lowest average score).

2. Calculate the Brand Perception Score. A response of "Worse Than Competitors" gets a value of −3. A response of "About the Same" gets a value of 0. A response of "Better than Competitors" gets a value of +3. Sum the individual response from customers and calculate the average score for your firm and for each of your competitors for each of the factors. Your values will range between a minimum of −3 and a maximum of +3.

3. Create the Perception Charts. Begin by selecting the two factors with the highest importance scores. Designate one of the factors as the horizontal or X-axis factor, and the second as the vertical or Y-axis factor (the two axes should cross at the 0 point; see Figure 17.1 for an example). Then, using the scores for your firm and for competitors, place each firm on the chart at the corresponding (X, Y) average values. Voilà! You have a simple, easy-to-interpret brand perception chart that compares your organization to competitors on key dimensions of the brand positioning, as shown in Figure 17.1.

4. Perform as many two-dimensional comparisons as you feel appropriate to have for a meaningful set of brand perception

analyses. In most cases, three charts are usually sufficient; once you start getting down to factors that are fourth or lower in importance, it is generally doubtful as to whether or not the analyses will be providing you with useful data. If you want to be somewhat sophisticated, you can create a three-dimensional chart using the top three factors in terms of importance. Just beware that while these look great, such charts can be difficult to interpret due to the limitations of depicting a three-dimensional chart on a two-dimensional space!

5. There is one caveat to this process, and that occurs when you are asking customers about some factor of the brand experience that doesn't exist yet. Customers will not be able to give you a perceptive response because they cannot perceive of the existence of the product or service. In these cases, you can educate the customer about the potential features and/or benefits, but without any actual experience with the factor, customers will largely be guessing. Brand perception analyses about innovative new products, services, features, or benefits are always going to be limited; after all, if a brand is a promise of an experience, and the customer hasn't had the experience, how can they evaluate the brand?

Key Strategic Questions

Good brand perception charts can lead to a host of strategic questions. Some of the noteworthy ones we've encountered include:

- What is it about our products/services that is causing customers to perceive us as better/worse than competitors?

- Is our strategic positioning aligned with the factors that customers consider to be most important when assessing brand perceptions?

- Is our desired strategic positioning reflected in customer perceptions?

- If we know that our products or services are superior to competitors on some factor but customers don't perceive us as significantly better, why not? Is it a failure of communication? A failure of messaging? A failure of information?

- What are the areas in which our products/services are perceived as superior to competitors? Which areas are we perceived as inferior? Why?

- What types of brand activities — advertising, sales, web or e-commerce, etc. — would be most effective at reaching customers with the desired brand message?

Our Favorite Anecdote Using This Tool

A few years ago, we had an experience while working with a not-for-profit organization, a local foundation that was part of a regional health care organization. In the process of trying to identify the strategic position, the strategic planning team — consisting of the Foundation Director and top executives, along with select members of the Foundation Board — discussed many issues that were potentially important to potential donors: ease of donation, awareness of the Foundation mission, whether or not donors knew anyone helped by the foundation, etc. A long list of 17 potential factors was developed by the group. How to cull this into some reasonable number for the purpose of setting strategy?

One of the Board members, a local attorney, came up during a break and shared her insights regarding the problem. She noted that she had served on numerous not-for-profit Boards, and she felt that ultimately the choice of whether or not to donate came down to just a few things: the donor's perceived importance of the organization's mission, the perception of how effectively and efficiently the organization delivered services, the perceived need for those services, and the perceived ability of the organization to secure funds. She suggested that these might be worth performing a brand perception analysis. A survey was put together in 2 hours by the team and was distributed to the organization's donor base via an online survey methodology.

The results were pretty stark and eye opening. After the initial review of the importance, it became clear that the two most important factors — by far — were the perceived need for the services in the community and the perceived ease with which the organization could secure funds. The higher the perceived need for the service, the likelier that the donor would make a contribution, unless the donor felt that the organization had other ways to raise funds, such as through second-hand stores, volunteer services, grants, or government aid. In these cases, the likelihood of a contribution decreased significantly. The resulting brand perception chart is shown in Figure 17.2.

What the analysis indicated was that the client organization (in the solid black above) had a fairly high perceived need for the services. Donors were aware that the types of health care services provided by the organization that were supported by the

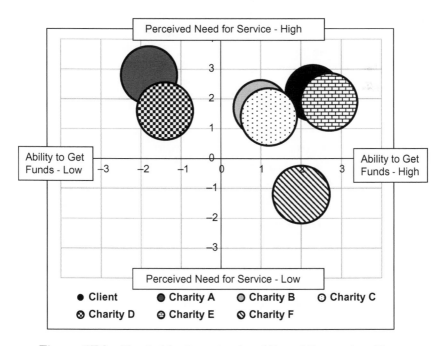

Figure 17.2: Charitable Organizations' Brand Perception Chart.

Foundation were needed in the community and were desirable. The problem was that the organization and the Foundation were perceived as the second highest in terms of the ability to secure funding through grants, fee for services, etc. As a result, donors saw little need to donate dollars to the Foundation, believing that the Foundation had plenty of ways of getting the necessary funds. Conversely, Charities A and D (in the upper left quadrant above) had comparable perceived need for the services, but both organizations were seen as having fairly low ability to generate funds on their own. As a result, donors felt more inclined to give to these organizations.

As a result of this brand perception analysis, the team decided to begin a promotional campaign that focused on three messages: the high value and effectiveness of the Foundation at producing the outcomes that were seen as important by the community, the emphasizing of the high perceived need for service, and the lack of state funding available as a result of changes in the financial situation of the state and other granting organizations which had resulted in fewer grant dollars available and fewer dollars for state aid. By addressing the brand perception, the Foundation was able to shift the competitive position more toward the left of the chart and increase the perceived need for donors to contribute. Within 6 months of the promotional campaign, the Foundation was able to launch an annual fund drive that yielded the highest amount of dollar donations in the organization's history.

A postscript: if you want to see the value of a simple brand perception chart, go to YouTube and search for Steve Jobs' presentation made in 2007 at the launch of the iPhone. It lasts a little over 50 minutes, but you don't need to watch the whole thing. Watch about the first 6 minutes. At about the 4:30 mark, Jobs uses a simple brand perception chart to demonstrate the intended strategic positioning of the iPhone. By the time he's done with the chart, you'll feel ready to buy one. That's the power of simplicity and brand perception.

The Opportunity Sourcing Matrix

Strategy Question: How can I prioritize among all the potential opportunities in front of me?

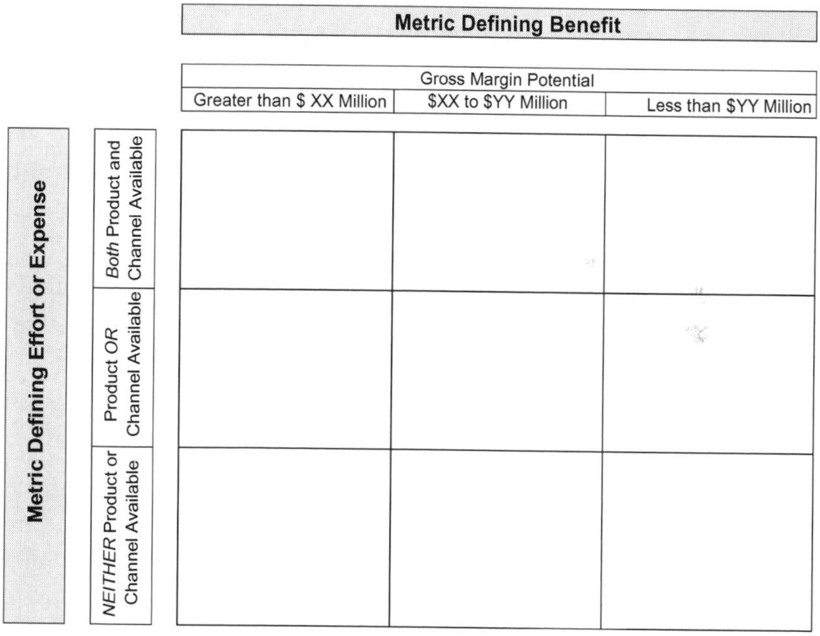

Figure 18.1: A Typical Opportunity Sorting Matrix Framework.

Overview

Many times, we face the need to make choices from numerous options when given imperfect, if not limited, information. A 9-box matrix is presented in a structured format that will help support a decision-making process. Key here is cleverly choosing the two sorting criteria best suited for your particular circumstance. In our example case, the matrix uses "expense" versus "benefit" sorting criteria. Using the chosen criteria, the group of options are plotted relative to each other toward creating some decision space and spread between them. The comparatively better and worse options can thus be discerned for your decision-making purposes.

Time to Complete the Tool

This matrix can be completed in 2–4 hours, especially if the data are more qualitative in nature.

Introduction

The nature of strategic management is decision-making in a condition of risk or uncertainty. It is given in today's environment that there will be more things to do than there are resources to do them. There will be choices you will need to make without the information you would like to have. The job of the strategist is to provide a direction, to give people a framework for action that will enable them to commit time, energy, and effort to produce desired outcomes. The reality of the job is that organizations always lack resources to do everything; in fact, that's one of the things that make a decision strategic. Strategic decisions always require a choice among exclusive alternatives. Investing in online marketing development means funds are not available to invest in product R&D. Directing the sales force to sell more of Product A means effort is diverted from Product B. Hiring a person to perform market analytics precludes hiring a person to deliver service. The fact that resources are limited and finite means the strategist is always having to make trade-offs. Often these decisions need to be made with imperfect information, either because getting the information would be too expensive, take too long, or simply isn't available. It is helpful to have a process to fall back on when you confront these situations.

That is what we've tried to do with the Opportunity Sourcing Matrix Tool. When confronting numerous opportunities, and an absence of solid information by which to evaluate them, we offer this solution. You can tell by now we're advocates of 9-box matrices. There is nothing particularly clever, unique, or fancy about these. The value of the matrices is the ability to cast the decision or sort the alternatives into terms that can really help you arrive at a decision. The criteria you can use is simply a function of your creative thinking and the decision parameters. Many times, we use this process to prioritize opportunities. Whenever we are deciding among alternative opportunities, there are generally two parameters that we're interested in: (1) if successful, what is the potential benefit or gain from this opportunity? and (2) How much will it cost to pursue this opportunity? Hence, we typically use a cost/benefit approach for sort criteria and use this as our example for the tool. (Do not be afraid to use it more broadly, though, whenever you need a sort among potential options.) So here is an example how you might approach a cost/benefit problem.

On the cost side, you can choose a number of general criteria. If you are capital-constrained, you may choose to segment by the magnitude of capital expenditure — is the capital investment required to pursue the opportunity high, moderate, or low? If you are personnel-constrained, you may segment by a manpower metric — does the opportunity require a major commitment of personnel time, a moderate commitment, or a low commitment? When considering strategic decisions from a market-based perspective, we have used a general indication of cost or expense by identifying whether the product or service is available, and whether access to the customer or the distribution channel is currently available. In the case shown in Figure 18.1, if *both* the product/service is already available, and the channel to deliver it already exists, the expense to pursue that opportunity will be relatively low. Conversely, if *neither* are available and you need to develop both a new product/service and a new channel to deliver it, the cost/expense for that option will be relatively high. And of course, development of either a new product/service *or* channel will fall relatively in the middle. The important point is to select criteria that reflect the costs associated with pursuing the various alternatives.

On the benefit side, you can choose whatever metric is appropriate. In our case, we usually default to gross margin dollars. You can choose revenue dollars, number of website clicks, patients served, etc., whatever makes sense for your situation. Then, defining a range for plotting the opportunities gives you perspective on the opportunity. You will likely be making a best guess at this point since information is likely scarce, but if you apply the same assumptions across all the opportunities, you should still get an apples-to-apples perspective.

What You Will Need to Construct the Tool

- A list of the options to be sorted.

- Choice of sort criteria (if not using the suggested approach). You will then need to break the sort criteria into three categories with increasing to decreasing attractiveness.

- Development of a ranking and plot points for each option to be evaluated.

Where to Get the Information

The list of options will come directly from the situation you are trying to get a handle on and the decision you need to make. The sorting criteria will also need to come from you. The better your choice of criteria, the more helpful the sort will be. You will need to be able to frame your sorting categories in three groupings. A helpful approach can be a "good, better, best" framework or a "positive, average, or negative" type of sort.

How to Construct the Tool

- Structure a 9-box matrix.

- Apply the sorting criteria for the x-axis and y-axis blocks.

- Rate each option (or items to be evaluated) by the two sorting criteria.

- Plot the points within the matrix. Note that plot points can also be structured to add depth and substance to the 9-box analysis. Much like the plot points in the Strategic Market Portfolio Matrix (Chapter 9), the plot points can be sized relative to opportunity size. They can also be color coded to reflect gross margin percent or some other relevant criteria pertinent to the sort. The ability to add information in a simple manner is limited by your own creativity and the nature of the decision, and it can enhance the decision process.

- Figure 18.2 shows a typical result from the Opportunity Sorting Matrix tool.

Key Strategic Questions

There are a number of questions that can be considered here, even noting that information is definition limited. Some questions that might arise from the use of the Opportunity Sorting Matrix might include:

- What are the potential benefits available to the organization, and how do these affect the firm's performance?

- Have we considered the right costs in making our decision? Are there additional resource commitments that might be required?

- How do the alternatives compare with one another? Are we comfortable with the comparisons?

- Are these alternatives mutually exclusive, or could we handle multiple options among the alternatives?

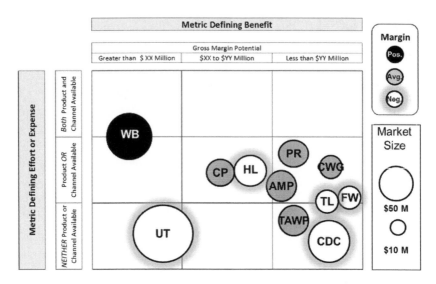

Figure 18.2: Typical Opportunity Sorting Matrix Tool Output.

- If the costs and/or benefits are high (or low), why is this the case? What does the sort tell us about our own capabilities as an enterprise?

For example, using Figure 18.2 as an example of an Opportunity Sort Matrix, questions we would likely raise for discussion might include:

- Why do most of the opportunities we've come up end up on the high expense-low return portion of the matrix? Are our markets so mature that we are facing limited future growth?

- If we are looking at opportunities needing new product and channel, why are we focusing on such small market sizes and such relatively low gross margin percent?

- Why haven't we been pursuing project WB earlier? Did it fall through the cracks?

- Which three of the opportunities should we pursue toward better definition?

Notice that the value of the Opportunity Sort Matrix is not only the ability to prioritize among alternatives, but also to guide discussion by asking the right strategic questions to drive sound decision making!

Our Favorite Anecdote Using This Tool

A manager helping to lead a strategic planning effort had just completed a process brainstorming session on potential product/ service projects. He was pulled into his boss's office mid-afternoon. He was told that the company's executives had to make some schedule changes and a key strategic plan meeting had been pulled ahead to tomorrow morning — at 8 am. Furthermore, the executives were anxious to understand his final product/service initiative recommendations. And, since his boss was trying to handle other aspects of the accelerated status review timing, he would be making the presentation himself.

The manager was frantic. He had just brainstormed the list — and in fact there were upwards of 20 programs that came out of that meeting! They were still working the timelines to evaluate them. There was no quantitative information available whatsoever and obviously no time to get any prior to the rescheduled meeting. The manager turned to the Opportunity Sorting Matrix tool.

He decided on the sorting criteria defined in Figure 18.1. He could put together a pretty clean assessment on the product and channel sorting criteria for the relative expense side and completed that portion with little effort. However, he still had a problem defining the benefit side. So, he took a proposed project with what he considered would have the median gross margin dollar return (i.e. exactly in the middle of the pack) and set it as a baseline. He then ranked the other projects relative to the median in three buckets — are they likely to have margin dollar returns better than, worse than, or equal to the median benchmark chosen. He was able to get enough differentiation, or spread, in the data points to display the three groups of projects within the tool.

Plotting the points, including sizing the opportunities to show market size and color coding the plot points for gross margin profitability, he had a decent picture of the potential projects — all with only qualitative data. The manager decided to use the one-page Opportunity Sorting Matrix tool characterization of the situation as the major supporting slide in his presentation (similar to Figure 18.2). He confessed immediately to the executives that he didn't have an absolute recommendation given the circumstances, but rather engaged them in his process, using the tool output, and took them through his analysis point by point. Sharing his logic, he concluded by choosing the top third of the most attractive potential projects from the sort for further evaluation, and he recommended immediately eliminating the least attractive bottom third from contention — freeing up resources to more quickly complete evaluations of the top third.

The executives reacted very favorably to the manager's "under the gun" presentation. They not only were impressed with his analysis and conclusions but were even more impressed with his ability to inform their understanding of the complex situation by using a single, one-page slide to do it.

Milestone Project Management Tool

Strategy Question: *How do we successfully manage our product/service improvement projects?*

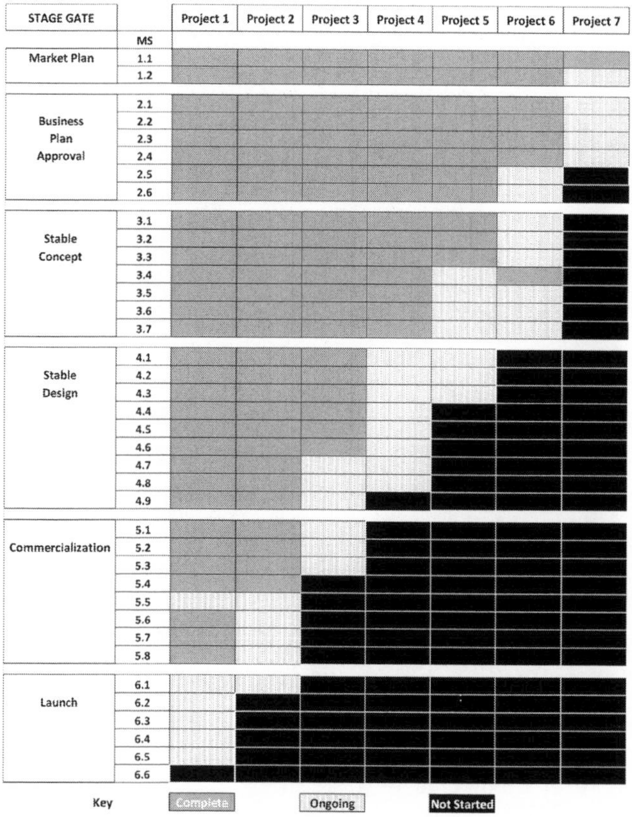

Figure 19.1: The Milestone Project Management Tool.

Overview

The Milestone Project Management Tool is a structured project management process. It is formatted after classic "stage gate" approaches, with some clever additions that allow it to serve as an overarching management tool. Each "Stage Gate" represents a major element of the development process. Individual "Milestones" or tasks supporting each stage gate, are grouped within that heading. Examples of stage gates and related milestones are provided should the user want to modify an existing or create a new Milestone Project Management Tool for their unique situation. Color coding the cells as completed (gray), ongoing (white fill), and tasks not started (black) when incorporating in the final matrix form provides a great visual management format for multiple ongoing projects.

Time to Complete the Tool

A solid draft can be completed in 2—4 hours given a reasonable understanding of the organization's development needs and capabilities.

Introduction

If you have been following the chapters in this book, or augmenting your own planning process, you are transitioning to an execution phase. Nothing is more frustrating than getting the environmental analyses right, getting the market analyses right, objectively evaluating the product/service offerings for action, defining a winning specification — and then having the project languish in the development stage due to poor execution.

There are some organizations that have no project management process whatsoever. We believe, and believe history has shown, that some type of project management structure will significantly improve your probability of project success. There are some organizations that have a loosely defined process or general framework. Some Fortune 500 companies with multiple subsidiaries have no formal corporate process and leave it to the individual business units, while others mandate a corporate process whether it fits individual business units or not. There are many examples of effective stage gate processes in business today. If you research the literature and find one you think makes sense for you, grab it. If not, we offer the following toward building your own hybrid that hopefully you can tailor for your individual circumstances. Our bias has been — where no system exists — to build a unique set of stage gates and an individual milestone for that unique circumstance. This allows us to design the process around our particular projects, current process, resources, strengths, weaknesses, and organization.

We like to think in terms of two components of a project management process:

Stage Gates: Many of the best project management systems, and the basis of our tool, consist of what are generally called "Stage Gates." These are simply logical phases of the development process one needs to pass through to begin the next step. They generally progress from some type of general definition of the project, specification development, product or service development, commercializing or getting the product/service ready for market, and the launch of the product or service. Hence, some functional areas will normally have more activity in certain stage gates than in others.

Milestones: These are individual tasks defined as necessary to support completion of each stage gate.

What You Will Need to Construct the Tool

- A set of stage gates appropriate for your situation.
- A set of milestones supporting each stage gate.
- An understanding of your organization's project/service strengths and weaknesses.
- A simple spreadsheet program.

Where to Get the Information

Stage Gate Selection

Stage gates are the guidelines for your Milestone Project Management Tool, so selecting the stage gates is important. You want to be sure you capture elements of your specific situation and your culture. You may have certain criteria that has been imposed by management or your Board of Directors that needs to be included, and by all means do that. The stage gates should capture the flow of the product/service development unique to your organization. They should also be helpful in separating the project into logical decision points for moving on to the next step of funding or capital spending.

Table 19.1 illustrates some stage gate structures we've seen in the past that may be of help to you. There are many more in business today. As you can see, they all have a similar theme, yet they all have a different language and approach for their specific situation.

Milestone Selection

Here is where the most individualization will likely occur. There are numerous milestones that can be added to each stage gate. If you are starting from a blank sheet, we provide below numerous milestone ideas for each general category of stage gates (some are similar with different language — simply provided to help spur the best definition for your individual circumstance). You are invited to pick and choose the ones that may resonate with your personal situation, or reshape them in your own words or company terminology.

(Authors' Note — If you are defining a stage gate and milestone system for the first time, we'd suggest you ease your organization into the concept. Do not hit your organization with 100 milestones — it might overwhelm them. We'd suggest maybe 5–10 milestones for each stage gate to begin with. You can add sophistication and more milestones as the team becomes familiar with your process; in fact, you will likely have each functional group suggesting additions.)

Table 19.1: Potential Stage Gate Structures.

Potential Stage Gate	Option 1	Option 2	Option 3	Option 4
Stage Gate 0	Charter		Approve Strategy	Strategic Planning
Stage Gate 1	Marketing Plan Approval	Market Study and Product Definition	Approve Program	Start Program
Stage Gate 2	Business Plan Approval	Charter Phase	Approve Business Plan	Fund Program
Stage Gate 3	Stable Development Concept(s)	Engineering Prototype Phase	Approve Capital Spending	Ready to Capitalize Program
Stage Gate 4	Stable Product/ Service Design	Pre-Production Prototype Phase	Approve Pilot Production	Ready to Produce
Stage Gate 5	Commercialization	Pre-Production Phase	Approve Production	Ready to Hand Off
Stage Gate 6	Managed Introduction	Production Launch Phase	Assessment	Program Success
Stage Gate 7	Full Production Project Audit			

Here are some typical milestones categorized by general stage gate phase of a product or service development project. We could make the list much longer but are generalizing to get you started. If (or better, when) you see a step we've missed that is relevant to your circumstance — add it. After all, it is your tool!

Charter Phase/Market Definition

- Define program objectives.
- Prepare preliminary proposal.
- Prepare marketing proposal or case for project.
- Define customer/market needs.
- Define internal project needs (manufacturing, quality, warrantyissues, etc.).
- Define preliminary and final quality function deployment (QFD) driven specifications (see Chapter 13 — The Poor Man's QFD Tool).
- Discuss concepts to be pursued.
- First-pass estimate on potential expense, cost, and capital needs by function.
- Define preliminary project financial summary (sales projections, project expense, capital requirements, and return on investment projections).
- Review meeting or approval step to move to the next stage gate.

Concept Development/Product Design

- Concept viability proven.
- Drawings/specifications released for development cost, time, and expense calculation.
- Patent analysis (potential infringements and new designs to protect).

- Costed bill of materials established to track product/service cost evolution.

- Operations approach defined.

- Supply chain approach defined.

- Testing or product/service validation program defined.

- Product safety review.

- Prototype units built.

- Technical validation of prototype.

- Market validation of prototype.

- Design Failure Mode Effects Analysis (Design FMEA — an analysis used to identify potential design flaws and rank those that are most severe via an RPN — ranked priority number).

- Operations Failure Mode Effects Analysis (Process FMEA — an analysis used to identify potential operations flaws in the production process and rank those that are most severe via an RPN).

- Review meeting or approval step to move to the next stage gate.

Stable Design/Commercialization/Launch

- Final concept chosen.

- Final drawings/specifications released for final costing.

- Parts/service plan.

- Final operations, supply chain, quality, and other internal group plans.

- Reduction in highest Design FMEA RPN scores (correcting the biggest identified failure modes).

- Reduction in highest Process FMEA RPN scores (correcting the biggest identified failure modes).

- Technical validation of product/service performance.

- Pilot build planning (quantity, timing, use for pilots).

- Supplier validation.

- Validation of product/service cost estimates.

- Confirm Marketing launch plan (advertising, collateral, website, etc.).

- Service materials development and publication.

- Launch definition (quantities, mix, timing, etc.).

- Sales and Service Training.

How to Construct the Tool

- Choose a spreadsheet program and construct the basic structure in the form of Figure 19.1.

- Choose a set of Stage Gates you feel appropriate for your organization and enter them into the spreadsheet.

- Choose the supporting Milestones you feel appropriate for each stage gate. Enter them into the spreadsheet as line items under the appropriate Stage Gate headings.

- Create columns for each project that you need to track.

- Enter the status of each project you need to track. Color code each cell status (in our example gray if the Milestone is already complete, white fill if it is ongoing, and black if it has yet to be started (note we often also use green, yellow, and red for cell shading).

- The final tool should look like Figure 19.1.

- Customize Your Tool — You can add extra information to the tool to personalize it further. We prefer to add a descriptor to each milestone, along with functional responsibility and even schedule commitments. In this way, we can optimize our time by maintaining only one chart for multiple purposes and meetings. (Figure 19.3 in the anecdote section below shows a real-world example of these extra descriptor columns.)

Key Strategic Questions

A well-constructed Milestone Project Management Tool should allow many good strategic questions. Some of the likely questions we'd pursue:

- Do your chosen "first-pass" stage gates and milestones make sense? Is the structure adequate to help you drive your projects and not miss key steps in your development process? Is it too simplistic or too complex at this stage of your organization's culture?

- How many projects are actively being worked? Is this too many? Or not enough; can you handle more?

- Are you having common issues at any particular stage gate over the course of many programs? If so, why?

- Do you have a resource bottleneck in a particular area or stage gate? Why?

- Is the activity (or deployment of resources) evenly spaced through all stage gates, or are many programs active in the same stage gate? By definition, each stage gate typically depends strongly on one functional area. For instance, Charter and Market Definition phases typically fall on Marketing and Sales, Concept Development and Product Design stage gates are typically Engineering-Intensive, and similarly Commercialization and Launch phases typically fall more heavily to Operations. Hence a concentration of "ongoing" activities across multiple project columns in one stage gate would be telling. Figure 19.2 illustrates how this tool can quickly identify this situation. The left side of the chart quickly shows a suboptimal situation where one or two

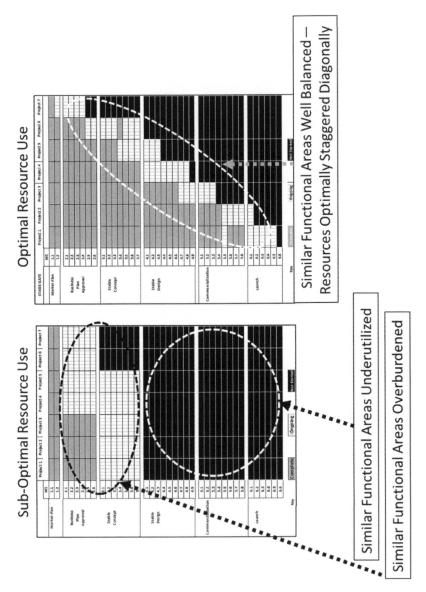

Figure 19.2: Ineffective and Effective Stage Gate Resource Use.

functions are constraining progress. The right side of the chart showing a diagonal nature of the "ongoing effort" distribution is optimal, as numerous projects are being advanced with each functional area in balance. (Note also the dates shown in Figure 19.3 as another way to schedule and keep track of functional balance; each project is staggered 2–3 months apart to ensure ongoing balance.)

Our Favorite Anecdote Using This Tool

A small manufacturing company was mired in a new product development (NPD) rut. The timeline to get new products to market was 30–36 months. When the products were launched, they were often obsolete, as markets had evolved and competitors had already reacted to the changes. Furthermore, when they were completed, there were numerous field issues that immediately plagued the launch. The organization was frustrated with this but couldn't pull themselves out of their funk.

A new CEO had been assigned to help rebuild the organization. When he got to the entire new product area, he did his data gathering within the company. Having experience in new product/service development in his past, he quickly surfaced in this company the two typical issues that beleaguer most new product/service programs: incomplete specifications and a flawed project management process.

Recognizing that both are critical, he worked with the organization using the techniques in Chapter 13 and the Poor Man's QFD Tool to start nailing down solid specifications. Resulting specification feature/requirement/metric combinations were then well defined and prioritized for the team so they knew exactly what they needed to accomplish. The specs were challenging given how stale the existing product portfolio was in the marketplace. Facing significant business urgency, the CEO set a mandate that each new product would be launched in 12 months or less.

With that he knew he also needed a strong project management process. He was not surprised when he asked to see the schedule

Stage Gate and Milestone	Definition	Functional Responsibility	Milestone	Project A	Project B	Project C	Project D
Stage 0 - Charter			Date				
Project Charter	Overview of project definition and market need	Marketing Product Manager	Charter				6/1
Stage 1 - Marketing Plan Approval			Date				
Marketing Justification	Strategic fit, synergy, reasoning for project	VP - Marketing and Sales	1.1			4/12	6/15
Marketing Plan	Definition of volumes, price points and payback potential	VP - Marketing and Sales	1.2			4/12	6/15
Preliminary CTC Project Specification	Critical To Customer (QFD) rank order specification	VP - Marketing and Sales	1.3			4/28	6/22
M1 Review and Approval		Executive Team	1.4			4/30	6/24
Stage 2 - Business Plan Approval			Date				
Concept Identification	Identify potential approaches to meet project need	Lead Engineering Team Member	2.1		3/7	5/5	7/31
Engineering Review	Preliminary review of concepts and likely development expenses, capital expense and product cost expectations	Lead Engineering Team Member	2.2		3/14	5/5	7/31
Manufacturing Review	Preliminary review of concepts and likely development expenses, capital expense and product cost expectations	VP Operations	2.3		3/14	5/12	8/10
Supplier Information Matrix	Plan for suppliers to be used and any strategy/action items that will be necessary	Purchasing Manager	2.4		3/14	5/12	8/10
Quality Review	Preliminary review of concepts and likely development expenses, capital expense and product cost expectations	VP - Operations	2.5		3/14	5/12	8/10
Engineering Validation Program Review	Review Test Program - cost, expense, timing and other issues	Engineering Team Member	2.6		3/8	5/12	8/10
Warranty History Analysis	Review Warranty - Incorporate fixes into new product design	Customer Service Manager	2.7		3/7	4/30	8/10
Patent Analysis	1) Will new design violate existing patents 2) What patent opportunities exist with new design	VP-Engineering	2.8		3/6	5/12	8/10
Business Plan Development	Revenue plan (Sales), Expense estimates (all), Project ROI and Capital summary (CFO)	All Functional Areas	2.9		3/15	5/21	8/17
Engineering Design Concept(s) Defined for Development	Prototype paths and top choice(s) to pursue	Assigned Engineering Manager	2.10		3/15	5/21	8/31
Final QFD driven Specification	Include external market and internal cost needs	Team	2.11		3/15	5/31	8/31
M2 Review	Multi-Functional Review to move to SG3	Executive Team	2.12		3/15	5/31	8/31
Stage 3 - Stable Concept			Date				
Engineering Design and Prototype Release	Release development drawings for concept(s) chosen	Assigned Engineering Manager	3.1	3/1	3/19	6/15	TBD
Tracking Costed BOM Development	Establish Costed BOM and monitor against spec	Cost Accounting Team Member	3.2	3/1	3/26	5/31	TBD

Legend: Not Started / In Process / Complete — Project Queue

Figure 19.3: Detailed Milestone Project Management Tool.

for the last new product project that was undertaken. There was no structure. Task definition from how to get from beginning to end was unclear. There was no definition of who was to do what and when. And the culture was apathetic to the whole idea. Not that they didn't want better products, they just didn't know how to get out of their own way to get it done.

The CEO took charge and identified himself as the project leader of the NPD effort. The first meeting called had one agenda: review the company's project management process. The intent was to resurrect and enhance the format the team already knew. It quickly became apparent that it would not work; there was so much misinterpretation by each member that it was obvious why the company had issues. Furthermore, there was significant pent-up animosity between groups from the last project.

The CEO decided he needed to start from scratch. He turned to the Milestone Project Management Tool and began to define the new company process. He chose a structure reminiscent of Option 1 in Table 19.1. He also knew he needed to guide the organization, so he added *task detail* and *team member responsibility* to each of the milestones he chose to support each stage gate. With his 12-month completion mandate, he wanted to ensure that he benefitted from time-saving cross-functional activity, so he also incorporated that rigor in each stage gate milestone.

Figure 19.3 shows a portion of the active Milestone Project Management Tool about 6 months after he introduced it to his team. Note the following:

- The added task definition and accountability detail are shown in the second and third columns of the tool.

- The full Stage Gate 2 is shown to provide perspective on how he added structure. Note that each major functional area is involved early in the project to ensure minimal surprises in later stages.

- Also note that the final QFD-driven spec (MS 2.11) is compiled with the benefit of internal needs as defined in prior completed milestones (MS 2.2–2.10).

- Six months after starting the first project, others followed. The CEO concluded a 3-month resource stagger was appropriate. Note how he used dates embedded in the cells to establish that target schedule to keep the projects moving.

- Also note how he used the dates to create and manage the ongoing resource "diagonal" to ensure no particular stage gate was bottlenecking the overall development efforts. This was key to maximizing his new product output by keeping his team members at high capacity without overburdening them.

The number, velocity, and effectiveness of the New Product development for this company, due in part to the Milestone Project Management Tool, was improved substantially. The CEO pulled together Figure 19.4 to show his team how effective they had really been. While the first Project A took every bit of the mandated 12 months to complete (with a few learning curve hiccups along the way), the team quickly got comfortable with the process. The CEO was able to rightly bow out of the leadership role in short order.

Using the Milestone Project Management Tool, coupled with the important Poor Man's QFD Tool to quickly define a winning

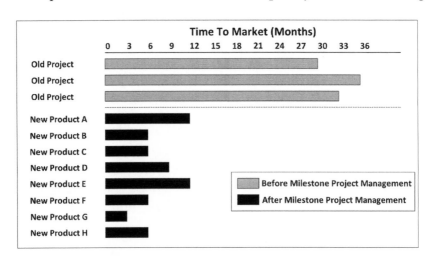

Figure 19.4: Positive Impact on Time to Market using the Milestone Project Management Tool.

project specification, the team continued to roll with a steady stream of timely new products. Their time to market was reduced by roughly 75%. Furthermore, all launches were staggered 3–6 months of each other — reminiscent of the stagger the CEO imposed within the stage gates and milestones. They took the market by storm, so much so that they entered "world class status" with almost 50% of sales coming from new products released in the past 3 years. And best of all, the design-related warranty failure rate for these new products hitting the field was significantly reduced — to 0.000%!!

Ordinary people. Simple tools. Extraordinary results.

The Visual
Waterfall Chart Tool

20

Strategy Question: How can I track the status of multiple initiatives in a timely and easily understood fashion?

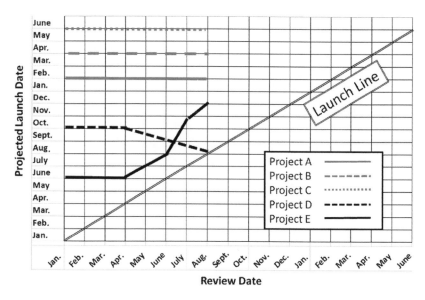

Figure 20.1: The Visual Waterfall Tool.

Overview

This one-page chart visually tracks progress of multiple projects or activities. By using the waterfall format, we can track schedule status in a quick and timely manner. The unique feature of this tool is the immediate highlighting of initiative status. The tool is constructed to represent an "on-schedule" project as a horizontal line. We show slips by a line moving parallel or away from the launch line (the line where the same x- and y-axis months meet on the graph), and conversely, we show accelerations of a project by a line moving toward the launch line. The Visual Waterfall Tool provides an efficient method to track and report on numerous initiatives in a format that can be reduced to management by exception if desired.

Time to Complete the Tool

This tool can be completed in less than 2 hours. Updates take 5−10 minutes each month.

Introduction

You are now working to execute on the numerous initiatives from your planning effort. There are lots of moving parts. How do you keep track of them all? If you have followed the tools in this book, you have likely seen our predisposition toward maximizing the effectiveness of the usually resource-constrained organization. We don't want to see the efficiency you've gained so far suddenly halted by bulky reporting formats. And as a strategy leader, you want your resources executing on the initiatives, not working on the update presentations.

We like to use this tool to capture the essence of our major initiatives on one page. With this tool, you and your teams instantly get a grasp on the most important initiatives you've chosen to follow. It is an offshoot of a waterfall chart. Waterfall comparisons have been used in business settings for some time. Our introduction to them was in finance reports, especially in tables tracking initially approved budget items over the course of subsequent monthly financial reporting periods. We like using the concept of tracking schedule performance over time, and we really like relaying it in the visual form of the Visual Waterfall Chart Tool.

You read the chart very simply: the y-axis "Projected Launch Date" is the date currently forecasted for project completion. The x-axis "Review Date" is the real-time update. So, Figure 20.1 is reporting as of August, in year 1. Focusing on Project E, the chart would read like this: in February of year 1, the projection was that Project E would launch in June of year 1. In April of year 1, the similar projection was that Project E would launch in June of year 1 (hence, on-schedule is a straight horizontal line). But in May, a 1-month slip occurred such that the new projected launch date was July (parallel line to launch line). Furthermore, as of August, the projection is that the project would launch in December of year 1 (movement away from launch line). Once your team understands how the chart works, it takes literally seconds to comprehend the changes in a newly presented update chart.

You can use this tool anytime you have initiative schedules to measure. You can further easily tailor the chart to your individual needs (different line colors or dashes for different categories or groups of initiatives, etc.).

What You Will Need to Construct the Tool

- A list of the initiatives you want to track.

- The original or currently scheduled completion date for each initiative to be tracked. (If you want to show a historical perspective you'll need the corresponding data for previous review dates.)

- The current forecasted completion date for each initiative to be tracked.

- Standard spreadsheet and slide presentation software.

Where to Get the Information

The information should come from your internal agreement on what items need to be tracked. The initial completion and forecasted completion dates come from the leaders of the internal projects or initiatives.

How to Construct the Tool

This tool is easy to construct. We have tried using spreadsheet programs for the entire chart and will admit there is likely a way to create a graph therein, but neither of us are enough of a super-user to have figured it out. We basically set the grid up in a spreadsheet program and import it into a slide presentation software (PowerPoint, etc.) to finish it. Here are suggested steps:

- Choose the period you want to track and in what increments (Figure 20.1 shows an 18-month period by monthly increments). This would imply 18 individual tracking points.

- Create a grid corresponding to the number of tracking points. For Figure 20.1, we use a grid of 18 rows and columns. If you wanted a two-year perspective by month, your grid would be 24×24. We like to use a spreadsheet program for sizing the rows and columns and labeling them. (Note anything above 24 increments begins to challenge clarity for the observer.)

- Label the rows and columns. The x and y axes start with the same date. So, if you want to start tracking from January 2018, each row and column would start from that date. Take the final grid and copy it to the slide presentation software (PowerPoint or other) program.

- Create the "Launch Line" by creating a solid bold line and connecting the points where the review date month equals the projected launch date month (we find this more easily done in the slide presentation software).

- Create the line for each initiative item. We simply use a generated line from the slide presentation software. If an initiative is envisioned to jump month to month, you can easily cut and paste the monthly line segment as needed. (Note that if you have over 10–12 initiatives, or several converge in a 2–3-month span, the chart might get crowded and you may need to adjust accordingly.)

- Place your "label description" for each line item below the launch line in the bottom-right half of the chart, where no plotting occurs.

Key Strategic Questions

Strategic questions from this tool tend to center around which issues are causing the slips. As our activities are integrated, the initiatives highlighted in the tool are also hopefully integrated — hence a slip in one may impact others. Additionally, the environment is constantly changing, and mid-course initiative corrections are sometimes necessary. This tool output provides great insight for the strategy leader or program manager. Some questions we'd likely explore given the scenario shown in Figure 20.2 are:

- What did we do right to accelerate Project D?

- Why is Project E slipping? What must we do to recover?

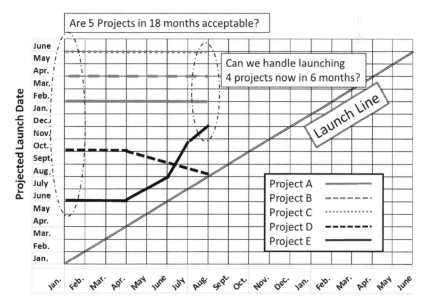

Figure 20.2: Strategic Information from The Visual Waterfall Chart Tool.

- If Project E is a higher priority, is there something we can do with the resources of Projects A, B, or C to delay them towards getting Project E back on track?

- Can we pull Projects A and B ahead into this fiscal/calendar year if we sacrificed the Project C timeline? (i.e. Have you ever had to pull ahead your Cap-Ex spending into the current year?)

- Referring to Figure 20.2, for the January review, is five projects in 18 months acceptable? Is this too many or not enough? Is one initiative launch per quarter a more realistic pace for our organization?

- Relative to the August (current) review date, with the slip of Project E to December, there are now four projects (E, A, B, and C, respectively) launching within a 6-month period. Can we handle that?

The 90-Day Bucket Tool

21

Strategy Question: How can I keep my performance goals relevant and continually driving proper action and achievement?

			Upcoming Fiscal Year				
		Q4	Q1	Q2	Q3	Q4	Q1
Prioritized Strategic	Strategic Initiative 1	Early Start	Task	Task	Task	Task	
	Strategic Initiative 2		Task	Task	Task	Task	
	Strategic Initiative 3	Early Start	Task	Task	Task	Task	Task
	Strategic Initiative 4		Task	Task	Task	Task	Task
	Strategic Initiative 5		Task	Task	Task	Task	Task
	Unexpected Disruption1						
	Unexpected Disruption2						
Sustaining	Function A Initiative		Task	Task	Task	Task	
	Function B Initiative		Task	Task	Task	Task	
	Function C Initiative		Task	Task	Task	Task	
	Function D Initiative		Task	Task	Task	Task	

Anticipated Quarterly MBO

Figure 21.1: The 90-Day Bucket Tool.

Overview

The 90-Day Bucket Tool describes an approach to ensure the organization is working the most important initiatives in a way that probability of on-time success is greatly enhanced. Our 90-day bucket approach focuses on three main elements:

1. *90-Day Objectives to Keep Goals Relevant* — Define for the organization, at the beginning of each quarter, the three most important tasks that must get done in the next 90 days to support the overall strategy.

2. *Cross-Functional and Cross-Pay Grade Alignment* — *All* Vice Presidents, Directors, and Managers (and even Supervisors if possible) are tasked with the exact same three objectives for the quarter.

3. *Incentivize Completion of Objectives to Ensure Execution* — Best case — modestly restructure a portion of existing incentive programs as suggested below. Less optimal but still effective is to weave the quarterly 90-Day Objective achievement into performance review criteria. (Note all levels, including VPs and Directors, would get the exact same rating for purposes of their performance review.)

This 90-Day bucket approach accounts for changing environmental conditions and unexpected business disruptions that must be addressed, and it encourages cross-functional participation to execute and get key objectives done. And it works, as we've used it to change culture and get results.

Time to Complete the Tool

The concept behind this tool is simple and can be adopted informally at any time. If incorporated into a formal compensation structure, it may take the time until your next incentive structure is set.

Introduction

We have never been smart enough to know at the beginning January of our fiscal year what goals will be business-critical in the latter months of the year. Our crystal ball is always too cloudy, our tea leaves too soggy, and even our magic-8 ball is stuck on "ask again later." Business settings change. Company situations change. Competitors take actions that may require immediate reaction. Business disruptions occur. Strategy needs to adapt to changing environments. Yet how many times do we find our organizations feverishly working in November or December on incentive-laden year-end goals that became obsolete in March or April? *We need a way to ensure our goals are focused on our most important initiatives, relevant to the changing environment, and adaptive to business disruption.*

Additionally, we've seen so many situations where incentive goals are not aligned. We especially see this in larger companies with a matrix management approach. The Finance function sets a goal of improving working capital, while the Sales function intends to improve revenues by extending payment terms. The Supply Chain function intends to reduce inventory levels, while the Operations VP intends to improve lead time by adding inventory buffers. Each functional VP and related executives are incented on achievement of their particular initiatives, but none are coordinated within the organization. The poor folks in the business unit entities have numerous functional VPs pulling them in equal and opposite directions, with little time to address their actual business needs. And when forces are equal and opposite, engineering science tell us that (1) nothing will move — the entity will remain static and (2) as the tensions ratchet up, the stress within the entity will increase until something breaks. *We need a way to ensure we align our most important objectives across the organization.*

Lastly, the best strategic plan is worthless if you don't execute it, and we'd suggest that having a good plan is maybe half of the battle. The other half is developing a great team with motivation toward a successful result. We see many strategy planning books superficially cover plan execution in the final few paragraphs of their writings. One we saw recently tickled us; the single line on execution stated, "Find a way to link strategy to performance." Well, that is easier said than done — at least for those of us living in the real world and not in a theoretical textbook. We've spent years trying to figure out *how best to ensure execution of our important strategic initiatives.*

We suggest the 90-Day Bucket Tool as an approach to address these universal needs to keep company initiatives relevant and to consistently achieve them. It accounts for changing business conditions and encourages cross-functional alignment and incentive to get them done. Following is more detail on each of the three elements and how we've successfully used them. Hopefully, it will spark your thinking relative to what you might be able to do in your organization

90-Day Objectives — If you have been following the chapters in this book, you now have a prioritized set of initiatives ready to go. You also have split your resources into "strategic" manpower to fulfill the plan initiatives and "sustaining" manpower to keep the company running. You should also have balanced the initiative manpower requirements with the resource bandwidth you have available.

Here is where many companies will likely assign functional incentive goals, while missing the more important cross-functional strategic goals. We agree that functional goals are important, but we suggest they should be relegated to the "sustaining resources" for achievement.

The next step we suggest is to take each prioritized strategic initiative and break it into four quarterly time frames. By having four points in the year to assess your situation, you have the ability to drive the strategy initiatives based on key shorter-term milestones to ensure their overall schedules stay on track. You now bring to bear a powerful focus in your organization to complete key goals in 90 days so you can move on to the next ones. Rather than an annual target, four shorter-term targets let you focus, tweak, and adjust during the year — with all goals remaining relevant.

Breaking the annual initiative into quarterly goals is not difficult. Make the quarterly tasks logical and ones the team can drive toward. Completion dates can come anywhere within the quarter as your initiative timeline dictates; the focus should be to *GET IT DONE* within the 90 days. See Table 21.1 for some simple examples.

Now, if (when) business disruptions arise that need to be addressed, you have a baseline set toward shifting reactive resources much more quickly to address them — and you know

Table 21.1: Examples of Defining 90-Day Bucket Tasks.

Priority	Typical Annual Objective	90-Day Bucket Task Suggestion			
		Q1	Q2	Q3	Q4
1	Complete New Product/Service by December 31	Complete Stage Gates 0 and 1 by March 15	Complete Stage Gates 2 and 3 by June 30	Complete Stage Gates 4 and 5 by September 30	Complete Stage Gate 6 and launch by November 1
2	Purchase, Install and Launch the new machine line by November 15	Capital Justification completed by February 26. Order by March 15	Monitor machine line construction at supplier	Install machine line by July 15. First pilot run by August 15	Production ready by October 31. First production run November 15
3	Migrate ERP system software by December 1	Data conversion — all functional areas complete by March 31	Test data base ready for trials by April 31. First pilot run by May 31	Final pilot testing by July 15. Ready to "go-live" by August 30	Switchover — Go live October 15 (or after Q3 books are closed)
4	Build a Sales Channel in Market Segment X by adding 12 Dealers by year end	Total of 3 new dealers by March 30	Total of 7 new dealers by June 30	Total of 10 new dealers by September 30	Minimum of 12 new dealers by December 1

where the resources are coming from. What disruptions are we talking about? Here are a few that may resonate with you:

- The price of this commodity (gold, silver, copper, oil, steel, corn, wheat, etc.) has suddenly spiked (dropped) on the world market and we need to react by _____

- Our Union suddenly reversed positions and is threatening a strike in 30 days. We need to protect the company by

  _____

- Our key competitor was just acquired by Moneybags, Inc. with the intention of _____

- Our only single-source supplier has just announced they are exiting our market _____

- The ERP system (hardware, software, both) has been neglected for so long it is now shutting down without warning and endangering our ability to do business. We need to immediately _____

Any of them sound familiar to you? They will occur. We've rarely had a year go by without at least one or two 90-Day Bucket Objectives coming from an outside business disruption. This approach allows you, the leader or team member, the opportunity to quickly address and get them behind you.

Figure 21.1 shows how you could capture this thinking in a structured form. Note a few things. The chart has three sections. First, the prioritized strategic initiatives at the top. Second, the functional initiatives (again to be completed from the "sustaining" resources) at the bottom. In the middle, we've left a spot for those unexpected disruptions. We like to highlight those areas (shaded in black) that are the most critical for completion in the quarter, and those would be likely candidates for the incentivized 90-Day Objectives.

Cross-Functional and Cross-Pay Grade Alignment — This is important! All functional VPs, Directors, and Managers are responsible for achievement of the same 90-day objectives. So what is wrong with the VPs or Directors being held accountable for actual results in the exact same way their underlings are? Talk about getting their attention and making sure their organizations are focused on the right things — this will do it. Cross-Pay Grade alignment is a very powerful way to ensure cross-functional cooperation too. If the VP of Engineering doesn't support an operations-heavy quarterly objective, she suffers along with the VP of Operations if it doesn't get done.

This really isn't so far-fetched. Think about it: you are picking objectives at the strategic level. Therefore, activities are complex, and all functions are relevant to completion. Having all functions and organization levels focused on these most important tasks just makes sense. And when those unexpected disruptions hit, and they are serious enough to warrant a quarterly objective toward resolution, you have the full focus of the company to get things back on track.

Incentivize Completion of Objectives — If you really want to get it done, incentivize it. It works. But changing compensation is usually emotional organizationally and something that should be done with care. While we don't want to get into a debate with Human Resource and Compensation experts, our experience is that allocating some portion of an annual incentive program provides significant motivation toward achievement. We have seen executives seriously protective of their resources suddenly transform when incentives structured as described above enter the picture. In fact, we often see those functional managers or VPs actually offer up their resources toward achieving an objective if another function is facing unexpected difficulty. Since you've chosen the most important quarterly tasks for the most important initiatives as your 90-day objectives, that is exactly what you want your organization doing!

Each manager, director, and vice-president usually have a bonus plan with their payout, commensurate with their level in the organization. Let's call each of their target levels 100%. We'd suggest carving out roughly one-quarter of each individual's annual incentive program target and dedicate it to achievement of 90-Day Bucket tasks. We've actually used 24%, with the remaining 76% dedicated to more normal revenue, profit, working capital, or other typical metrics. Of that 24%, we then allocate 6% for each of four quarters. The 6% per quarter is then broken down to three objectives at 2% each. Hence, each objective is worth 2% of each

Manager, Director, and VP's annual individual target incentive bonus. That is pretty substantial — and <u>BOOM</u>, each member of the team can easily comprehend the monetary impact of successful achievement. And since the 90-day Bucket Objectives will likely be focused on your highest-priority initiatives (likely fueling revenue and profit growth), you automatically put yourself in position of better success on the metrics for the remaining 76%.

If adding formal incentive compensation is not possible, as suggested earlier, you can include 90-Day Objective attainment in the normal performance review process. We feel it is important that each of the team members be given the same rating. If you believe that the achievement of six of the annual 12 90-Day tasks is failing, each team member (VP, Director, and Manager) would have that same failing rating reflected in their review. Hence, everyone has the same skin in the game.

One note on the objectives themselves. We suggest that the objectives be defined and chosen by the executives themselves at the beginning of each quarter; they know best what needs to happen. The CEO, president, or appropriate leader (who is rightly incented by overall performance of the organization and <u>not</u> incented by the 90-Day Objectives) should have the final say on the objectives selected and goals defined at the beginning of the quarter and judge achievement of the goal at the end of the quarter. We feel it is important the objectives have stretch goals. Our definition of a stretch goal is "just out of reach — but not out of sight." It is up to the leader to ensure that the proper objectives and targets are chosen to move the organization forward. In our experience, and the way we set these goals, achievement of 8 or 9 out of 12 objectives is a pretty good year.

What You Will Need to Construct the Tool

- A simple spreadsheet program.

- The prioritized list of organizational initiatives.

- An action-oriented task breakdown of said prioritized initiatives in 90-day buckets.

- A defined group of executives and managers key to success of the initiatives.

- An executive committee (with the organization leader to break the ties) to help set/choose the quarterly initiatives, and to score the prior quarter's objective completion. This group will also determine if any business disruptions rise to the level that warrant definition as a quarterly objective for the next quarter.

Where to Get the Information

Prioritized list of organizational initiatives — If you have been following the chapters of this book, you already have those well defined — and the fact they are already integrated will be a big advantage to you at this point. If this is your starting point in the book, you will need to get the prioritized list from your existing plan, or from the executives driving the initiative definition. It is important that you know what the priority is.

Action-oriented 90-day bucket task breakdown of prioritized initiatives — These are key events in the project timeline. If you have implemented the principles of Chapter 19 (Milestone Project Management Tool), use this resource to help. If not, turn to the development schedules for your planned projects. You will need to similarly pose task structure for addressing any disruptions serious enough to warrant consideration as a quarterly objective. Again, Table 21.1 is a good reference.

Key leaders to set priorities and incentive definition — This needs to come from the leaders of your organization.

How to Construct the Tool

- Put together a spreadsheet in the format of Figure 21.1.

- Import the list of prioritized initiatives.

- Import the defined quarterly tasks envisioned for each prioritized initiative.

- Shade or somehow designate which of the 90-day bucket tasks are initially seen as most critical to the organization. Again, in theory you have already balanced the resources and all should be achievable. But in many cases, there are slack or wait times inherent in a schedule (lead times for purchased capital items, reliability testing, customer surveys, etc.) that allow concentration toward resource-intensive phases of other initiatives.

Key Strategic Questions

At the beginning of each quarter, you need to reassess your tactical plan and determine whether there are any major changes necessary in your overall strategy. Here are questions we'd likely pursue:

- Have the environmental conditions changed enough that we need to reassess our strategic initiatives or direction? Do we need to reprioritize initiatives or add new ones?

- Are the quarterly objectives defined still relevant to moving the most important initiatives forward?

- Are we continually besieged by business disruptions? If so, do we have some remedial tasks in the functional areas that need to be addressed? Should those be prioritized to get them out of the way?

- If so, what are the initiatives we need to keep moving regardless of the disruption, and are we setting our 90-day objectives appropriately?

- Is there enough incentive in place to ensure the organization's full attention?

- What is the "hit rate" for objective completion? If too high, are the objectives stretched enough? If too low, are objectives set too high and are you losing motivation from the team?

- Have any unanticipated business disruptions risen to the point that they need to supersede your most important strategic initiatives? How are you reallocating resources to do this?

Figure 21.2 shows how the tool can help you monitor and reallocate resources. Figure 21.2 differs from Figure 21.1 only in that two disruptions have been added, and resources shifted from anticipated quarterly MBOs of strategic initiatives 4 (in Q2) and 5 (in Q3) to address the unexpected disruptions in the business. In this example, the company continued to move the three most important strategic initiatives forward without delay — but immediately knew they could shift resources from the lower two strategic initiatives to bring to bear the entire force of the company to solve the disruption issues and get both quickly behind them. Note that some resources could have been shifted up from the sustaining initiatives if more appropriate. But again, you have a tool that you can quickly use to make decisions and to *ACT* in an intelligent and timely fashion.

Our Favorite Anecdote Using This Tool

This tool and philosophy has a number of applications. While we use it routinely to schedule quarterly objectives, the 90-Day Bucket approach can be adapted for practical use in many other ways, and at other levels. Consider the case of a CEO who, upon taking on a new business, began to quickly uncover numerous organizational issues. His compensation was tied exclusively to growth in the value of the failing company.

His immediate priority was to do the company's first strategic plan — and that defined his first 90-day bucket. As he proceeded through the plan (using many of the tools in this book), he got a clear dose of organizational reality. Among a cast of earnest, hardworking people, there were issues.

There were leaders who were not qualified to hold the positions they currently held, and resulting shortcomings due to that subsequent poor management. There were situations where process

Upcoming Fiscal Year

		Q4	Q1	Q2	Q3	Q4	Q1
Prioritized Strategic	Strategic Initiative 1	Early Start	Task	Task	Task	Task	
	Strategic Initiative 2		Task	Task	Task	Task	Task
	Strategic Initiative 3	Early Start	Task	Task	Task	Task	Task
	Strategic Initiative 4		Task	Task	Task	Task	Task
	Strategic Initiative 5		Task	Task	Task	Task	Task
	Unexpected Disruption 1			Disruption 1			
	Unexpected Disruption 2				Disruption 2		
Sustaining	Function A Initiatve		Task	Task	Task	Task	
	Function B Iniaiative		Task	Task	Task	Task	
	Function C Initiative		Task	Task	Task	Task	
	Function D Initiative		Task	Task	Task	Task	

Figure 21.2: Using the 90-Day Bucket Tool to Adjust and Monitor Resource Allocation.

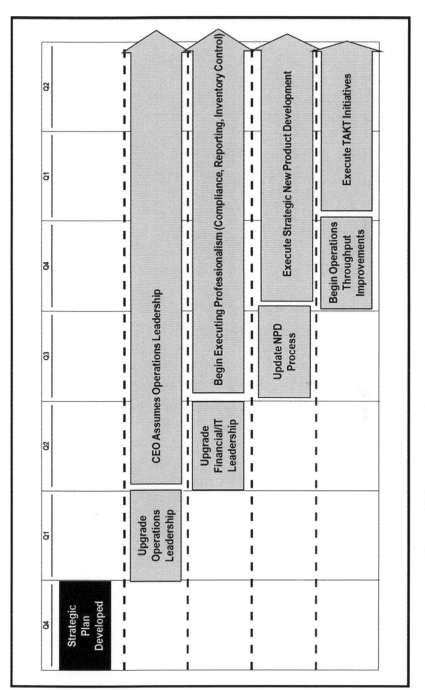

Figure 21.3: 90-Day Buckets for CEO Organizational Transformation.

rigor was simply missing, and adding it would help. There were blocking and tackling issues at a basic level, too. Unfortunately, time was of the essence. With so many areas of improvement necessary, the CEO fell back to his 90-Day Bucket Tool. He had to devise an improvement roadmap and prioritize exactly what he wanted to do and when. Then he had to make sure he got the tasks done in 90 days each. He took a swim-lane approach to his 90-Day Bucket Tool and presented his prioritized initiative thinking to his Board. Figure 21.3 is a representation of that result.

Quarter by quarter, he laid out a tough set of prioritized tasks to achieve. After the top priority strategic plan, he needed to make some organizational changes in operations (Q1) and add financial competence (CFO in Q2) just to right the ship. Then he challenged himself to begin introducing key process rigor in the areas most in need of change. He needed to get his New Product Development team going with specification development and design focus (Q3) so he could then begin to concurrently work in the next step of operations growth (Q4), after stabilizing the shop floor in the previous three quarters. Concurrently, the CEO fashioned 90-day bucket goals for his organization in the form of Table 21.1 and Figure 21.2 to help achieve key initiatives within the swim lanes.

The point here is that the CEO used the same 90-day philosophy and tool approach of Figure 21.1 at his higher organizational level to keep his tasks focused, relevant to the business, and aligned with the organization toward getting the results he needed. It was not easy, and there were a lot of late nights, but the philosophy of "get it done in 90 days so you can move on to the next task" was paramount (and each task indeed got done in the quarter designated).

The Communication Matrix Tool

22

Strategy Question: *How do I keep everyone on the same page?*

Table 22.1: A Typical Communication Matrix.

Formal Communication Type		CEO/President	VP/Director	Manager or Supervisor	Employees
Quarterly	All Employee Meetings	Leader			
Monthly	Key Leader Meeting	Leader			
Weekly	Staff Meeting	Leader			
	Staff Meeting		Leader		
	Staff Meeting			Leader	
Daily	Stand-up Daily Review (15 minutes)			Leaders	
	Daily Floor Meeting			Leader	

Overview

Communicating with your people is one of a leader's biggest responsibilities. Ensuring communication is flowing throughout an organization is critical to ensuring the intended messages are being delivered. We suggest a basic skeletal template for routine communication plan. Both formal and informal methods are discussed. You are encouraged not only to add and delete to best suit your circumstance, *but to adopt one if you haven't already*.

Time to Construct the Tool

You should be able to construct a template for formal scheduling and organizational use in at most a day or two.

Introduction

You hear it all the time: "I don't have a clue what is going on." And when your leaders say it, you pretty much know your organization's morale arrow is pointing due south. People want to be included. People want to be informed. Communication is a lynchpin for execution. When it comes to your strategic plan, it is equally important that each of the major groupings of your organization (executives, key leaders, managers/supervisors, and general workforce employees) understands where you are going and why.

We advocate for a standard schedule of *formal* communication. That way, you can get into a routine. This should include a form where each employee hears from their immediate supervisor or manager and has the opportunity to hear from their functional heads (directors or vice-presidents), as well as the organization leader. While we abhor meetings sucking up most of our day, we encourage you to make room for this effort.

Table 22.1 shows a suggested format for a quarterly, monthly, weekly, and daily communication plan. The groups involved and the leader of each effort is clearly shown. Again, this is a good template from which to evolve your individual needs. Use it, modify it, or create your own — just have one.

One thing we strongly encourage is the question-and-answer portion of our meetings — especially the quarterly all-employee meetings or our Key Leader meetings. In some cases, people are hesitant to ask questions. One way we encourage them to speak their mind is to mandate three good questions be asked before adjournment. So, somebody first asks an innocuous question, spurring one that is a little more on-topic. Once the ice is broken, we find we get down to business. While a leader can get these questions individually, it is really helpful to see how many employee heads are shaking in the group setting when a question or topic is being raised. (The last one we remember is an employee asking if the reimbursement for safety shoes could be addressed, as it hadn't kept up with inflation. Just about every audience head nodded. We were completely unaware of the issue. Easy fix, and the workforce is happy and comfortable that they can voice a problem and it will be seriously considered.) Don't get us wrong, there are some all-employee meetings where issues are teed up and we'd like to limit it to three questions only. But the point is to encourage the interaction in the large, all-employee settings. You see what your group is made of, and they can see what you are made of as well.

We also believe that *informal* communication is equally important. Keeping items forefront in employee's minds is beneficial. The more interactions that can occur in-person and the more employees can interface with leaders outside of formal meetings, the more human both groups will become to each other (hopefully in a good way). Informal communications can happen in a variety of ways. We note a few here for consideration (recognizing you will be much more creative in your list):

- Company-sponsored events.
- Community events.
- Lunches with smaller employee groups.
- Company newsletters.
- Monthly business summary and bonus update posted on company bulletin boards.
- Refrigerator magnets with key numbers (attendance, medical provider, 401K administrators, etc.).
- Paycheck or paystub envelope stuffers.
- Setting up a company Facebook site for employees only.
- Company intranet.

- All-employee e-mails when the need arises.
- Visiting employees in their break areas during break time.
- Simple walks around the shop.

What You Will Need to Construct the Tool

- A list of key employee groups
- A list of key manager/employee meetings you are currently holding
- A list of same meetings you want to see in the future
- Rollout of the new structure.

Where to Get the Information

This is pretty simple; it comes from your organization and your desires.

How to Construct the Tool

The spreadsheet of Table 22.1 is as easy as any to construct. Use it as a guideline.

Strategy Implications

The biggest implications to your communications strategy is whether or not it is effective, and you can get a sense of that quickly from your employees.

Our Favorite Anecdote Using This Tool

A new leader of a manufacturing facility wanted to have his first all-employee meeting shortly after his arrival. He inquired on how the organization usually conducted them and got a chuckle in response; it turns out they really didn't do all-employee meetings because they simply didn't have any place to do them. The leader then toured the shop floor and found two or three areas where square footage would seem to accommodate all the employees, and he chose one for the meeting location. Then he had to get down to basics. Since they had nothing to sit on, his purchasing folks found a salvage sale with folding chairs for $2 each, and they bought all 150. Similarly, he had to buy a simple PA system and a projector to display his presentation. But what to project on? He asked his maintenance folks to figure out a way to mount a screen in the chosen area. They actually thought the request was a joke and didn't even pursue the request.

The leader learned 3 hours before meeting time that there indeed was no place to project the presentation. A bit frustrated, he asked his (now embarrassed) maintenance personnel to position one of the overhead cranes at a certain point in the space he decided to use. Then he sent them to the scrap pile and told them to cut a 3/8-inch diameter steel rod and a section of 2-inch square pipe that could be drilled through, both 9-feet long. Then he drove to the local Wal-Mart and bought the cheapest 300-thread count, king-size bed sheet (which happens to be roughly 108-inch long). They cobbled up a screen by attaching the rod to the bottom for weight and clamping the sheet through the drilled holes at the top of the square pipe. Pulling the thingamajig up with the overhead crane gave them a screen to project on.

The new leader lamented his "Rube Goldberg" contraption as the most unprofessional of his career. The screen was a bedsheet that still had wrinkles, having just been pulled from its packaging. He figured he'd get laughed out of the place. But he pressed forward. Come meeting time, he had all the employees in one place (for the first time), all settled in an arrangement conducive to receiving his presentation where they could actually see, hear, and question the message.

Well, it turned out to be one of the best meetings the leader had ever held. The employees were receptive, asked great questions, and good-naturedly ribbed him about buying an iron for next quarter's meeting. But on the serious side, they couldn't believe a leader would take the time and effort to actually try to communicate with them — and that made a huge impression on his workforce.

What did the leader learn? The communication effort didn't have to be fancy, it just needed to be genuine.

The 10-Quarter Tool

23

> **Strategy Question:** *Is there a way to help me follow through on the changes I personally need to make?*

Overview

We have discussed numerous tools to improve your organization through a better strategy and plan. We thought we'd leave you with one tool to help you improve yourself. The 10-Quarter Tool deals with personal change management. The user picks an area they want to work on or a behavior they want to change. The repetition in the 10-Quarter Tool puts you on course to make your intended change a habit.

Time to Complete the Tool

As long it takes you to identify the area you want to work on.

Introduction

You are not doing yourself or your organization a favor by neglecting changes you need to make to be more effective. You know what you really need to work on. If not, your boss, Board or peer group can probably help you. Or in our cases, our wives!

Anyway, conventional wisdom says it takes 21 days to make a behavior change a habit. This ties back to Maxwell Maltz and his 1960's self-improvement book titled *Psycho-Cybernetics*. In that book, he observes an empirical timeframe of 21 days for a change to set in (time it takes living in a new residence for it to feel like home, time it takes for plastic surgery patients to become accustomed to their new faces, etc.). The nominal 21-day rule of thumb just seemed to stick for all these years. Other experts comment change takes much longer. Some studies cite 28 days, others 66, others up to 1 year. The one noteworthy commonality is that some type of repetition is important to the process.

The 10-Quarter Tool provides you a simple method to identify a behavior you want to change, forces you to be aware of it throughout your day, and gives you a method to reinforce repetition. Here is how it works: you determine the behavior you want to improve. You take 10 quarters and put them in your left pocket. Your goal is to do the new behavior 10 times each day. Every time you do it, you move one quarter from your left to your right pocket. At the end of the day your goal is to have all 10 quarters in your right pocket. Kind of simple, right? Yup (hopefully, like most of our previous tools). Yet it works. You jingle a bit when you walk, but the weight of 10 quarters and the noise emanating from your pocket reminds you of the task at hand.

Now when we share this tool with others, we get all sorts of comments. One in particular we get from our female peers is that they don't always have pockets — so what do they do? We always respond to get creative. They can use 10 small bracelets or rubber bands around their wrists, or re-arrange small Post-It notes or paper clips attached to the planner they usually carry, or create some sort of reminder on their smartphone, etc. The point here is to raise the importance of the area you want to work on and finding a way to remind yourself in the flurry of each day to not forget it.

Try it. See if it works for you. We'll wager you'll be passing this tool along to friends and family before too long.

Our Favorite Anecdote Using This Tool

A CEO we know of was in the middle of his latest annual strategic plan development. Things were going well; the previous strategic plans had helped turn the business around, and he wanted to continue that trend. There were many positive initiatives to investigate, and the market segments were healthy and growing.

In his zeal for addressing the opportunities before them, he didn't realize he had essentially sequestered himself in meeting rooms and planning sessions. He started sensing something was wrong when he happened to be out on the shop floor and one of his employees good-naturedly teased him about being on vacation for the last two months. In thinking about the comment, he knew he had recently fallen short on his responsibility to be available and visible to his people.

So he pulled out one of the methodologies he occasionally used when he found himself needing to make a change: he chose his 10-Quarter Tool. With his 10 quarters in his left pocket, his objective was to talk with 10 people outside his office each day. It didn't need to be a long conversation — 3–5 minutes, or even 30 seconds — but just enough to catch up with the folks in the organization he was separated from, one at a time. After one week, he had talked with 50 people. After two weeks, over 100. After one month, 250 (he actually added quarters). He felt more energized, and the folks outside the executive office felt better about the connection with their leader. Like anything else it was a time commitment — a whopping half hour out of each busy day for this CEO. But in our experience, the investment of time with your people pays pretty strong dividends.

About the Authors

Aaron Buchko earned his PhD from Michigan State University following a successful career in sales and marketing. He is currently Professor of Management in the Foster College of Business at Bradley University, where he teaches graduate and undergraduate courses in Strategy, Executive Development, Management, and Ethics. He is also a confidential advisor to executives in numerous organizations, and serves as a Director for several companies. He has authored numerous articles and a textbook in academic and professional publications. He lives in Peoria, Illinois with his wife, Kathy. Outside of his professional activities, he is focused on his faith and on being a husband, father, and fly fisherman — generally in that order.

Steve Fairbanks is a seasoned executive with over 18 years serving at President/CEO/Board of Directors level. He has successfully taken over and worked on numerous engineered product manufacturing businesses out of distressed situations in Private Equity and Fortune 500 settings. He received his MBA from Baldwin Wallace University and his BS in Mechanical Engineering from Michigan Technological University. He earned his Professional Engineer's License, has been awarded eight United States patents, and is a trained six-sigma black belt. He has also been involved with and is certified as a facilitator with the Lead Like Jesus organization and has a passion for leadership development. He recently relocated to Rockford, Michigan, where he lives with his wife Lori. He loves being a husband, father, and grandfather, singing in the church choir, reading, and enjoying the outdoors.

Index

Actions, 8–9
Allegiant Air, 159
American Airlines, 160
Analysts, 66
Apple, 76, 223
Application knowledge, 30
Art of War, The (Sun Tzu),
121
Attention to prioritized list of
processes, 213
Attractiveness metric, 65

B2B (business to business),
39–40
B2C (business to consumer), 38
Big Data, 72
Bills of material (BOM), 146,
201
Board of Directors, 1
Boston Consulting Group
(BCG), 104, 110
Product Portfolio Matrix,
103
Bottom-Up Market Sizing Tool,
23–34

case study, 34
chart construction, 31–33
key strategic questions,
33
overview of, 26
requirements for, 27
sources of information,
27–30
Brand Perception Tool,
221–232
case study, 230–232
completion time for,
224–225
gathering information,
226–227
information analysis,
228–229
key strategic questions,
229–230
method of construction,
228–229
overview of, 224
requirements for, 226
British Airways, 160
Brother, 125

Caesar, Julius, 122
Case study
Bottom-Up Market Sizing
Tool, 34
Brand Perception Tool,
230–232
Communication Matrix Tool,
281–282
Critical to Customer Mindset
Tool, 215–219
Customer Value Analysis
Tool, 138–141
Market Map Tool, 69–70
Market Segmentation Tool,
45–47
Milestone Project
Management Tool,
251–255
90-Day Bucket Tool,
273–276
Opportunity Sourcing
Matrix, 239–240
Process Improvement
Guidance Tool,
195–196
Product/Service Portfolio
Matrix Tool, 166–170
Product Volume Margin
Chart Tool, 97–99
Quality Function
Deployment Tool,
185–187
Segment Niching Tool, 58–59
Strategic Environmental Scan
Tool, 86–90
Strategic Market Portfolio
Matrix Tool, 117–119

Strategic Outsourcing Matrix
Tool, 205–208
10-Quarter Tool, 285–286
Willingness to Pay Ranking
Tool, 152–155
Caterpillar, 223
Cause and Effect Diagram, 216
Charter phase/market
definition, 246
Check sheet, 216
CINDBWA, 210
Cluster analyses, 135
Coca-Cola, 223
Communication Matrix Tool,
277–282
case study, 281–282
completion time for, 278
method of construction, 280
overview of, 278
requirements for, 280
sources of information, 280
strategy implications, 281
Competitive advantage, 9
Competitive environment,
9–10
Competitive position analysis,
161
Compound Annual Growth
Rate (CAGR), 2
Concept development, 246–247
Conjoint Analysis, 176
Cost(s), 201
competitiveness, 175
elements, 201
metric, 145–147, 149, 153
per transaction, 198
see also Price

Cost of Goods Sold (COGS),
  145–149, 152
Cost reduction, 190–191
  external, 191
  internal, 191
Critical to Customer (CTC)
  Mindset Tool,
  209–219
  case study, 215–219
  method of construction, 214
  overview of, 209
  requirements for, 211
  source of information,
  211–214
  strategy implications,
  214–215
Cross-functional agreement,
  200, 201
Cross-Functional Alignment,
  264, 268–269
Cross-Pay Grade Alignment,
  264, 268–269
Customer Value Analysis
  (CVA) Tool, 121–141
  arraying the data, 133–137
  case study, 138–141
  completion time for, 130
  gathering information,
  132–133
  key strategic questions,
  137–138
  overview of, 126–130
  requirements for, 130–131

Data triangulation, 41
Daytona Beach, 141
Decision Matrices, 176, 177

Deming, W. Edwards, 191
Distinctive competence, 9, 198

80/20 rule, 130
Engineering costs, 145
Environments of organizations,
  75–77
Execution, 18
External experts
  data triangulation, 41
  Segment Niching Tool, 56
  technical competency rating,
  201
  for validating assumptions, 30

Failure mode effects analysis
  (FEMA), 247
Federal Express, 125
Fishbone Diagram, 193, 216
Forced ranking approach, 176,
  179–180
Ford, Henry, 191
Form 10-K, 66
Form 10-Q, 66
Formal communication,
  278–279
Four P's model, 16–17, 36, 158,
  159, 191, 209
  case study, 18–21

General Electric (GE), 103–104
Google, 34
Great Recession, 2
Gross margin (GM), 20, 21, 63,
  94–96, 111, 117
  calculation, 144, 145, 148–149
Group meetings, 201

High value–high cost offering, 159

Home office costs, 145

House of quality, 173

"How they buy?", 51

Incentivize completion
    of objectives,
    269–270

Industry experts, 29

Industry leaders, 66

Industry or trade associations,
    28–29

Informal communication,
    279–280

Innovation, 133

Integration, 7

Internal costs, 176

Internal experts
    data triangulation, 41
    Segment Niching Tool, 56
    technical competency rating,
        201

Ishikawa, Kaoru, 191

Ishikawa Diagram, 216

Jobs, Steve, 125, 232

Key Strategic Issues (KSIs), 83

Kodak, 72–73, 122–123

Kutcher, Ashton, 125

Lafley, A. G., 210

Lean Approach/Lean
    Manufacturing
    Approach, 190–195,
    214, 216–217

Lifestyle approach, 39–40

Low value–low cost offering, 159

Macro-economic metrics, 28

Maltz, Maxwell, 284

Margin enhancement, 180

Market, 16
    case study, 34
    competitiveness, 158
    forecasts, 29
    map, 20
    method of construction,
        161–163
    portfolio matrix, 20
    segmentation, 19, 37–38,
        138–139
    segment attractiveness,
        160–161
    sizing, 19, 23–34

Market Map Tool, 61–70
    case study, 69–70
    completion time for, 62
    method of construction, 67
    overview of, 62
    requirements for, 64–65
    sources of information,
        65–67
    strategy implications, 68–69

Market Segmentation Tool,
    35–47
    case study, 45–47
    construction of, 43–44
    overview of, 36
    requirements for, 37
    sources of information, 37–42
    strategy implications for,
        44–45

McDonald's, 129
McKinsey Company, 103
Mekko Graphics, 56
Milestone Project Management
        Tool, 241–255
    case study, 251–255
    completion time for, 242
    method of construction,
        248–249
    overview of, 242
    requirements for, 243
    sources of information,
        244–248
    strategy implications, 249–251
Milestones, 243
    selection of, 244
Military background of
        strategy, 121–122
Moments of Truth, 210, 211
Motorola, 191
Multiple regression, 135

NAICS (North American
        Industry Classification
        System) code, 38
Napoleon, 122
Niche focus, 159
90-Day Bucket Tool, 263–276
    case study, 273–276
    completion time for, 264
    examples of, 267
    method of construction,
        271–272
    overview of, 263–264
    requirements for, 270–271
    sources of information, 271
    strategy implications, 272–273

Olsen, Ken, 125
Opportunity Sourcing Matrix,
        233–240
    case study, 239–240
    completion time for, 234
    key strategic questions,
        237–239
    method of construction, 237
    overview of, 233–234
    requirements for, 236
    sources of information, 236
Outsourcing candidates, 198

Paired Comparison
        Evaluations, 176
Palo Alto Research Center
        (PARC), 125
Pareto Chart, 194, 216
Performance competitiveness,
        175
Placement (channel), 17
Poor Man
    Quality Function
        Deployment Tool,
        171–187, 251, 254–255
Position, 9, 159
Price/cost position, 17, 158, 159
Price
    distinguished from value, 127
    metric, 145–147, 153
    per unit/service, 30
    see also Cost(s)
Process improvement
        approach, 213–214
Process Improvement Guidance
        Tool, 189–196
    case study, 195–196

completion time for, 190
overview of, 189–190
Product, 16–17, 20
Product/Service Portfolio
      Matrix (PPM) Tool,
      157–170
  case study, 166–170
  completion time for, 158
  key strategic questions,
      163–166
  method of construction,
      161–163
  overview of, 158
  requirements for, 160
  sources of information,
      160–161
Product design, 133,
      246–247
Products/services
  breakdown of, 161
  cost competitiveness, 175
  deficiencies, 158
  performance
      competitiveness, 175
Product Volume Margin
      (PVM) Chart Tool,
      91–99
  case study, 97–99
  completion time for, 92
  construction of, 95–96
  overview of, 91–92
  requirements for, 93–94
  sources of information,
      94–95
  strategic questions, 96–97
Promotion, 17

Psycho-Cybernetics
      (Maxwell Maltz),
      284
Psychographics, 38
Public Company segment, 66
Purchase Criteria, 128, 129,
      132–138
Purchased market studies, 29
Purchase Process, 128–129,
      132–138
PVM Tool, 20

Quality Function Deployment
      (QFD) Tool, 171–187,
      251, 254–255
  case study, 185–187
  completion time for, 172
  key strategic questions,
      183–185
  method of construction,
      179–183
  overview of, 171–172
  requirements for, 174–175
  sources of information,
      175–179
QWIP machine technology,
      124

Ranked priority number (RPN),
      247
Rank order of features/
      requirements/metrics,
      177–179
Resource commitments, 8
Resources, 17–18
Ryanair, 159

Sales, General, and
Administrative
(SG&A) expenses, 94,
99, 145–149, 153, 176
Segmentation, 19, 37–38,
138–139
Segment Niching Tool, 49–59
case study, 58–59
completion time for, 50
method of construction,
56–57
overview of, 50
requirements for, 53
sources of information,
55–56
strategy implications for,
57–58
Service business health, 20
Service satisfaction, response
on, 211–213
Seven Basic Tools of Quality,
190–194, 214, 216
Sharp, 125
SIC (Standard Industrial
Classification) code, 38
Six-Sigma Approach, 132–133,
190–195, 214
Smith, Fred, 125
Sorting methodology, 176–177
Southwest Airlines, 123
Stage Gates, 243
selection of, 244
structure of, 245
Starbucks, 129
Strategic alliances, 198
Strategic environment, 19

Strategic Environmental Scan
(SCS) Tool, 71–90
case study, 86–90
completion time for, 80
forecasting the effects, 84
gathering information,
81–82
key strategic questions, 85
overview of, 78–80
requirements for, 80
sorting the information,
82–84
Strategic leadership, 2
Strategic Market Portfolio
Matrix (SMPM) Tool,
101–119
case study, 117–119
completion time for, 106
key strategic questions,
116–117
method of construction,
110–116
overview of, 104–106
requirements for, 106
sources of information,
106–110
Strategic Outsourcing Matrix
Tool, 197–208
case study, 205–208
completion time for, 198–199
key strategic questions,
203–205
method of construction, 202
overview of, 198
requirements for, 200
sources of information,
201–202

Strategic questions
  Bottom-Up Market Sizing
    Tool, 33
  Brand Perception Tool,
    229–230
  Customer Value Analysis
    Tool, 137–138
  Opportunity Sourcing
    Matrix, 237–239
  Product/Service Portfolio
    Matrix Tool, 163–166
  Product Volume Margin
    Chart Tool, 96–97
  Quality Function
    Deployment Tool,
    183–185
  Strategic Environmental Scan
    Tool, 85
  Strategic Market Portfolio
    Matrix Tool, 116–117
  Strategic Outsourcing Matrix
    Tool, 203–205
  Visual Waterfall Chart Tool,
    261–262
Strategic vulnerability, 198
Strategy
  actions, 8–9
  competitive environment,
    9–10
  defined, 5–11
  integration, 7
  position, 9
  practical tools, 11–14
  set of resource
    commitments, 8
  superior performance,
    10–11

Strategy implications
  Communication Matrix Tool,
    281
  Critical to Customer Mindset
    Tool, 214–215
  Market Map Tool, 68–69
  Market Segmentation Tool,
    44–45
  Milestone Project
    Management Tool,
    249–251
  90-Day Bucket Tool, 272–273
  Segment Niching Tool,
    57–58
  Willingness to Pay Ranking
    Tool, 150–151
Sturgis, 141
Sun Tzu, 121
Superior performance, 10–11
Suppliers, 30
Supply chain personnel costs,
    145

Technical competency rating,
    201
10-Quarter Tool, 283–286
  case study, 285–286
  completion time for, 284
  overview of, 283–284
3M
  QWIP machine technology,
    124
Total market allocation, across
    defined segments,
    40–41

U.S. Postal Service, 124

Value
  distinguished from price,
    127
  price or value per unit/
    service, 30
  see also Customer Value
    Analysis (CVA) Tool
Value added costs, 145
Value Stream Map, 201
Visual Waterfall Chart Tool,
    257–262
  completion time for, 258
  key strategic questions,
    261–262
  method of construction,
    260–261
  overview of, 257–258
  requirements for, 259
  sources of information,
    259
Von Clausewitz, Karl, 122

Wal-Mart, 127, 281
Walt Disney World, 123–124, 223
WHY question, 132–133
"Why they buy?", 51
Willingness to Pay (WTP)
    Ranking Tool, 143–155
  case study, 152–155
  completion time for, 144
  method of construction,
    147–150
  overview of, 143–144
  requirements for, 146
  sources of information,
    146–147
  strategy implications,
    150–151
Wozniak, Steve, 125

Xerox, 125

Yellow Pages, 34